Jesuit Studies

Contributions to the arts and sciences

by members of the Society of Jesus

Jesuit Studies

JESUIT STUDIES

The Presidential Election
of 1880

Herbert J. Clancy, S.J.

LOYOLA UNIVERSITY PRESS

Chicago, 1958

PREFACE

I dedicate this book out of a sense of deep gratitude to Catherine and Frank Heller. Their interest and support made this monograph possible.

This study has for its primary object an analysis of the presidential election of 1880. A brief introductory chapter has been used in the hope that it will help clarify the issues that confronted the nation during the contest between General Garfield and General Hancock. The final chapter, besides discussing the election results, also treats of the assassination of President Garfield and its effects upon the country.

I wish to record with a very grateful heart the many kindnesses of my dear friend, Dr. Charles C. Tansill, whose large fund of historical knowledge has always been of great service to me. Dr. Tibor Kerekes, professor of history at Georgetown University, gave me the benefit of his deep knowledge of history. I owe a special debt of gratitude to the Reverend Joseph Durkin, S.J., of Georgetown University for the assistance he gave me when I came to Washington to begin research on this book. Mr. David C. Mearns, chief of the Division of Manuscripts in the Library of Congress, and his entire staff have been exceedingly helpful. I am indebted to Mr. Robert Hill, chief of the Division of Manuscripts in the New York Public Library and to his able assistant, Mr. Edward B. Morrison, for courtesies unnumbered. Mr. Watt P. Marchman, curator of the

Rutherford B. Hayes Memorial Library in Fremont, Ohio, has been a rare example of courtesy and efficiency. I also wish to recognize the help afforded me by Miss Elizabeth C. Biggert, documents librarian of the Ohio State Archaeological and Historical Society. She was kind enough to send me typed copies of several important letters in the Allen G. Thurman Collections. I cannot forget the invaluable aid of Mrs. Emily M. Jahn, Mr. John Hunt, and Mr. John S. Deporry of the Library of Congress. I shall always be grateful to the Very Reverend Robert F. Grewen, S.J., president of Le Moyne College, for his unfailing encouragement. The Reverend Francis J. Fallon, S.J., dean of Le Moyne College, was most gracious in arranging a teaching schedule that permitted time for research and writing. His Excellency, Walter A. Foery, D.D., bishop of Syracuse, has helped me more than he will ever know. The Reverend Harry Sievers, S.J., of Bellarmine College, and Dr. Louis M. Sears of Purdue University were two close friends whose counsel meant very much to me. I wish to express my appreciation to the Very Reverend Thomas E. Henneberry, S.J., provincial of the New York Province of the Society of Jesus, for the consideration which he showed of the time-consuming nature of the work. Finally, my mother's prayers and advice were quite vital in the completion of this book.

H. J. C.

August 15, 1957
Feast of Our Lady's Assumption

CONTENTS

Senator Louis T. Wigfall of Texas, addressing a Senate gallery filled with ardent secessionists, said: "South Carolina has laid her hands on the pillars of Union and she will shake it till it totters and topples."[1] It was December 1860. But Wigfall, Toombs, Davis, and their fellow Southern statesmen were ultimately unsuccessful. The Union was preserved. Richmond fell on April 3, 1865, and Lee surrendered to Grant on April 9 at Appomattox Village. The eleven states over which defeat spread its black wings in that spring of 1865 contained about five million white inhabitants and three and a half million Negroes.[2] When Lee laid down his sword, Lincoln was in Virginia, not far from Appomattox, and he appeared anxious over the fate of these eight and a half million souls. Now that the war was over, he returned to Washington and on April 14 addressed his Cabinet:

> I hope there will be no persecution, no bloody work after the war is over. No one need expect me to take any part in hanging or killing these men, even the worst of them. . . . We must extinguish our resentments if we expect harmony and union. There is too

[1] Henry L. Stoddard, *Presidential Sweepstakes*, p. 76. New York: G. P. Putnam's Sons, 1948.

[2] Allan Nevins, *The Emergence of Modern America, 1865-1878*, p. 1. New York: The Macmillan Company, 1927.

much of a desire on the part of some of our very good friends to be masters, to interfere with and dictate to those states, to treat the people not as fellow citizens; there is too little respect for their rights. I do not sympathize with these feelings. . . . If we are wise and discreet we shall reanimate the states and get their governments in successful operation, with order prevailing and the union reestablished before Congress comes together in December.[3]

Before these words of hope could reach a defeated and dejected South, the author of them lay dead and buried. Lincoln was shot on the evening of April 14 and died the next morning. The bullet that killed Lincoln also killed his mild reconstruction plans for the South.

Andrew Johnson of Tennessee at once quietly took the oath of office as president and immediately undertook to carry out the policy of Lincoln. But it was not to be. The Republican radicals were intent upon blocking the Lincoln-Johnson plan. Johnson naturally did not possess the power and prestige of Lincoln. No one knew that better than Thaddeus Stevens of Pennsylvania and Charles Sumner of Massachusetts. These two men, the leaders of the radical Republicans, were to suffer a severe shock when under the Lincoln-Johnson plan Congress convened in December 1865.

Among the delegates elected to Congress were a half dozen former members of the Confederate Congress, five colonels, and four generals. In addition there was Alexander Stephens, former vice-president of the Confederacy, still under indictment for treason. This spectacle not only shocked the radicals but also worried them. In 1860 a Negro had counted as three fifths of a man in apportioning congressional representation. Eman-

---

[3] The text of Lincoln's talk to his Cabinet does not exist. His address was summarized by Gideon Welles, secretary of the Navy, and was published in *Galaxy* 13:506, April 1872. I have followed the *Galaxy* account. See also William S. Myers, *The Republican Party: A History*, p. 154 (New York: Century Company, 1928).

cipation made him five fifths of a man. The South, although it lost the war, was now entitled to twelve more votes in Congress. Thirty of these were based on Negroes who as yet could not cast a ballot.

Northern radicals were asking themselves the question: Who won the war? If the Southerners joined hands with ex-Copperheads and discontented farmers of the North and West, they might win control of Congress. These ex-Confederates might then proceed to destroy the industrial and financial foundations of the Republican party. They would have the power to abolish excessive land grants to the railroads, repeal the Homestead Act, curb monopoly, reduce high war tariffs.

The radicals were successful in drawing many moderates to their side when they pointed out that these "whitewashed rebels" might go so far as to repudiate the national debt and re-enslave the Negro. With the radicals, thought was action. On December 4, 1865, therefore, the first day of the session, they refused to recognize the credentials of the newly elected Southern delegates.

With the door effectively shut against Southern representation, the radicals undertook to write the principles of the Civil Rights Act—which they had passed over Johnson's veto—into the Constitution as the Fourteenth Amendment. The suggested revision disclaimed all Confederate indebtments while underwriting the federal debt; ex-Rebels who as officeholders had once taken an oath to support the Constitution of the United States were barred from state and federal offices; the Negro was granted civil rights but not the right to vote; and finally the representation of a state in both the Electoral College and Congress was reduced proportionately if it refused the Negro the franchise.

Some historians have suggested that, if Johnson had been farsighted, he would have urged the Southern states to accept the Fourteenth Amendment in the spirit of compromise. But he encouraged them to vote against it. All of the secession states, except Tennessee, spurned the amendment.

The radicals now forged a pen from a saber and wrote the Military Reconstruction Act of March 2, 1867. This new act destroyed the Southern state governments and created five military districts, each commanded by a Union general and policed by thousands of blue-coated soldiers.

New state constitutions, drafted under federal bayonets, disfranchised additional tens of thousands of Southern white leaders. Rigid conditions were adopted for readmission to the Union. Ratification of the Fourteenth Amendment was compulsory, and in addition the Southern states were obliged to include in their state constitution a guarantee of full suffrage for their former slaves.

Beginning in 1867, and under the observant eyes of Northern guns, new state governments gradually reappeared below the Potomac. By 1870 all the Southern states had reorganized their governments and had been granted full rights. The hated troops were withdrawn from a state only when the radicals seemed in full control. Finally, in 1877, the last federal bayonets departed.[4]

When the time for the presidential election of 1868 came around, political prognosticators were not betting on the chances of the Democratic party. With Negro suffrage fully protected by the Federal Government and with the disfranchisement of thousands of Southern whites an accomplished fact, a Republican triumph in Dixie seemed fairly certain. General Grant carried

---

[4] For details on Reconstruction see Claude G. Bowers, *The Tragic Era,* pp. 198-219 (Boston: Houghton Mifflin Company, 1929); Walter L. Fleming, *The Sequel of Appomattox,* pp. 221-42 (New Haven: Yale University Press, 1921); John W. Burgess, *Reconstruction and the Constitution,* pp. 195-221 (New York: Charles Scribner's Sons, 1902). *The Harvard Guide to American History,* p. 401 (Cambridge: Harvard University Press, 1954) lists the standard works on this topic.

all the Southern states save Georgia and Louisiana. The latter two states were won by the Democrats, mainly because of the efforts of the Ku Klux Klan.[5] In Texas, Mississippi, and Virginia, still "unreconstructed," no elections were held at all. Grant obtained 214 out of 294 electoral votes and a popular majority of approximately 300,000. The most interesting feature in the North was that the Democrats captured New York for the first time since 1856. Seymour carried the Empire State by an exact majority of 10,000 votes. The Tammany Tweed Ring was accused by the Republican Stalwarts of engineering this very neat surplus.[6] Even though Republican success was assured in the Electoral College, still the Democratic total popular vote rose from 45 per cent in 1864 to 47½ per cent in 1868.[7]

The election of 1868 showed a remarkable contrast in the conventions of the two major parties. The Republicans convened in Chicago on May 24. General Grant was nominated by General John A. Logan. The roll of the states was immediately called. The convention possessed 650 votes in all. Ulysses S. Grant received every vote on the first ballot.[8] The Democrats held their convention in Tammany Hall, New York, on July 4. In spite of the fact that prospects for success were slim in the coming campaign, the struggle for the nomination was bitter and long. General George H. Pendleton of Ohio was the leading aspirant. President Johnson was a distinct possibility and the Democratic platform endorsed his course and thanked him for his efforts against the aggressions of Congress. When it became evident that neither New York nor Pennsylvania would accept

---

[5] Myers, *Republican Party*, pp. 187-88.
[6] Frank R. Kent, *The Democratic Party: A History*, p. 233. New York: Century Company, 1928.
[7] Edward A. Stanwood, *A History of Presidential Elections*, p. 269. Boston: Houghton Mifflin Company, 1896.
[8] Charles H. Coleman, *The Election of 1868: The Democratic Effort To Regain Control*, p. 92. New York: Columbia University Press, 1933.

Pendleton because of his soft-money theories, the contest narrowed down to Thomas A. Hendricks of Indiana and General Winfield Scott Hancock of Pennsylvania. But neither seemed acceptable to the New York delegation. A dark horse appeared in the person of Governor Seymour. As presiding officer of the convention, he seemed far removed from the conflict. For twenty-one ballots his name was not even mentioned in the convention. On the twenty-second ballot the Seymour sensation was sprung. He became the unanimous nominee with 317 votes. Scenes of great enthusiasm and excitement followed. With the Republicans holding a fair measure of control in the South and with the magnetic Grant opposing Seymour, it is hard to understand the high hopes of the Democratic party.[9]

The record shows Seymour's easy defeat by Grant, whose victory, however, was ultimately to endanger Republican ascendancy in national politics. Henry Adams tersely sums up the cause of President Grant's many failures by remarking that "Grant avowed from the start a policy of drift; and a policy of drift attached only barnacles."[10] Grant was always grateful to his friends, even though those friends turned out to be a horde of grafters, place hunters, and more or less disreputable demagogues. He was thoroughly honest himself; but for the multitude of corruptions that took place during his administration he must take the blame, since the responsibility of the office was his.[11]

---

[9] Robert S. Mitchell, *Horatio Seymour of New York*, pp. 410-32 (Cambridge: Harvard University Press, 1938). Professor Mitchell tells how, on the evening before Seymour's nomination, the latter dined with Tilden, John Kelly, and Hewitt, and agreed to nominate Chase. Seymour did not desire the nomination and accepted it with reluctance. John Kelly and Abram S. Hewitt, both Tammany Democrats, worked with Tilden in smashing the Tweed Ring.

[10] Myers, *Republican Party*, p. 190.

[11] Allan Nevins, *Hamilton Fish: The Inner History of the Grant Administration*, p. 641 (New York: Dodd, Mead and Company, 1936). Professor Nevins draws a graphic picture of the political bankruptcy of Grant's administration, and Grant's responsibility for it. See also William B. Hesseltine, *Ulysses S. Grant, Politician*, pp. 190-206 (New York: Dodd, Mead and Company, 1935).

As Grant's first administration was drawing to a close, strong opposition was forming against him within his own party. As early as September 30, 1871 Carl Schurz, Republican senator from Missouri, told Charles Sumner of his opposition to Grant and urged energetic action to block the latter's re-election. The nomination, he felt, could not be prevented. Schurz was confident that a movement could be put on foot, powerful enough to beat both Grant and the Democrats. He declared he was already laying the groundwork for such an offensive.[12]

Both Sumner and Schurz were strong old-line Republicans; and besides being appalled by the rampant corruption in high places, they were both stirred to action by Grant's gross ignorance of the principles of foreign policy. The president's clumsy attempts to annex the Dominican Republic, which he did not seem to realize would enrich such adventurers as General William L. Cazneau and Colonel Joseph W. Fabens, disgusted the better element in the Republican party.[13]

Schurz's dreams were partially realized, for at Cincinnati, on May 1, 1872, the revolt which he had so ardently sponsored took place. On that day the Liberal Republican party came into being and held its first convention. Its initial mistake, as well as its most damaging, was the choice of Horace Greeley as its presidential nominee.[14] That "Wizard of the Lobby," Thurlow

---

[12] Carl Schurz to Charles Sumner, September 30, 1871; in Frederic Bancroft and William A. Dunning, editors, *The Reminiscences of Carl Schurz*, Vol. 3, pp. 338-39. New York: McClure Company, 1908.

[13] Charles C. Tansill, *The United States and Santo Domingo, 1798-1873*, pp. 344-45 (Baltimore: The Johns Hopkins Press, 1938). Professor Tansill tells how Cazneau and Fabens had secured title to some of the most valuable portions of the Dominican Republic and how, realizing that their holdings would increase tremendously in value if annexation came about, they turned to some prominent businessmen in New York City and through them sought to interest Grant himself.

[14] Earle D. Ross, *The Liberal Republican Movement*, pp. 100-03 (New York: Henry Holt and Company, 1919). Professor Ross gives an excellent summary of the reasons why Greeley received the nomination.

Weed, felt that no considerable group of men outside a lunatic asylum would nominate such a man. The *Nation,* on May 9, 1872, soberly observed that there was a greater degree of incredulity and disappointment caused by the Cincinnati nomination than was the case when the Northern states received the first news of the Battle of Bull Run. Edwin L. Godkin, editor of the *Nation,* concluded by commending the platform but pronouncing the convention a complete failure. On May 4, 1872 the *New York Times* reported that the news of Greeley's nomination was received in Washington with "a general laugh," and its editorial comment was headed, "The End of a Farce." Charles Francis Adams had been an unsuccessful contender for the nomination, and his son Henry Adams, with his usual caustic wit, commented: "If God insists on making Mr. Greeley our President, I give up."[15]

On July 9, in Baltimore, the Democratic convention was held. Greeley was nominated, and the Liberal Republican platform was adopted *in toto.* Greeley's advocacy of high protective tariffs, together with his prewar abolitionism, provoked a split in Democratic ranks. At Louisville, on September 3, a "straight" Democratic National Convention nominated Charles O'Conor for president. O'Conor was the first Roman Catholic to run for the presidency.[16] As editor of the *New York Tribune,* Horace Greeley enjoyed a nationwide reputation. His prewar editorials found a certain sympathy among those who held that secession was a constitutional right. For Greeley had not been in favor of coercing the South. In his mind the Constitution was not clear on the point of the rightness or wrongness of secession, and on

---

[15] Leon B. Richardson, *William E. Chandler, Republican,* p. 132 (New York: Dodd, Mead and Company, 1940). All that is said here about Greeley's nomination is taken from Professor Richardson's work. See also Glyndon G. Van Deusen, *Thurlow Weed: Wizard of the Lobby,* p. 338 (Boston: Little, Brown and Company, 1947). Weed supported Grant in the election of 1872.

[16] Kent, *Democratic Party,* p. 235.

November 2, 1860 he dared the fire-eaters to submit the question of secession or no secession to the popular vote of their own people. If the latter should vote themselves out of the Union, he was in favor of "letting them go in peace."[17]

And so the Democrats went to the polls in November 1872 in an attempt—their second since the war's end—to put a Democrat in the White House. The election took place on November 5, and the result was an overwhelming defeat for Greeley. The devastating campaign caricatures of Nast, coupled with the vast barrage of abuse heaped on Greeley from all quarters, led the defeated candidate to say that he was the worst-beaten man who ever ran for high office.[18] He barely knew, he averred, whether he was running for president or for the penitentiary.[19]

The Union comprised thirty-seven states in 1872. All of them voted for the first time since 1860. Grant carried every Northern and Western state. Greeley carried but six states: Georgia, Kentucky, Maryland, Missouri, Tennessee, and Texas. The electoral vote was 272 to 66. The popular vote was 3,597,-132 to 2,834,125. O'Conor polled less than 30,000 votes and did not affect the election in any state.[20]

The strain proved to be too great a one for Greeley. As one commentator put it: "Within a month he lost his wife, the election, his job, his mind and his life."[21] With Greeley's defeat and death, the Liberal Republican party vanished from the arena of national politics.

---

[17] Jeter A. Isely, *Horace Greeley and the Republican Party, 1853-1861*, p. 305. Princeton: Princeton University Press, 1947.

[18] Albert B. Paine, *Thomas Nast: His Period and His Pictures*, pp. 216-20 (New York: Harper and Brothers, 1904). Nast considered the Schurz Liberals to be mere politicians using the slogan of reform to gain office for themselves.

[19] Harold U. Faulkner, *American Political and Social History*, p. 395. New York: F. S. Crofts and Company, 1943.

[20] Myers, *Republican Party*, p. 207.

[21] Thomas A. Bailey, *The American Pageant*, p. 492. Boston: D. C. Heath and Company, 1956.

The easy victory of 1872, like a strong wine, went to the heads of the Republican Stalwarts. Their leaders became reckless, and lapsed into the pleasant belief that the question of dispensing the loaves and fishes of political patronage was settled forever. They paid little heed to the cries of political reform which continually reached their ears, not only from the Democrats, but also from the liberal elements within their own party ranks. The panic of 1873, the dissatisfaction with the monetary system, the failure of Reconstruction, the Crédit Mobilier exposures, the Salary Grab Act, the Sanborn contract, and other scandals—all these proved to be the opening wedge for "the Democracy," as it was often called in those days. The elections of 1874 resulted in a great tidal wave. Thirty-five states held elections in that year. Twenty-three of them went Democratic, and such dyed-in-the-wool Republican states as Wisconsin, Ohio, Pennsylvania, and Massachusetts were counted in the Democratic column. Only a comparative handful of Republicans were returned to the House. In fact, when the representatives convened in 1875 the Democrats controlled that body by a vote of 198 to 94.[22] Even though the party of Jefferson had only one third of the Senate, it was in a stronger position than it had been since 1856. Barring some accident, the tidal wave of 1874 seemed a sure indication that the Democracy would triumph in the next presidential election.

The time for the Republican convention of 1876 was fast approaching. For the first time since 1860 there was real uncertainty as to who would be chosen to lead the Republican party. In 1875 there was much debate in the newspapers and magazines about a third term. In the spring of that same year the Pennsylvania Republican state convention passed a resolution against a third term. Grant, who in the past, as at Fort Donelson

---

[22] Paul L. Haworth, *The Hayes-Tilden Election*, p. 3. Indianapolis: Bobbs-Merrill Company, 1906.

and elsewhere, had always possessed a marked ability for clear expression, now permitted himself some diplomatic double talk. Writing to General Harry White, chairman of the Pennsylvania convention, the hero of Vicksburg denied that he wished the renomination. He did not seek it, he protested, any more than he had sought it the first time, nor would he accept it "unless it should come under such circumstances as to make it an imperative duty—circumstances not likely to arise."[23]

Many regarded this letter as a declination with a string to it. As a consequence the discussion of Grant's availability was kept up. The knockout blow to the third-term talk came in December 1875. The House then passed a resolution by a vote of 233 to 18 reaffirming the precedent established by Washington and regarding any departure from it as being unwise, unpatriotic, and fraught with peril to our free institutions.[24]

With Grant thus disposed of, the field was further cleared by the famous Fifth Avenue conference. Held in New York City at the Fifth Avenue Hotel on May 15 and 16, 1875, it was in reality a meeting of the liberal element in the Republican party. Carl Schurz, Theodore Woolsey, Horace White, William Cullen Bryant, Alexander H. Bullock, and Charles Francis Adams were among the more prominent Republicans who attended. The conference issued an elaborate "Address to the American People." This paper, coming from the able pen of Schurz, deplored the corrupt practices of the last two administrations and declared that the Independents would support no candidate in whom the impulses of the party manager had shown themselves predominant over those of the reformer.[25]

The pith and substance of the address was contained in the conclusion, where it was stated that they would refuse support

---

[23] *Ibid.,* pp. 10-11.
[24] *Congressional Record*, 44th Cong., 1st Sess., 228.
[25] Claude M. Fuess, *Carl Schurz: Reformer*, p. 222. New York: Dodd, Mead and Company, 1932.

to any candidate about whom there was any question of his being "really the man to carry through a thorough going reform in the government."[26]

The address was a direct warning from the Independent Republicans to the Stalwart Republicans that they would not accept Blaine, Conkling, or Morton. For Blaine's friends, although dissatisfied with the administration, were by no means reformers.[27] Then, too, the disclosure—not too long before the convention met—of the celebrated Mulligan letters, which purported to make some uncomfortable revelations regarding Blaine's dealings with the Little Rock and Fort Smith Railroad, did not help the Plumed Knight in the eyes of Schurz and his Liberal reformers.[28] Senator Oliver P. Morton of Indiana had called the civil service "the best upon the planet."[29] That remark erased his name from the roll of the Schurz worthies.

When the Republican convention met in Cincinnati on June 14, Benjamin H. Bristow of Kentucky was the leading reform candidate. As secretary of the treasury he had conducted a ruthless warfare against the Whiskey Ring and had not feared to expose the personal friends of President Grant. Cincinnati was the scene of a four-way race between Blaine, Morton, Bristow, and Conkling. Some maintain that Blaine would undoubtedly have won the nomination on the first ballot had it not been for the trickery of the Conkling-Cameron Stalwarts. The Conkling-Blaine feud went back to 1868 when Blaine, on the floor of the House, had compared Conkling to a turkey gobbler. The Stalwarts never forgot or forgave. "Anyone but Blaine" was a creed

---

[26] Haworth, *Hayes-Tilden Election*, p. 16.

[27] George F. Hoar, *Autobiography of Seventy Years,* Vol. 1, p. 378. New York: Charles Scribner's Sons, 1903.

[28] *Ibid.*, p. 379.

[29] Haworth, *Hayes-Tilden Election*, p. 13. See also William D. Foulke, *Life of Oliver P. Morton,* Vol. 2, pp. 387-402 (Indianapolis: Bowen-Merrill Company, 1899).

with them. But they would have to think fast and act still faster
if they were to deprive Blaine of the nomination, for Colonel
Robert G. Ingersoll of Illinois in nominating Blaine had captured the imagination of the convention in words that would
long be remembered:

> Like an armed warrior, like a plumed knight, James G. Blaine
> marched down the halls of the American Congress and threw his
> shining lance full and fair against the brazen foreheads of the de-
> famers of his country and the maligners of his honour. For the
> Republican party to desert this gallant leader now is as though an
> army should desert their general upon the field of battle.[30]

At the conclusion of this speech the tide in favor of Blaine
was running so high that the Stalwarts determined to press for
an adjournment until the next morning. There is an interesting
but probably apocryphal story concerning the adjournment.
Suddenly the lights refused to work, the Stalwarts Robert W.
Mackay and Matthew S. Quay having cut off the gas supply.
Thereupon the convention adjourned until ten o'clock the next
morning. Blaine's chances, so the story says, had been extin-
guished with the lights. Actually, contemporary newspaper ac-
counts show that the motion to adjourn was put and voted on
without any such dramatics.[31]

On the fifth ballot Hayes entered the four-way race by jump-
ing from 68 to 104 votes. The crisis came on the seventh ballot.
It seemed to many that the tide was turning toward Bristow, but
the Kentucky delegates, realizing that Bristow was cordially

---

[30] Cameron Rogers, *Colonel Bob Ingersoll*, pp. 206-07 (New York: Doubleday,
Page and Company, 1927). See also Clarence H. Cramer, *Royal Bob, The
Life of Robert G. Ingersoll*, pp. 14-15 (Indianapolis: Bobbs-Merrill Company,
1952).

[31] Haworth, *Hayes-Tilden Election*, p. 22. See also Charles R. Williams, *The Life of
Rutherford Birchard Hayes*, Vol. 1, p. 466 (Boston: Houghton Mifflin Com-
pany, 1914) for Liberal Republican approval of Hayes. See also Harry
Barnard, *Rutherford B. Hayes and His America*, p. 553 (Indianapolis: Bobbs-
Merrill Company, 1954). I am relying on Mr. Barnard's account.

hated by the Blaine faction, voted unanimously for Hayes. A dark horse had again triumphed in a political convention. The nominee represented a victory for the Liberal Republicans, for Hayes was definitely a reform candidate.

As the campaign of 1876 approached, the Democrats were in a much more sanguine mood than their opponents. Elated by their victory in the congressional elections of 1874 and encouraged by the fact that all but three of the Southern states had at last been redeemed from Carpetbag rule, they felt confident that for the first time in twenty years a Democrat would be president of the United States.

Reform and the electoral vote of New York would be important factors in the coming contest. These two factors made Governor Samuel J. Tilden of New York a logical candidate for the presidential nomination of the Democratic party. In his early years he had been intimately associated with that prince of politicians, Martin Van Buren. Tilden had won distinction as a lawyer, and through his success as a railroad reorganizer he had amassed a fortune of several millions. In 1866 he obtained the chairmanship of the Democratic state committee in New York. As chairman he had been associated more or less with unscrupulous leaders of the party in New York City. His chance for renown on a national scale came in 1871, when the *New York Times* and *Harper's Weekly* exposed the Tweed Ring. At the eleventh hour he threw himself into a desperate struggle against the ring. The ring was smashed; and by thus playing a conspicuous part in the defeat of Boss Tweed, Tilden became allied in the minds of many people with reform. Despite the opposition of Tammany he was the party's candidate for governor of New York in 1874. He was triumphantly elected over John A. Dix by a plurality of about fifty thousand.[32]

---

[32] Alexander C. Flick, *Samuel Jones Tilden: A Study in Political Sagacity*, pp. 215-25, 250. New York: Dodd, Mead and Company, 1939.

The eight years of Grant rule had seen America reach a new low in political corruption. Reform was to be the issue in the presidential campaign of 1876. The Republicans had acknowledged this by their nomination of Hayes. The Democrats, equally alive to the situation, declared in the very first plank of their platform:

> We, the delegates of the Democratic party of the United States, in national convention assembled, do hereby declare the administration of the Federal Government to be in urgent need of immediate reform.[33]

When the Democratic convention assembled in St. Louis on June 27, the Tilden forces were admirably organized. Henry Watterson, Montgomery Blair, and others were able to convince many delegates that the proper candidate to lead a reform campaign was the reform governor of New York. They insisted that a reform campaign without Tilden would be like the play *Hamlet* with Hamlet left out. Their persuasive tactics achieved results, for Tilden obtained the necessary two-thirds majority on the second ballot. He was accordingly nominated, and the choice was enthusiastically made unanimous.[34] Tilden's program, said Blaine some years afterward, embraced three features: his steppingstone was the governorship, his shibboleth was administrative reform, his method was organization to a degree which has never been surpassed.[35]

Although Tilden captured the nomination rather handily, nevertheless in the preconvention analysis the political forecasters had singled out four men who were considered to be quite

---

[33] *Official Proceedings of the Democratic National Convention, Held in St. Louis, Mo., June 27-29, 1876*, p. 94. St. Louis: Woodward, Tiernan and Hale, 1876.

[34] Haworth, *Hayes-Tilden Election*, pp. 31-34. Henry Watterson was the editor of the *Louisville Courier Journal*. Blair was Tilden's counsel before the Electoral Commission.

[35] James G. Blaine, *Twenty Years of Congress*, Vol. 2, p. 574. Norwich: Henry Bill Publishing Company, 1893.

definitely presidential timber. These were Senator Thomas F. Bayard of Delaware, Senator Allen G. Thurman of Ohio, General Winfield Scott Hancock of Pennsylvania, and Governor Thomas A. Hendricks of Indiana. Bayard was undoubtedly one of the ablest Democrats in the Senate, and was acceptable to the South because he had been an ardent champion of their rights during Reconstruction; yet his availability in the convention was greatly impaired by the smallness of the state from which he came.[36] Senator Thurman was a top-ranking constitutional lawyer, and because of his hard-money views he was regarded with favor in the East. Soft-money theories, however, were permeating Ohio at the time, and consequently Thurman did not receive the support of his own state. General Hancock—four years later to be the party's candidate against Garfield—was looked upon as a possible dark horse. He had been a strong competitor for the nomination in 1868. He was popular with the war veterans, but in the convention he received little support outside his own state. Next to Tilden, Governor Hendricks' fortunes were pushed with the greatest vigor. As a congressman, senator, and governor he had been prominent in state and national politics. He had been one of the leading candidates in the convention which nominated Seymour. His following was strong in Indiana and in some other states of the Middle West, but in the East his views on money were considered unsafe. He did win the vice-presidential nomination and was expected to win the soft-money votes of the West.[37]

As the summer of 1876 faded, the world little realized that it was about to witness an election which was to be the most unique in all American history up to that time. November 7 was

---

[36] Charles C. Tansill, *The Congressional Career of Thomas Francis Bayard, 1869-1885*, p. 122 (Washington: Georgetown University Press, 1946). Professor Tansill presents facts that show on the one hand the loyalty of the South for Bayard and on the other Tilden's finesse in manipulating the convention.

[37] Haworth, *Hayes-Tilden Election*, pp. 26, 27, 28.

election day, and when the votes had been counted it seemed quite apparent that Samuel J. Tilden had been elected president. Even the Stalwart Republican organ, the *New York Tribune,* conceded the defeat of Hayes. Hayes himself accepted his defeat with good grace and assured his son Rutherford that he and Mrs. Hayes were not disappointed in the result, no matter how much they had hoped it would be otherwise. Hard times and the cry of reform had carried the day. He felt the defeat had spared him a heavy responsibility. While it would have been a great gratification to try to establish civil-service reform, he bowed cheerfully to the will of the people.[38]

Hayes's lieutenants, however, did not accept defeat with such detached philosophic calm. In the early hours of the evening of November 7 the *New York Times* had sent to the pressroom an editorial which was in effect a practical concession of the election to Tilden. But later that evening the *Times* was the recipient of certain notes from Democratic headquarters. These notes were nothing more than requests for information concerning the votes of Louisiana, South Carolina, Oregon, and Florida, but they were interpreted by John C. Reid, editor of the news department of the *Times,* to mean that the Democratic leaders were in a doubtful frame of mind. After a hurried consultation with his colleagues Reid recalled the pessimistic editorial and prepared a new one in which all the doubtful states were claimed for Hayes. This was equivalent to saying that Hayes had won the election by one electoral vote.

It was after midnight. There was no time to lose. So in the early morning hours of November 8 Reid made his way to the Fifth Avenue Hotel. He was in search of Zachariah Chandler, chairman of the Republican National Committee. In the lobby of the hotel he encountered William E. Chandler, one of the

---

[38] Rutherford B. Hayes Memorial Library, Rutherford B. Hayes MSS, Rutherford B. Hayes to Rutherford (Ruddy) Hayes, November 8, 1876.

smoothest politicians in the Republican party. This meeting was
to change the political history of the United States. On hearing
Reid's story, William E. Chandler thought out a plan that was
to win the presidency for Hayes. At that moment the Republicans were sure of 166 votes. The Democrats had 184 certain
votes, needing but one more to win. William E. Chandler realized that if the 19 votes of South Carolina, Louisiana, and
Florida could be listed in the Republican column, Hayes would
win by 185 to 184. He determined that the votes of the three
states in question should be cast for Hayes.

Together with Reid he rushed to the room of "Old Zach."
After arousing him from his slumbers and explaining the situa-
tion, they obtained from Zachariah a blanket permission to do
what they thought necessary. Armed with this authority, Reid
and Chandler made straight for the telegraph office in the hotel.
Telegrams were immediately sent to Republican leaders in the
lower South. The telegram to Governor Chamberlain of South
Carolina was typical: "Hayes is elected if we have carried
South Carolina, Florida and Louisiana. Can you hold your
State? Answer immediately."[39] Chandler then prevailed upon
President Grant to send federal troops into the three states to
"protect the Republican canvassers." Both parties sent agents
with ample funds into the disputed states. Two sets of returns,
one Republican and one Democratic, were sent to Washington
from the three states in question.[40]

Congress was now faced with the perplexing problem of
counting the votes. The Senate was controlled by Republicans

---

39 *New York Times*, June 15, 1887.
40 See Library of Congress, William E. Chandler MSS, Vol. 43, nos. 8683-88 for a
   long and undated account of the election of 1876. Most of what has been said
   above is based on this account. See also the *New York Times* for June 15,
   1887 for an account by John C. Reid of the strategy used by Republican
   leaders on the night of November 7-8, 1876. I have also utilized this report in
   my own paragraphs on the Republican methods that seated Hayes in 1876.
   See also Barnard, *Hayes*, pp. 316-23 for an excellent account.

and the House by Democrats. It was obvious from the start that the one would nullify the other and that an indefinite and hopeless deadlock would prevail. Something had to be done quickly, for the danger of another civil war was imminent. After careful research Paul Haworth concluded that more people in that winter of 1876-1877 expected an armed conflict than had anticipated war as a result of the secession movement of 1860-1861.[41] Senator Hoar felt that there would have been a resort to arms had it not been for the bitter experience of a few years before.[42] Murat Halstead, editor of the *Cincinnati Commercial,* swore that he had definite and accurate information that Tilden was ready for war in 1876-1877. Halstead asserted that Tilden told a group of Southern members of Congress that he could depend on the militia of New York, which he thought would amount to about 22,000 men; that he could also count on troops from Connecticut, New Jersey, Delaware, and Maryland; and that if necessary he would seize the $14,000,000 in the subtreasury at New York.[43]

The net result of the ensuing deadlock, coupled with the awful fear of another civil war, was the passage of an act by Congress, proposed by the Republicans and acquiesced in by the Democrats. This act created an Electoral Commission to decide the election. The commission was composed of five members chosen by the Senate, five by the House, four justices of the Supreme Court designated in the bill, and the fifteenth member

---

[41] Haworth, *Hayes-Tilden Election,* p. 168.

[42] Hoar, *Autobiography,* Vol. 1, p. 369.

[43] Hayes MSS, L. C. Weir to Hayes, February 7, 1877. Weir recounts the story he had just heard from Halstead. I have given the substance of the story above. Hamilton J. Eckenrode in his *Rutherford B. Hayes, Statesman of Reunion,* p. 233 (New York: Dodd, Mead and Company, 1930) expresses the opinion that "civil war would not improbably have followed if Tilden had actually been allowed to take his seat and govern." Samuel L. Barlow congratulated Bayard for aiding "in averting a civil war" (Library of Congress, Thomas F. Bayard MSS, Samuel L. Barlow to Thomas F. Bayard, April 3, 1877).

to be selected by the four justices thus named. Before the justices selected the fifteenth member the line-up of the commission was seven Republicans and seven Democrats.[44] The four justices finally selected Joseph P. Bradley, a New Jersey Republican. On learning of Bradley's appointment, Abram S. Hewitt, speaking for Tilden, wrote that absolute reliance could be placed upon the judicial fairness of Judge Bradley. When Bradley, however, joined the seven Republicans and Hayes was seated by an eight-to-seven vote, Hewitt changed his mind and felt that Bradley had been "reached."[45]

The selection of Bradley had been somewhat unexpected. According to Hewitt the Democrats had approved the plan of an Electoral Commission idea on the assumption that Judge David Davis "would have the casting vote, and that he could be relied upon to see that the will of the people as expressed in the election of Mr. Tilden should not be thwarted."[46] But this assumption was shattered when the news arrived in Washington that the Illinois legislature had elected Judge Davis to the United States Senate.

---

[44] The give-and-take between Republicans and Democrats during this period of crisis is usually referred to as the Compromise of 1877. Hayes, acting through intermediaries, made the following concessions to Southern conservatives: an end to Carpetbag rule, a government subsidy for the Texas and Pacific Railroad, at least one Cabinet post as well as other patronage favors, and federal aid for education and internal improvements in the South. For these promises the South agreed to the peaceful seating of Hayes. The famous Wormley conference, held at Wormley's Hotel in Washington, D.C., was "actually . . . only a last minute meeting to reassure worried southerners that the terms already agreed upon would be respected" (Eugene H. Roseboom, *A History of Presidential Elections*, pp. 248-49 [New York: The Macmillan Company, 1957]). For further details see C. Vann Woodward, *Reunion and Reaction: The Compromise of 1877 and the End of Reconstruction*, pp. 3-21 (Boston: Little, Brown and Company, 1951) ; also Barnard, *Hayes*, pp. 387-93.

[45] With regard to Bradley's having been "reached," Barnard states that "nothing was ever proved one way or another" (*ibid.*, p. 373).

[46] Abram S. Hewitt, "Secret History of the Disputed Election, 1876-1877"; in Allan Nevins, editor, *Selected Writings of Abram S. Hewitt*, p. 171. New York: Columbia University Press, 1937.

When Davis refused to be a candidate for a place on the Electoral Commission, many persons believed "that a bargain had been made by the Republicans by which Judge Davis, in consideration of his being made Senator should decline a position upon the Electoral Commission."[47] Three years after the election Hewitt observed:

> If Senator Davis had remained on the bench and acted as the 15th member of the Electoral Commission in lieu of Judge Bradley, the Democratic Party would have owed him a debt of gratitude. As it is, it is due to him, and to him alone, that Mr. Tilden was not inaugurated in the office to which he was elected by the people.[48]

Who was the choice of the people in 1876? "The truth never was and never will be told," writes Harry Barnard. It never will be known how many ballots were fraudulently cast or fraudulently counted. As Barnard indicates, the Electoral Commission was but an extension of the presidential campaign of 1876. "The Republican Party had the greater power—and it had used it as the Democratic Party also would have done. In private Democratic leaders admitted this."[49]

---

[47] *Ibid.*

[48] New York Public Library, Abram S. Hewitt MSS, Abram S. Hewitt to J. H. Cleveland, December 11, 1879.

[49] Barnard, *Hayes*, pp. 316, 395. An interesting picture of the struggle in 1876 is given in an undated letter from Samuel Barlow to Manton Marble: "I only wish you had succeeded!—that Mr. Tilden was elected is plain, was plain when you were in Florida. That he was likely to be cheated out of his election by the hypocrites, who talk about honesty and good faith, was then as plain as it is now—you were willing in the emergency to purchase the honest action of a Republican blackguard, who knew the right, but would still the wrong pursue, unless he was paid for doing his duty. . . . But I am ashamed of your company. To concoct even justice with the help of Johnny Coyle and Pelton is too much. Uncle Sammy deserved to be beaten for his choice of friends" (Library of Congress, Manton Marble MSS, Vol. 52, no. 11361).

CHAPTER I

The Struggle
for the
Republican Nomination

March 5, 1877 was significant for two reasons. It saw
the peaceful inauguration of Hayes and heard the opening gun
in the bitter war for the Republican presidential nomination of
1880. Hayes had stumped Ohio in 1872 for the corrupt Grant
machine. In spite of this he had been accepted by the Schurz
faction as a reform candidate. If Hayes was anxious for a second term, he carefully concealed his intentions, for he immediately alienated both the Conkling Stalwarts and the Blaine
Half-Breeds. Conkling had ambitions for the Department of
State for himself and had asked for the Post Office Department
for his lieutenant, Thomas C. Platt. Neither he nor Platt entered
the official family of Hayes. Blaine had urged his friend William P. Frye for the Cabinet, only to be ignored. Simon Cameron of Pennsylvania had demanded the retention of his son,
Don Cameron, as secretary of war. Hayes refused to respond to
this pressure. Instead of Conkling, Evarts got the State Department. Schurz, secretary of the interior under Hayes, suggested
Evarts. Instead of Platt, David M. Key, ex-Confederate and
Tilden Democrat from Tennessee, became postmaster general.
Instead of Cameron, George W. McCrary of Iowa became secre-

tary of war. John Sherman, who had done so much to nominate Hayes, was rewarded by being given the Department of the Treasury. Not only had Hayes antagonized Blaine by refusing to elevate Frye, but the Sherman appointment was salt to Blaine's wounds. For Sherman, more than anyone else, had hurt Blaine at Cincinnati in 1876.[1]

Hayes lost no time in recalling the federal troops from the South. As a consequence, by April 1877 the Republican administration in both South Carolina and Louisiana had been ousted. Democratic governments were quickly installed in their places. To the regular Republican Stalwarts, as well as to the Blaineites, this action on the part of Hayes was nothing less than treason to the Grand Old Party. With the pacification of the South an accomplished fact, "His Fraudulency," as Roscoe Conkling styled Hayes, turned his attention to a reform program.[2] By June 1877 Schurz had appointed a board to investigate the Bureau of Indian Affairs. The government was paying $6,000,000 a year in an effort to solve the Indian problem. Schurz's investigating committee reported that the bureau was "simply a license to cheat and swindle the Indians in the name of the United States of America."[3] Officeholders on small salaries were performing the miracle of getting rich. Scandals and small wars were commonplace. Schurz dismissed the Indian commissioner and effected a complete reorganization of the Indian bureau. The decline in Indian disturbances was immediately apparent.[4] June was hardly over when Hayes turned from the thieves who

---

[1] Eckenrode, *Hayes*, p. 244. See also Donald B. Chidsey, *The Gentleman from New York: A Life of Roscoe Conkling*, p. 237 (New Haven: Yale University Press, 1935). McCrary had been one of Hayes's chief counselors before the Electoral Commission. For Sherman's antipathy to Blaine see Matthew Josephson, *The Politicos: 1865-1896*, p. 215 (New York: Harcourt, Brace and Company, 1938).

[2] Josephson, *Politicos*, p. 238.

[3] Eckenrode, *Hayes*, p. 266.

[4] Fuess, *Schurz*, pp. 255-57.

preyed on the Indians to Roscoe Conkling and the New York customhouse. Conkling had conveniently contracted malaria during the campaign of 1876 and had not hesitated to assert that Tilden had really been elected. This of course did not endear him to Hayes and his reformers. John Sherman, acting for Hayes, appointed a commission in the summer of 1877 to investigate the customhouse service in New York. The collector of the customs in New York was Chester A. Arthur. The naval officer was Alonzo B. Cornell. Both belonged to the Conkling machine. The Sherman investigation revealed abuses. Hayes was determined to oust both Arthur and Cornell. This would violate what Senator Conkling called "senatorial courtesy." In practice this meant that the chief executive usually acceded to the wishes of the senators with regard to appointments in their states. The real issue came down to the control of federal appointments. Would the president control them or would the senators? Conkling blustered and fumed. He coined new expressions of contempt for the president; he became "Granny Hayes with his Snivel Service."[5] Lord Roscoe, as Conkling's enemies frequently called him, campaigned in the cloakroom of the Senate and speedily won the sympathy of his fellow senators. By a majority of thirty-five to twenty-one the Senate upheld Arthur and Cornell. Conkling's victory, however, was but a temporary one; for when Congress adjourned in the late summer of 1878, the executive arm struck again in an effort to destroy the New York machine. In a special message to the Senate on January 31, 1879 Hayes regarded it as his plain duty "to suspend the officers in question and to make the nominations now before the Senate, in order that this important office may be honestly and efficiently administered."[6] Under the impact of this message

---

[5] Stoddard, *Presidential Sweepstakes*, p. 85.

[6] James D. Richardson, editor, *A Compilation of the Messages and Papers of the Presidents*, Vol. 7, p. 512. Washington: Government Printing Office, 1898.

the Senate reversed itself, and on February 3, 1879 upheld the new nominees: E. A. Merritt and Silas W. Burt.[7] The new officers took up their duties on July 20, and Arthur and Cornell moved out. Conkling seethed with anger. It was war to the death between himself and the Hayes coterie.

The senator from New York was not alone in his criticism of the new administration. Both John Hay and Whitelaw Reid, ardent supporters of Blaine, entertained serious doubts concerning the new reform. Hay was sure that not even Boss Tweed himself had ever attempted to run an administration in the interest of his own crowd as this "model reformer" had done. Reid felt that it was not the president so much as the greenhorns in his Cabinet who were causing all the trouble. It was his conviction that the administration was in deep water, and that the storm would break first on Schurz, who he felt certainly first deserved it.[8]

John Hay's reflections on Hayes were to be shared by others a few months later. For in November 1879 Conkling, eager to prove that he still retained the leadership in his own state, supported the recently chastened Cornell for governor of New York. The administration heads, John Sherman, secretary of the treasury, and William M. Evarts, secretary of state, immediately stumped New York for Cornell. The fact that Cornell had but three months previously been removed for dishonesty as naval officer of the port of New York was conveniently forgotten by Hayes and his reformers. More than a few eyebrows were raised and at least one Republican expressed his disbelief that the administration would go so far.[9] Cornell was elected;

---

[7] George F. Howe, *Chester A. Arthur: A Quarter-Century of Machine Politics*, pp. 90-92. New York: Dodd, Mead and Company, 1934.

[8] Royal Cortissoz, *The Life of Whitelaw Reid*, Vol. 1, p. 389. New York: Charles Scribner's Sons, 1921.

[9] Library of Congress, Carl Schurz MSS, John P. G. Smith to Carl Schurz, October 30, 1879.

and a few months later George W. Curtis, editor of *Harper's Weekly*, stressed the crucial importance of the vote of New York in the presidential election of the coming year.[10] Conkling and Cornell, because of their influence in a state with so many electoral votes, would indeed be very important in Republican plans to retain the White House in 1880.

Conkling had made a governor. Why couldn't he make a president? If Grant would only let him, Lord Roscoe would see to it that the general was nominated and elected for a third term. But the hero of Appomattox had already defied orders and committed a serious political blunder. In spite of the importunities of Conkling, Grant had returned from his world tour six months sooner than had been planned. The reason he always assigned for this was that his wife wanted to see her children.[11] Grant arrived in San Francisco late in September 1879 after a twenty-six months' absence from the United States. The man who twenty years before had pawned his watch for the Christmas holidays had just finished spending over $100,000 in visiting the world capitals.[12] His remark that Venice would be a pretty city if it were only drained has never failed to provide a good-natured laugh. News of the great American railroad strikes reached Grant while in England. He remarked, half hopefully, that what America needed was a strong man and that he felt he might be called back by the emergency.[13]

From his landing in San Francisco in September 1879 until the following January, Grant moved across the country in a slow triumphal procession. Hamilton Fish, his former secretary of state, remarked that General Grant's return was calling out a

---

10 *Harper's Weekly* 24:2, January 3, 1880.

11 Adam Badeau, *Grant in Peace: From Appomattox to Mount McGregor. A Personal Memoir*, p. 317. Hartford: S. S. Scranton and Company, 1887.

12 Badeau (*ibid.*, pp. 307-14) gives an interesting and intimate account of Grant's world tour.

13 Hesseltine, *Grant*, pp. 430-31.

very enthusiastic reception in every part of the country that he visited, very much to the disturbance of Democratic hopes.[14]

George S. Davis, Republican congressman from Illinois, expressed the feelings of the majority of Americans when he said: "I believe that if the nomination were to be made tomorrow Grant would be the nominee, but I don't see anything that is liable to occur between now and the day of the nomination that will decrease his strength."[15]

But by the first of the year there were visible signs of change in the political skies. Elihu B. Washburne, former minister to France and considered by many to be Grant's political protégé, heard of a decided reaction to the Grant flood tide, with prospects of an imminent ebb. Some said that Grant's early homecoming had damaged his presidential chances, while others blamed it on his lengthy stay in Philadelphia.[16]

If Grant objected to the boom that was being manufactured for him, he managed to maintain a discreet silence. George Jones, editor of the *New York Times,* quoted a "near personal and political friend" of Grant's to the effect that Grant did not desire the nomination. But, added the friend cautiously, Grant would deem it his duty to accept if the Republican nominating convention so desired.[17]

The *Times,* along with the *Chicago Tribune,* the *Boston Advertiser,* the *Hartford Courant and Post,* and the *Providence Journal,* were asserting that the people were looking to Grant "to extinguish smouldering animosity" and "silence partisan cries of hatred and distrust." The *Springfield Republican,* reputed to be one of the most impartial of late-nineteenth-century

---

[14] Library of Congress, Hamilton Fish MSS, Letter Book, Hamilton Fish to Nicolas Fish, November 13, 1879.

[15] *New York Times,* October 2, 1879.

[16] Library of Congress, Elihu B. Washburne MSS, Charles H. T. Collis to E. B. Washburne, January 14, 1880.

[17] *New York Times,* February 10, 1880.

newspapers, commented that such expressions amounted to but a "beautiful fiction of sentiment to dress up Grant's candidature as something else than a revival of stalwartism."[18]

Murat Halstead, editor of the *Cincinnati Commercial*, was, together with Carl Schurz, ready to abandon the Grand Old Party for the Democratic party should Grant be nominated. He believed that the politicians were deceiving themselves in thinking that the people were for Grant. Sherman and Blaine, he was sure, were not conceding the fight to the general.[19] John W. Frazier was sure that Sherman would be chosen, and wrote:

> As there is [sic] not likely to be any idiots in the Chicago Convention I fail to see how Hayes is to get his name again placed in the nomination. . . . John Sherman is the only Republican that can carry New York.[20]

Hayes was not anxious for a repeat performance, and formally announced his retirement from politics before the Chicago convention. John Sherman, the administration candidate, was confident that the contest between Grant and Blaine in New York and Pennsylvania was so bitter that the inexpediency of the nomination of either would soon be acknowledged. Sherman was determined to stand firmly on his candidacy. He thought that it was the aim of Grant and Blaine to force his withdrawal from the contest. He would rely on the support of business to defeat this move.[21]

Sherman was correct in his assumption that he would have the backing of big business in his drive for the presidency. Samuel B. Dick, a Pennsylvania banker, gave assurances that such support for Sherman would be forthcoming.[22] The *London*

---

[18] *Springfield Republican*, December 24, 1879.

[19] *Cincinnati Commercial*, November 16, 1879.

[20] Library of Congress, John Sherman MSS, John W. Frazier to John Sherman, December 31, 1879.

[21] *Ibid.*, John Sherman to George C. Tichenor, February 19, 1880.

[22] *Ibid.*, Samuel B. Dick to John Sherman, November 23, 1879.

Times, which was so often a spokesman for British banking interests, declared:

> The claims of Secretary Sherman to popular support are on
> the whole deserving of sympathy . . . the revival of business is now
> a fact . . . if the Government had not pursued a prudent and steady
> course in dealing with the currency . . . the revival would have
> been delayed.[23]

The thought persisted in the minds of many people both here
and abroad that the prosperity that revisited America in 1878
was almost wholly due to Sherman's cleverness in bringing
about a resumption of specie payments. The panic of 1873 left
in its wake widespread unemployment and financial instability.
The credit of the United States in the early seventies was none
too good. As a remedy Congress enacted a law in January of
1875 by which the resumption of specie payments would be
accomplished by January 1, 1879. This resumption was necessary, as Sherman pointed out, to restore European confidence
in American credit. The popular conception of resumption was
that, as soon as the government paid out gold for greenbacks,
there would be a general rush for the yellow metal, thus neces-
sitating the redemption of the entire paper currency at once.
Sherman sold $140,000,000 of bonds for gold; that is, about
40 per cent of the outstanding greenbacks. Having done this, he
felt quite sure that he had secured ample coin for all his needs.
He was right. For on the first day of 1879, while a skeptical
Europe looked on, windows opened in the appointed places for
exchanging good gold for worn-out paper. There was no rush
at all. The people, satisfied that they could get gold if they so
desired, preferred paper as more convenient. American credit
was on the heights again after the immense expenditures of the
Civil War period. The credit belonged mainly to Sherman, but

---

23 *London Times*, October 15, 1879.

no historian can fail to record the part played both by a bountiful nature and by war in the restoration of American prosperity. Our crops were full in 1878; and the Russo-Turkish War, starting in March 1878 and ending in the summer of that same year, created a European demand for our breadstuffs and cotton.[24]

On October 10, 1879 George C. Tichenor, a Sherman agent in the New Orleans treasury department, reminded his chief that the resumption of specie payments was an immense boost to the prestige of the Republican party and a great impetus to prosperity. It was natural, then, that the needs of the hour called for the wise man who had achieved this boon.[25]

Besides the backing of big business, Sherman possessed a mighty weapon in his control of a large patronage. This was no inconsiderable means by which loyal delegates could be obtained for the coming convention in June. The followers of James G. Blaine believed that they were being slowly but surely decimated by Sherman's powerful but "invisible" methods. William E. Chandler was informed in a letter of January 30, 1880, from W. E. Horne that Cuney went out of the treasury because he was inimical to Sherman's presidential aspirations.[26] The W. E. Chandler papers contain numerous letters of which

---

[24] James F. Rhodes, *History of the United States*, Vol. 8, pp. 98-99. New York: The Macmillan Company, 1920.

[25] John Sherman MSS, George C. Tichenor to John Sherman, October 10, 1879.

[26] Chandler MSS, W. E. Horne to William E. Chandler, January 30, 1880. Horne continues: "This Department [the Treasury] for some time past has been made to feel the chilly air from aeolian caverns where Sherman holds his court. This invisible agent has been effective in stifling all opposition, and where it has manifested itself political suffocation and death follows. . . . If John Sherman has a real, honest, manly supporter I do not know him. . . . He will come to grief in the convention and be found without other than a purchased support. His treatment of Cuney and others of similar status, will at the proper time become a calcium light and his lean lank cadaverous carcass will be left without a shadow to hide it from the closest scrutiny." The Cuney referred to was J. Cuney, deputy collector of internal revenue, Texas, First District. See *Official Register of the United States*, p. 95 (Washington: Government Printing Office, 1879).

this one is typical. Many thought that Sherman was following literally the advice of M. M. Shelly, the editor and publisher of the *American Pathfinder,* who counseled him in these words:

> If you wish to compete in the coming Presidential contest you must first get rid of every man in the departments who favors any other candidate . . . if you do not know how to distinguish friends from enemies I could tell you in five minutes and it can be done in such a manner that they would never know it. . . . My only reason for writing you is to benefit you for the good you have done the Country in a financial sense.[27]

Blaine, the man from Maine, after having served for six years as the acknowledged leader of the House, was sworn in as a member of the United States Senate in December 1876. With the opening of the Forty-fifth Congress in March 1877, he moved up into the Senate chamber only two seats away from Roscoe Conkling. When in the autumn of 1877 Lord Roscoe poured out his sarcastic invective against "Rutherfraud" B. Hayes for his assault on the Republican party in the name of reform, the Plumed Knight gave tacit approval. For Blaine, as Garfield recorded in his diary, believed civil-service reform to be so much humbug.[28]

When the House passed the Chinese Exclusion Act on January 28, 1879, by a vote of 155 to 72, Blaine, with his eyes on California delegates to Chicago, gave the bill his hearty support in the Senate.[29] Garfield, who strongly advised Hayes to veto the bill, was sure that Blaine had made a great mistake in his advocacy of it.[30] A half-century later a competent American historian

---

[27] John Sherman MSS, M. M. Shelly to John Sherman, December 26, 1879.

[28] Library of Congress, James A. Garfield MSS, Diary, December 1, 1872. Charles A. Dana, editor of the *New York Sun,* is responsible for the word "Rutherfraud." Robert Ingersoll had majestically referred to Blaine as the Plumed Knight in his famous nominating speech in the convention of 1876.

[29] *Congressional Record,* 45th Cong., 3d Sess., 800-01, 1299-1303.

[30] Theodore Clarke Smith, *Life and Letters of James Abram Garfield,* Vol. 2, p. 677. New Haven: Yale University Press, 1925.

wrote: "To gain friends on the Pacific Coast he [Blaine] had ostentatiously espoused the cause of the rabble in California against the Chinaman."[31] But the most spectacular event of Blaine's senatorial years, and the one which was to make him an available candidate for the presidential nomination, occurred far from the halls of Congress.

In the September 1878 elections in Maine a fusion of Greenbackers and Democrats had elected a Democratic governor, Alonzo H. Garcelon. At the next annual election on September 8, 1879 the Republicans received a clear majority in the legislature. The fusionists then set about to falsify the returns. In their eagerness to retain control of the statehouse and re-elect Garcelon, they threw out the names of thirty-seven Republicans duly elected to the legislature. Blaine, who for twenty years had been chairman of the Maine Republican committee, and who was accustomed to predict with uncanny accuracy the Republican majorities, saw his dictatorship threatened. Leaving the Senate floor, he made straight for Augusta, determined to dislodge the fusionists and to preserve Maine for the Republicans in the approaching presidential campaign of 1880.

The usually quiet capital on the banks of the Kennebec seemed transformed into a Charleston, South Carolina, during the dark days of Reconstruction. The fusionists posted armed men in front of the statehouse as an effective barrier against any Republican who might aspire to take his recently won seat. Just across the street was the Blaine mansion, where armed Republicans took counsel with their leader. Although Blaine vetoed the use of force, there was still imminent danger that a shot from either of the hostile factions would precipitate a bloody riot. The tension was finally removed when Governor Garcelon, sensing the rising tide of indignation against his bogus legisla-

---

31 Ellis P. Oberholtzer, *A History of the United States since the Civil War*, Vol. 4, p. 61. New York: The Macmillan Company, 1931.

ture, agreed to a legal settlement. The case was submitted to the Supreme Court of the state. The judges upheld the Republican claims, and the excluded members took their seats and promptly elected a Republican governor.

The Plumed Knight returned to Washington wearing the laurels of the Maine victory. The "Blaine legion" throughout the country felt that they had a magnificent new issue which would go a long way toward obliterating the memory of Little Rock and Fort Smith Railroad bonds and the Mulligan letters.[32] The Republican nominating convention was but five months away. Yet William E. Chandler was anxious and wrote to Mrs. Blaine that he had not yet recovered from the shock of Don Cameron's election. The subservience of the Pennsylvania legislature in electing the younger Cameron for the remaining two years of his father's term as senator meant that the Camerons and therefore the Conklingites controlled the Keystone State. If Cameron had been defeated, Blaine's forces, he felt, would have very nearly captured the Pennsylvania delegation. But the anti-Grant, pro-Blaine men were fighting without a leader. They were very valiant but were flopping about like chickens with their heads cut off. Chandler expressed the hope that Blaine would "mount the saddle instead of running alongside holding on to Grant's stirrup."[33]

Just as the *New York Times* gave Grant its wholehearted support, so the *New York Tribune* was a staunch advocate of Blaine. Wrote Whitelaw Reid, the *Tribune's* editor:

> Halstead is extremely anxious to have the National Convention meet in Cincinnati, on the ground that this is the best place to

---

[32] David S. Muzzey, *James G. Blaine: A Political Idol of Other Days*, pp. 156-57. New York: Dodd, Mead and Company, 1934.

[33] Library of Congress, James G. Blaine MSS, William E. Chandler to Mrs. Blaine, January 17, 1880. Don Cameron was elected to the United States Senate from Pennsylvania. He was the son of Simon Cameron, who had been secretary of war under Lincoln.

check the Grant movement and that it will be as good a place as
any other for Mr. Blaine . . . [and for] feeling . . . enthusiasm . . .
which might be helpful by way of demonstration in the galleries
beforehand. He says frankly that he is for Sherman, but that Sherman and Blaine ought to be each for the other as against Grant.[34]

The Blaineites and the Conklingites saw eye to eye on both
the civil-service and the Southern questions. Their feelings were
expressed by Harman C. Westervelt, who wrote that the Republican party ought to be "shorn of its Tylers and Johnsons." The
need was for "reliable men, those that will not trick us after a
victory, in establishing platforms of their own."[35]

It is not surprising, then, in view of the common ground
occupied by the Blaine and Conkling followers, that there
should be an attempt at rapprochement between these two factions of the Republican party. Mrs. H. C. Ingersoll, commenting
on a letter published by Blaine's manager in the *Cincinnati
Commercial*, asserted that, while every line suited her remark-
ably well, there were two points that were outstanding. The first
was that Chandler gave Sherman a blow that would eliminate
him as a presidential candidate. The second was the fact that
Chandler, the friend of Blaine, came out for Conkling as his
second choice, for Mrs. Ingersoll thought that Conkling was
"head and shoulders above the other candidates in ability."[36]

But the "turkey-gobbler" speech still rankled, and Conkling
was as intransigent as Blaine was adaptable. By March the

---

[34] Chandler MSS, Whitelaw Reid to William E. Chandler, December 13, 1879. The
brackets and insert are mine. Murat Halstead, editor of the *Cincinnati Commercial*, was so anti-Grant that he proposed to support the Democrats if Grant
were nominated.

[35] *Ibid.*, Harman C. Westervelt to William E. Chandler, December 2, 1879. Westervelt was a Republican attorney, for many years a trusted employee of the
United States Treasury at Washington.

[36] *Ibid.*, Mrs. H. C. Ingersoll to William E. Chandler, December 5, 1879. The
"blow" consisted in calling attention to Sherman's allegiance to the Southern Democrats. Mrs. H. C. Ingersoll was not related to the well-known
Robert G. Ingersoll.

"Blaine brigade" was convinced that William E. Chandler's suggestion not to conduct his fight in a way that would antagonize the Grant supporters must be at once abandoned. The Grant men must be fought. They would go for Blaine as soon as it was seen that he had a reasonable chance to win.[37]

Having failed to unite with Conkling, Blaine then moved in the direction of Sherman. A. N. Cole, a member of the New York Republican Reform League, acted as a sort of liaison officer between Sherman and Blaine. Cole confessed that he was "fearfully tried" with both Sherman and Evarts for coming to New York and saving "that scandalous ticket." Yet, upon reflection, his cooler judgment told him that they had acted wisely in doing so.[38]

After a series of protracted conferences between himself and Blaine, Cole was finally able to construct some sort of an *entente cordiale*. He exclaimed gleefully to Sherman:

> Thank Heaven for the agreement between your friends and those of Mr. Blaine. . . . I am morally certain that if Mr. Blaine becomes convinced that he cannot this time succeed, he will ask his friends to go over to you in a body.[39]

Blaine might well have kept this bargain, but a dark horse appeared at Chicago and overshadowed Sherman. Prior to the Republican nominating convention in June 1880, the press of the country was convinced that there were but three possibilities: the Stalwart Grant, the Half-Breed Blaine, or the administration candidate Sherman. But an examination of the private papers of the leading politicians of the time reveals that there was a strong movement afoot to nominate Garfield. No one was more aware of this than Garfield himself, and his straddling role of

---

37 *Ibid.*, William H. Kemble to William E. Chandler, March 1, 1880.
38 John Sherman MSS, A. N. Cole to John Sherman, May 22, 1880. The reference is to the Conkling-sponsored Governor Cornell.
39 *Ibid.*, A. N. Cole to John Sherman, May 31, 1880.

assuming the responsibility of delegate at large for Sherman, as well as that of introducing Sherman's name before the convention, has long been a subject of controversy. As early as January 9, 1880 Garfield was receiving messages in support of his candidacy. One correspondent thought that "with John Sherman President, W. T. Sherman commander in chief of the Army, Don Cameron Dictator of Pennsylvania, chairman of Republican committee, etc., [it] is *too much* of one family *at one time.*" The same writer, although "quite a Blaine man," believed that Blaine and Conkling would denounce each other.[40]

J. P. Robinson, a wealthy Cleveland packing-house owner, flattered the hopes of Garfield by suggesting that "the dark horse" might pull ahead in the homestretch, and that Sherman stock was on the wane in the Cleveland sector while Blaine's prospects were improving.[41]

On January 6, 1880 Garfield was overwhelmingly elected United States senator from Ohio. J. W. Tyler summed up the situation when he wrote that John Sherman wanted Garfield to be senator and the result was Garfield's unanimous nomination and election. Reciprocity would seem to oblige Garfield to work hard for Sherman's nomination in the coming Republican presidential convention. At least this would appear to have been Sherman's thinking.[42]

In late January, Garfield recommended to Senator R. A. Horr that Ohio should back the nomination of Sherman at the Chicago convention.[43] The reverberations were immediate. So persistent were Garfield's friends in denouncing the idea of

---

[40] Garfield MSS, S. P. Wolcott to J. A. Garfield, January 9, 1880. In 1878 Don Cameron married Elizabeth Sherman, niece of John and William T. Sherman.

[41] *Ibid.*, J. P. Robinson to J. A. Garfield, February 16, 1880. Blaine "raided" Ohio and captured nine delegates there. Senator Garfield did not even win his own district, the nineteenth, for Sherman.

[42] John Sherman MSS, J. W. Tyler to Sherman, January 15, 1880.

[43] Garfield MSS, Diary, January 25, 1880. Senator Horr was a state senator in Ohio.

Sherman's candidacy that he became hesitant in putting his political shoulder to the wheel for Sherman.[44] This hesitancy apparently showed itself, for the thoroughgoing Shermanites evinced their anxiety at what appeared to be Garfield's cooling toward the cause. A member of the Ohio state legislature sought to obtain from Garfield an explicit avowal of his intentions relative to the re-election of convention delegates from one of the districts. Would Garfield, he asked, cooperate in returning Sherman delegates or would he not?[45] There were certain Ohio Republicans who were becoming increasingly nervous about Garfield's loyalty, and who endeavored to bring him back to the "general line."[46]

Murat Halstead was evidently not in the confidence of the powerful and wealthy machine that was studiously working for Garfield's nomination. He remarked caustically that Garfield, if he intended to give Sherman a "send-off" at Chicago, had better look to his own district. A man who possessed no influence at home, as was true of Garfield, said Halstead, would not make too much noise as a delegate at large.[47]

Ohio's Governor Charles Foster and Garfield were close friends, but neither was wholeheartedly supporting Sherman in his quest for the Republican nomination. Although both Foster and Garfield were committed to Sherman, Foster advised Garfield that "when the time comes (if it does come) to support another, then Ohio should wheel into line solidly for him." Foster was certain that from the foregoing Garfield would "un-

---

[44] An unknown correspondent wrote to Garfield: "Your letter relative to Hon. John Sherman I have read. I am sorry you wrote it. Mr. Sherman will never be President of the United States! . . . he cannot be elected . . . he is too far from the people . . . he has no elements of popularity and sympathy with the masses. . . . Ohio will never name another president until she names James A. Garfield!" (Garfield MSS, January 28, 1880).

[45] *Ibid.*, J. E. Thorp to Garfield, January 29, 1880.

[46] For example, see Garfield MSS, B. A. Hinsdale to Garfield, April 23, 1880.

[47] *Cincinnati Commercial*, May 9, 1880.

derstand why I have advised against the Cleveland Meeting in Sherman's interest at which you were to speak."[48]

Although the press of the country was almost certain of the nomination of Grant, Blaine, or Sherman, the Garfield diary revealed that in a talk with Governor Pound the Garfield candidacy appeared as a strong possibility.[49] A few weeks after this entry Wharton Barker, a Philadelphia banker, during a visit to Garfield, pointed out the improbability of the nomination of any of the three leading candidates and asserted that he and his friends were in favor of nominating Garfield.[50]

Even though John Sherman was the administration candidate, it is now apparent that he did not enjoy the support of President Hayes. For Hayes told Wharton Barker that Sherman was in the field only to prevent the nomination of Grant or Blaine. Hayes felt that the candidacy of Garfield would more probably result in a Republican victory.[51] Yet Sherman, in his political naïveté, was unable to perceive the forces behind the nomination machinery, for he revealed to one of his loyal supporters that he was sure of the solid support of Ohio.[52] Privately his own party leaders had expressed some doubt about this.

Secretary of the Interior Schurz, like President Hayes, gave Sherman mere lip service. Both Schurz and Hayes were fully

---

[48] Garfield MSS, Charles Foster to Garfield, February 23, 1880. At the time this letter was written Garfield had already been informed by Governor T. C. Pound and Barker that they intended to nominate him. Pound had been lieutenant governor of Wisconsin in 1870-1871. At this time he was a congressman from Wisconsin and the right-hand man of Elisha W. Keyes, the boss of the Republican machine in Wisconsin. Foster, governor of Ohio in 1880, was a delegate at large in the Republican convention in the same year.

[49] Garfield MSS, Diary, February 4, 1880.

[50] *Ibid.*, February 18, 1880. In his *Recollections* John Sherman says he never considered "the contingency of Garfield's nomination" (John Sherman, *Recollections of Forty Years in the House, Senate and Cabinet*, Vol. 2, p. 778 [New York: Werner Company, 1895]). In the Sherman papers there is no mention of shifting his support to Garfield.

[51] Garfield MSS, Diary, April 24, 1880.

[52] John Sherman MSS, John Sherman to George C. Tichenor, April 14, 1880.

informed of the Barker-Lea Committee for Garfield. As early as December 1879 Lea informed Schurz that he had lost confidence in Sherman.[53] Had Sherman been informed, by either Hayes or Schurz, of the Barker-Lea movement, he would have never chosen Garfield to represent him at Chicago. Barker, with Lea, constituted the heart and soul of the Union League, which supposedly represented the old Liberal Republican movement of the Greeley-Schurz days. It had been expected that the league would endorse the administration candidate. But Lockwood, writing from Philadelphia, warned Schurz that "Barker and Lea said we must defeat Sherman."[54]

There is no question that Sherman's availability was impaired by the fact that he was considered by many persons to be pro-Catholic. One of Garfield's closest friends and supporters, Edwin Cowles, editor of the *Cleveland Leader*, was "crazy on the subject of Catholicism," and any action that looked like favoring the Catholics shocked him into a mild panic. He was "nearly crazed by the conversion of his daughter to the Catholic faith," and "it took him nearly all night to tell . . . the story to a friend."[55]

Besides being editor of the *Cleveland Leader*, Cowles was the president of the Order of the American Union. The bias of this secret organization was brought to the attention of Rome, and on August 22, 1878 Cardinal Simeoni, prefect of the Propa-

---

[53] Schurz MSS, Henry C. Lea to Carl Schurz, December 8, 1879. Lea was a well-known medieval historian who entered the field of politics.

[54] *Ibid.*, E. D. Lockwood to Carl Schurz, January 22, 1880. T. J. McLain hinted that Sherman realized the extent of Garfield's presidential possibilities and felt that the best way to sidetrack Garfield would be to have him give the Sherman nomination speech. Writing to Garfield, McLain said that "it seems friend Sherman was bound to have you, whether or no, which evinced, from his standpoint, his usual political sagacity" (Garfield MSS, T. J. McLain to Garfield, May 25, 1880).

[55] John Sherman MSS, C. W. Moulton to John Sherman, January 8, 1880. Moulton was Sherman's brother-in-law. The Edwin Cowles papers are in the possession of the Cowles family.

ganda, wrote Cardinal Gibbons and asked him to investigate the OAU. Since Gibbons apparently knew nothing about this society, he inquired of Bishop Richard Gilmour of Cleveland. Gilmour reported that he had tried in vain to secure a copy of the order's constitution. He stated that the organization was so anti-Catholic that he was sure that no practicing Catholic held membership. Gilmour concluded by paying his respects to the *Cleveland Leader* which he said was a sheet of such a kind that there was "nothing too vile nor too false for its columns."[56]

William H. Van Nortwick, a member of the OAU, warned Sherman that "much of the active opposition to your Presidential candidacy, particularly in your own state of Ohio, comes from the organization known to the public as the O.A.U. I do not guess at this matter. . . . I know it."[57] He then quoted from a speech given at a recent meeting of the OAU:

> Political Romanism aims to destroy our system of public education—that system once overthrown, the destruction of civil and religious liberty must inevitably follow. If Sherman should attain to the Presidency, his brother's wife the most bitter and active Catholic in the country would have unlimited influence with the Administration and the politico-religious organization of Rome would profit thereby.[58]

Letter after letter appears in the Sherman collection advising him that his presidential possibilities were seriously weakened by the fact that his sister-in-law, Ellen Sherman, was a

---

56 John T. Ellis, *The Life of James Cardinal Gibbons*, Vol. 1, pp. 444-45. Milwaukee: Bruce Publishing Company, 1952.

57 John Sherman MSS, William H. Van Nortwick to John Sherman, March 22, 1880. Cowles asked Garfield to bring pressure on Sherman to reinstate a member of the OAU in the Treasury Department. Cowles cautioned Garfield not to "wait till your return from Chicago for then Mr. Sherman will not be so anxious to gratify you" (Garfield MSS, Edwin Cowles to Garfield, May 25, 1880).

58 John Sherman MSS, William H. Van Nortwick to John Sherman, March 22, 1880. For a short description of the Order of the American Union see Albert C. Stevens, editor, *The Cyclopaedia of Fraternities*, p. 317 (New York: Hamilton Press, 1907).

Catholic. Sherman was aware that Cowles was doing him "real harm by making honest people believe that I am more than half-Catholic." The "imputation of Cowles that I am at all under the control of Catholics is entirely false." Sherman pointed out that his sister-in-law Ellen Sherman had refused to write to him during the past three years on the grounds that he was prejudiced against herself and Catholics in general.[59]

It was being said that Sherman was a "Catholic bigot."[60] The charge was made that his appointment clerk was a Catholic and that no one could receive an appointment in the Treasury Department unless he was favorable, or at least acceptable, to the Catholic element. Sherman stated that he did not believe that among the appointments to the Department of the Treasury Catholics comprised as much as 2 per cent.[61]

As an evidence of his immunity to Catholic influence Sherman declared his strong opposition to "certain dogmas" of the Church. He believed that the wooing of the Democratic party by the Church was harmful to the country. He felt that Catholic opposition to the public-school system should be met with the most determined resistance. But, he asserted (mixing his theology with a bit of practical politics), the Catholic Church was most dangerous when it adopted the dogmas of the Democratic party.[62] The secretary of the National Sherman Committee warned that the Methodists were greatly concerned at the number of Catholic appointments made by Sherman's department. Sherman suggested that the blame for this should be laid to President Grant.[63] This seemed to satisfy the Methodists.[64] Sher-

---

[59] John Sherman MSS, John Sherman to James M. Hoyt, March 22, 1880.
[60] *Ibid.*, H. S. S. to John Sherman, January 3, 1880.
[61] *Ibid.*, John Sherman to James M. Hoyt, March 22, 1880 and Sherman to Hon. George H. Foster, March 1, 1880 (Sherman, *Recollections*, Vol. 2, p. 768).
[62] John Sherman MSS, John Sherman to William H. Van Nortwick, March 27, 1880.
[63] *Ibid.*, B. D. Fearing to John Sherman, April 11, 1880.
[64] *Ibid.*, B. D. Fearing to John Sherman, April 13, 1880.

man suffered also from his lack of an attractive personality, a deficiency which did not endear him to Hamilton Fish.[65]

Senator George F. Edmunds of Vermont had a considerable following in the New England states and represented, in the eyes of many, the real successor to Horace Greeley. He retired as a candidate, however, in favor of Grant just before the opening of the convention.[66]

Elihu B. Washburne was playing a role somewhat similar to Garfield's. As minister to France during the Franco-Prussian War, Washburne had ingratiated himself with the Germans of the Midwest by his efficient service to the German nationals trapped in Paris during the war. As early as October 1879 Murat Halstead—whose slogan was "Beat Grant at any cost"— wrote Washburne a significant if somewhat vague letter. He said: "Thou canst not say I did it. But I did what I could. It's Grant's turn now to do you a good turn. Don't you forget that."[67] It is possible that Halstead was referring to an assertion that the Associated Press had ascribed to Washburne:

> This morning's Tribune has an interview with you, wherein you affirm that an Associated Press dispatch was sent from Washington some weeks ago, in which it was stated that you had received from General Grant a letter declaring that he would not under any circumstances become a candidate for the Presidency. . . . No dispatch has ever been sent out to the Western Associated Press, from Washington or any other city, containing the statement that you had received a letter like that referred to. . . . A dispatch

---

[65] Fish MSS, Letter Book, Hamilton Fish to Henry G. Connor, May 7, 1880.

[66] Library of Congress, Justin S. Morrill MSS, J. S. Morrill to Governor Smith, May 20, 1880. See also *Cincinnati Commercial*, June 1, 1880. At the last minute Edmunds' name was proposed at the convention. He polled about thirty votes until the thirtieth ballot, when he was reduced to eleven (Stanwood, *Presidential Elections*, p. 361). Governor John Gregory Smith had been governor of Vermont during the Civil War. In this letter Vermont's Senator Morrill assures him that, if Edmunds could secure the nomination, all doubt of his election would be removed.

[67] Washburne MSS, Murat Halstead to E. B. Washburne, October 16, 1879.

was sent from this city to the Western Press at a subsequent date
setting forth the truth in the matter, namely that you had not received from the General a letter of the character alleged.[68]

If Grant had retired, it was felt by many that his strength
would have gone to Washburne. Washburne, like Garfield, was
referred to as a dark horse. The *San Francisco Bulletin*, under
the caption, "The Dark Horse in Politics," informed its readers
that Washburne would not run against Grant, nor would he decline the nomination if Grant was unsuccessful.[69]

But the friends of the two Galena gentlemen, Grant and
Washburne, did not work together. Washburne apparently could
not control his friends. In Cook County, Illinois, they united
with the Blaine men to block a solid delegation for Grant.
George Jones, editor of the *New York Times*, asked Washburne
to manifest his intentions.[70] Just as Garfield did next to nothing
in organizing his district for Sherman, so Washburne was
equally apathetic with regard to Grant. Emery A. Storrs pleaded
with Washburne to start working for Grant.[71] Adam Badeau,
Grant's intimate friend and secretary for many years, recorded
that the general always believed that Washburne had played
him false.[72]

According to William H. Smith, Washburne had been nurs-
ing a grudge against Grant for several years. Smith informed

[68] *Ibid.*, W. H. French (agent of the Western Associated Press) to E. B. Washburne, 1879 (month and day omitted in original).

[69] *San Francisco Bulletin*, February 18, 1880. Washburne informed the Long Island
Historical Society of his labors for the Germans in Paris. A month later,
when he should have been winning the Cook County, Illinois delegation for
Grant, he "took sick" and had to retire to Hot Springs. The delegation was
lost to Grant.

[70] *New York Times*, February 15, 1880. See also Washburne MSS, George Jones to
E. B. Washburne, May 14, 1880.

[71] Washburne MSS, Emery A. Storrs to E. B. Washburne, April 6, 1880. Storrs, a
Grant Republican from Chicago, was chief counsel for General Babcock. See
Isaac E. Adams, *Life of Emery A. Storrs* (Chicago: Hubbard Brothers, 1886).

[72] Badeau, *Grant*, p. 322.

President Hayes that at a dinner in March 1877 Washburne had been most outspoken against Grant, and had asserted that he would no longer be kicked about by the general.[73]

Senator William Windom of Minnesota was one of the last to cast his hat into the presidential ring. He was friendly to Sherman, but at the opportune moment in the convention went over to Garfield.[74] He replaced Sherman as secretary of the treasury. Before the Chicago convention the *Springfield Republican* thought that the Minnesota senator was "an honest but rather superficial and showy man."[75] Windom never received more than ten votes in the convention.[76]

On May 4, 1880 James Gordon Bennett, fiery editor of the *New York Herald,* proposed the name of Hamilton Fish for the presidency.[77] Grant's former secretary of state was agreeably surprised.[78] Hamilton Fish was not a "scratcher." He was for the Republican party, first, last, and always. Just before the Republican convention opened he declared his belief that the election would be hotly contested and that the result was doubtful. The Republican party was experiencing the pangs of age that befell all parties after long ascendancy in power. It was not so important, he said, whom the party elected, but it was vitally necessary that it elect someone.[79]

The next day E. B. Martindale, editor of the *Indianapolis Journal,* echoed Fish's sentiments perfectly: "The *Journal* is

---

[73] Hayes MSS, William H. Smith to Rutherford B. Hayes, November 1, 1879. For twenty-two years Smith was general manager of both the New York Associated Press and the Western Associated Press. He had acted as chief agent for Hayes in the Compromise of 1877. See Roseboom, *Presidential Elections,* p. 248.

[74] John Sherman MSS, John Sherman to George J. H. Baker, April 26, 1880. See also *San Francisco Bulletin,* March 25, 1881.

[75] *Springfield Republican,* May 7, 1880.

[76] Stanwood, *Presidential Elections,* p. 361.

[77] *New York Herald,* May 4, 1880.

[78] Fish MSS, Letter Book, Hamilton Fish to Henry G. O'Connor, May 7, 1880.

[79] *Ibid.,* Hamilton Fish to E. R. Hoar, May 27, 1880.

neither for Grant nor for Blaine nor for Sherman nor for any other man. It is for either of these if nominated at Chicago and for the Republican Party, first, last and always."[80] The *Springfield Republican*, however, would sign no blank check, and insisted that the nomination of either Grant or Blaine would be as disastrous to the party as to the nation.[81]

Carl Schurz, secretary of the interior, differed from Fish, Martindale, and the *Springfield Republican*. He apparently would take the devil himself rather than Grant.[82] There is abundant evidence that Schurz, in the event of Grant's nomination, was ready to campaign for the Democratic party.[83] The very mention of Schurz's name among Grant's loyal followers was enough to send them into an angry rage. The hero of Appomattox had a considerable Southern following. "General Grant whipped us like a brave soldier," proclaimed Stonewall Jackson, Jr., "but on our surrender treated us in the spirit of a Christian gentleman; and today the South honors him as their best of friends within the Ranks of the Republican Party." Jackson was in earnest. "Should General Grant be defeated through your vile calumnies," he declared to the secretary of the interior, "I will shoot you on sight."[84]

Schurz received Jackson's letter while he was contemplating an answer to the following query from Halstead: "Would it do any harm if I stated . . . that in case of the nomination of Grant you would instantly resign and take the stump in Ohio against him?"[85] Whether or not young Stonewall's admonition was one of the determining factors in Schurz's refusal to allow

80 *Indianapolis Journal,* May 28, 1880.
81 *Springfield Republican,* May 8, 1880.
82 Chandler MSS, Murat Halstead to W. E. Chandler, December 25, 1879.
83 Schurz MSS, Murat Halstead to Carl Schurz, May 3, 1880.
84 *Ibid.,* Stonewall Jackson, Jr., to Carl Schurz, May 26, 1880. The writer was not related to the great Stonewall. It may well have been just another crackpot letter.
85 *Ibid.,* Murat Halstead to Carl Schurz, May 3, 1880.

the *Cincinnati Commercial* to make his intentions public is not known for certain.

This popularity of Grant in the South disturbed some of the old-guard Republicans. Thurlow Weed was among the worried. He unbosomed himself on the subject to Simon Cameron, then one of the high-ranking officers in the Grant phalanx. Grant's systematic and adroit appeal to the Rebel element was, in his opinion, most unfortunate. It raised the possibility of his being elected as a result of concessions made to those very forces which were the traditional enemies of Republican principles. Weed felt that those who had been avowedly in rebellion were still rebels at heart.[86]

By this time Garfield had received and rejected the logic of Professor Hinsdale, and was torn between his pledged devotion to Sherman and his desire for the presidency. Charles Foster, governor of Ohio and delegate at large, was in a similar state of vacillation. In substance, Hinsdale's advice was that Garfield could not have it both ways. He was pledged to Sherman and therefore should work wholeheartedly for him. He could not at the same time work for himself.[87]

Although Sherman was sure that the Blaine men were willing to "make almost any arrangement," yet he had no way of knowing that the arrangement might mean the nomination of Garfield.[88] William E. Chandler, Blaine's manager, was indeed

---

[86] Library of Congress, Simon Cameron MSS, Thurlow Weed to Simon Cameron, April 29, 1880. Thurlow Weed desired the nomination of John Sherman. See John Sherman MSS, Thurlow Weed to Charles Foster, April 28, 1880.

[87] Continuing, Burke A. Hinsdale, a professor of philosophy at Hiram College and a lifelong friend of Garfield, advised him thus: "If your party wants you to go to Chicago, I think you should go; why not? You have published a letter saying Mr. Sherman should be Ohio's candidate for the nomination. . . . If you are sincere . . . your published letter logically involves your going to Chicago. . . . Austin was afraid you might get hurt . . . but that is simply part of the current cant and insincerity." See Garfield MSS, Hinsdale to Garfield, April 23, 1880 and Charles Foster to Garfield, May 10, 1880.

[88] John Sherman MSS, John Sherman to Nelson A. Miles, May 21, 1880.

not overlooking the possibilities of Garfield's nomination. There were others who encouraged Chandler in toying with this hope.[89] The fact that Chandler was enthusiastic over General Garfield's chances would seem to indicate that the Blaine men were aware of the Barker-Lea movement. On May 23, 1880, during the course of a long walk together, Blaine told Garfield that he did not expect the nomination at Chicago and would not have become a candidate but for his belief that he, more than anyone else, could block the nomination of Grant. On the whole he thought Grant's victory quite probable.[90] This represented a change in Blaine's thinking of a month before, when he had termed Grant's nomination "impossible" and expressed firm confidence in his own chances.[91] Garfield must have overcome his distrust of Blaine, inasmuch as he subsequently made him his secretary of state.

The Grant machine overlooked nothing that might increase its chances of success. It sought support from every faction except Blaine's. John Russell Young, who had accompanied General Grant on his world tour in the capacity of a reporter for Bennett's *New York Herald,* made an emotional appeal to William Tecumseh Sherman:

> I shall never forget when he came into my room at our palace . . . in Tokio, one morning very early, I only half dressed, and said "Read this letter from Sherman." It was the long letter you wrote him about the Presidency, when you spoke about the cruel position in which destiny seemed to be forcing you. John Sherman and Ulysses Grant as possible rivals in a Republican convention. . . . He was very much affected. The tears seemed to be in his eyes. Certainly he spoke like a man under deep emotion. "People may

---

[89] Chandler MSS, George O. Odlin to W. E. Chandler, April 14, 1880.
[90] Garfield MSS, Diary, May 23, 1880. Garfield's diary for this period shows his distrust of Blaine.
[91] *Ibid.,* April 14, 1880. A few days before this, William E. Chandler waxed enthusiastic over Garfield's chances.

wonder he said why I love Sherman—how could I help loving Sherman—and he has always been the same during the thirty-five years I have known him. He was so at West Point."

Young added in a postscript:

> Grant's election would be a great gain to the country. He would return to his high place with the inestimable advantage of knowing the whole world as no man living knows it. . . . The coming canvass . . . promises to be the most important in our history.[92]

Before this heart-to-heart correspondence with General Sherman, Young had tried his skill with General Benjamin F. Butler, who was told that General Grant held him in the highest esteem.[93] The compliment was reinforced with a check for $1,000 to Butler.[94] Simon Cameron, one of the Grant Stalwarts, was the sender of the donation, which was to aid Butler in the coming gubernatorial contest in Massachusetts. Butler failed to win; but the $1,000, in addition to Young's soft words, did not harm Grant's cause.

Those politicians who owed no allegiance either to the Blaine or Sherman camp and yet who vigorously opposed General Grant, were more inclined to follow Blaine than Sherman. For, as Frazier informed Sherman, that which gave Blaine his greatest hold on the politicians was the absolute certainty in every man's mind that, if elected, he would turn out the men whom Grant had commissioned in 1869, 1870, and 1871. For some unexplained reason Hayes had retained these men by reappointing them as their commissions expired.[95]

As late as May 1880 many of the leading newspapers in New York and in the Eastern states felt that John Sherman

---

[92] Library of Congress, William T. Sherman MSS, Letter Book, John R. Young to William T. Sherman, February 14, 1880.

[93] Library of Congress, Benjamin F. Butler MSS, John R. Young to Benjamin F. Butler, November 19, 1879.

[94] *Ibid.*, Simon Cameron to Benjamin F. Butler, October 28, 1879.

[95] John Sherman MSS, John W. Frazier to John Sherman, April 7, 1880.

would win the nomination as a compromise candidate. Sherman himself felt quite confident of this result.[96] His relations with Grant and Blaine were of a friendly character; and in case of a deadlock between these two, Sherman's chances of victory were extremely good. By the middle of April 1880 General John A. Logan, whose task it was to garner the solid vote of Illinois for Grant, was considering the possibility of the defeat of Grant. William H. Smith, a Sherman supporter who interviewed Logan for Sherman, concluded by saying that Logan finally remarked with some "emphasis and significance" that this "does not run counter to your interests and we may all get together and agree on the candidate who can defeat Mr. Blaine."[97] George C. Tichenor wrote from New Orleans and discussed the possibility of cooperation between the friends of Blaine and Sherman.[98]

It was May 1880, and the Republican convention was just one month away. Most American newspaper editors and many American politicians were convinced that Grant would be the nominee. On May 4 Hamilton Fish was of the opinion that General Grant would have a "decided majority in the Republican Convention."[99] Blaine, as late as May 23, had said that Grant's nomination was "quite probable."[100] The next day the *New Orleans Times* felt that there was very little question now about the nomination of Grant at Chicago.[101] On the following day Henry Watterson asserted that the nomination of Grant could be assumed.[102] On May 21 the *San Francisco Bulletin*, commenting upon the expert manner in which General Logan carried the

---

[96] Sherman, *Recollections*, Vol. 2, pp. 772-75.
[97] John Sherman MSS, William H. Smith to John Sherman, April 16, 1880.
[98] *Ibid.*, George C. Tichenor to John Sherman, May 28, 1880.
[99] Fish MSS, Letter Book, Hamilton Fish to Nicolas Fish, May 4, 1880.
[100] Garfield MSS, Diary, May 23, 1880.
[101] *New Orleans Times*, May 24, 1880.
[102] *Louisville Courier Journal*, May 25, 1880.

Illinois state convention for Grant, made a mathematical tabulation of votes and concluded that Grant, at that time, lacked only eight votes of the number required for the nomination.[103] The calculations of the *Bulletin* were based on the not unreasonable assumption that the unit rule would prevail at Chicago.[104] Senators Conkling, Cameron, and Logan had successfully applied the unit rule, in the interests of Grant, to the states of New York, Pennsylvania, and Illinois. George Jones became a veritable zealot in his defense of the rule.[105]

When on May 21 the Illinois Republican convention instructed its delegation to vote as a body for Grant, there were the usual animadversions by the anti-Grant factions on the wickedness of the unit rule. E. B. Martindale, however, did not think the rule was a particularly wicked one, and on May 22 taught his readers a lesson in history which he had learned from the proceedings of the Illinois state convention of 1860:

> Resolved that Abraham Lincoln is the choice of the Republican party of Illinois for the Presidency and the delegates for this State are instructed to use all honorable means to secure his nomination by the Chicago Convention and to vote as a unit for him.[106]

What was all right for the Great Emancipator was certainly all right for the greatest of his generals. At least so the "old guard" argued. The *San Francisco Bulletin,* while admitting that the unit rule was well established both by tradition and precedent, argued against it. "There can be no doubt," the *Bulletin* asserted, "of the right of a State Convention to instruct

---

[103] *San Francisco Bulletin,* May 21, 1880.

[104] *Ibid.,* May 28, 1880.

[105] *New York Times,* February 26, 1880. Wrote Jones: "The 70 delegates to the Chicago Convention who were chosen in Utica today are pledged absolutely to the support of General Ulysses S. Grant, and bound by every consideration of honor to obey their instructions and carry out the will of the Convention by which they are commissioned as was the case at Harrisburg a few weeks ago."

[106] *Indianapolis Journal,* May 22, 1880. Martindale was editor of this paper.

the four delegates at large which it has the power to elect." But delegates chosen by the congressional districts are not subject to the control of the convention. The *Bulletin* continued:

> The theory is . . . that they are elected by the people of their districts to go to the National Convention . . . the district delegates are seized as it were by the State Convention, in their passage to the National Convention, and are transformed into its representatives.[107]

Conkling, Cameron, and Logan finally succeeded in getting control of the Republican National Committee, with Cameron chosen as chairman. Prospects were favorable both for the unit rule and a Grant triumph. But to many, a Grant victory was synonymous with the establishment of a monarchy. The presence of Prince Leopold, son of Queen Victoria, at the convention was played up as an evidence of Grant's support by the crowned heads of Europe.[108] The observation of Curtis was more accurate. It was already evident, he said, that no candidate was the spontaneous choice of the party as Lincoln had been in 1864 and as Grant had been in 1868 and 1872, and the decision must be made on a careful calculation of expediency.[109]

As June 2 drew near, it was obvious to the politicians that, if the machine could enforce the unit rule, Ulysses S. Grant would be the nominee on the first ballot.

---

[107] *San Francisco Bulletin*, May 3, 1880.

[108] John Sherman MSS, James Harvey to John Sherman, May 29, 1880.

[109] *Harper's Weekly* 24:322, May 22, 1880. When Conkling opposed the administration on the issue of the removal of Cornell and Arthur from their positions as officials of the port of New York, Curtis, editor of *Harper's*, lashed out at the boss of New York in editorial after editorial.

CHAPTER II

Democratic Struggles
for Nomination

Samuel Jones Tilden might well have been the nineteenth
president of the United States. Many feel that he was really
elected to that office. When in 1879 he was urged to run for
governor of New York, he refused on the ground that it would
be incongruous for a president-elect to run for a state office.[1]
After Hayes took his inaugural oath on March 5, 1877, it would
have been platitudinous to assert that Tilden would be the Democratic candidate in 1880.[2] For, as the Democratic party argued,
how could the American people undo the great fraud of 1876
unless they elected the one who had been defrauded?

But Tilden had lost more than the presidency in 1876. From
the strain of the contest he emerged with a shattered constitution. His left hand was paralyzed by arthritis. He suffered from
"numb palsy" or paralysis agitans, a disease which increased

---

[1] Flick, *Tilden*, p. 445.

[2] March 4 was a Sunday. Hayes had received anonymous letters warning him that
he would never be inaugurated. In February 1877, while Hayes was taking
dinner with his family, a bullet entered the parlor window. Missing Hayes,
it passed through two parlors and an open door to burrow into the library
wall (Williams, *Hayes*, Vol. 2, pp. 1-2). An attempt was also made to
assassinate Hayes on the day of his inauguration. The would-be assassin was
disarmed before he could fire (Rutherford B. Hayes Memorial Library,
Thomas C. Donaldson MSS, Memoirs, April 7, 1880).

in violence during the remainder of his life. His gait was slow and shuffling, and his face bore an unhealthy, yellowish appearance. His voice, never resonant, was now but little more than a hoarse whisper. Physically he was a broken-down old man; but mentally he was still keen, and his eyes reflected his sharp intellectual reactions. All his life he had relied inordinately on drugs, and at this period he was constantly looking for some new nostrum for an upset stomach, a headache, trembling hands, or swollen joints.[3] Tilden's medical adviser, Dr. Austin Flint, recommended rest and moderate exercise for his patient, and Tilden sailed for England on July 18, 1877.

Grant was at this time being feted in England, and some of the Democratic leaders thought that Tilden should not make the trip. They feared that the whole American diplomatic corps would be instructed to see to it that there were no Tilden demonstrations in England and on the Continent, and this might weaken Tilden's candidacy for 1880.[4]

Tilden returned to New York on October 25, 1877. On the following evening he was given a dinner by the Young Men's Democratic Club. His address to the group was a veritable clarion call to a dispirited party. After referring to the "great fraud" of 1876, which had "stabbed the very foundations of free government," he called upon the young men to unite with him in the defense of their sacred inheritance of democracy. Would they, he asked, "mark those wrongdoers of 1876 with the indignation of a betrayed . . . and sacrificed people?" Would they support the cause which he represented, "which has embraced the largest and holiest interests of humanity"?[5]

---

[3] Flick, *Tilden*, p. 417.
[4] New York Public Library, Samuel J. Tilden MSS, A. C. Beach to S. J. Tilden, June 7, 1877.
[5] John Bigelow, editor, *Letters and Literary Memorials of Samuel J. Tilden*, Vol. 2, pp. 562-65 (New York: Harper and Brothers, 1908). Tilden's will commissioned Bigelow to publish such letters as he thought expedient.

Henry Watterson, editor of the *Louisville Courier Journal* and the recipient of frequent subsidies from Tilden, congratulated his chief on the speech, but added that he should have castigated the traitors in his own party.[6] By traitors Watterson meant the presidential aspirants Bayard and Thurman, for these two gentlemen had taken part in the Electoral Commission against the wishes of Tilden.

If Tilden did not heed this advice, he at least permitted his friends to speak for him. For in April and June 1878 Watterson directed a barrage of accusations against Bayard, Thurman, and Hewitt.[7] Manton Marble, another close adherent of Tilden, published a letter in the *New York Sun* on August 5 which increased the violence of the assault. The letter recounted the alleged treachery of the Electoral Commission and told of the stab in the back the "great reformer" had received from Bayard, Thurman, and Hewitt. It was Marble's charge, in brief, that Hewitt and his partners of the Senate committee had railroaded the Electoral Commission bill through without consulting Tilden until the deed was accomplished.[8]

Three days after the appearance of Marble's letter the editor of the *New York World* telegraphed to Bayard and re-

---

[6] Tilden MSS, Henry Watterson to Samuel J. Tilden, November 5, 1877. For Watterson's debt to Tilden see *ibid.*, H. W. to Samuel J. Tilden, August 2, 1880.

[7] Nevins, *Writings of Hewitt*, pp. 183-92.

[8] *New York Sun*, August 5, 1878. It reads in part: "Before he read the new bill Mr. Tilden was told by Mr. Hewitt that the Democratic members of the Senate Committee were already absolutely committed to it, and would concur with their Republican associates in reporting it to the Senate, whether the House Committee should concur or not. Isn't it rather late, then, said Mr. Tilden, to consult me? They do not consult you, replied Mr. Hewitt. They are public men and have their own duties and responsibilities. I consult you." Dana was the editor of the *Sun*. He owed Tilden $45,000. (See Tilden MSS, Dana to Tilden, August 4, 1880.) In Allan Nevins, *Abram S. Hewitt, with Some Account of Peter Cooper*, pp. 334-35 (New York: Harper and Brothers, 1935) there is an account of Tilden's meetings with Thurman and Bayard. According to Nevins, Tilden left the two senators with the impression that the only course open was one of arbitration.

quested an interview for the purpose of discussing the charges.[9]
Bayard sent a terse reply: "Interview undesirable. The history
and motives of my actions on electoral commission seem above
the comprehension of Mr. Tilden and his agents."[10]

The lights in the Tilden camp began to burn brighter and
brighter. The Tildenites were not content with these attacks upon
distinguished Democrats. Their purpose was to cloud as much
as possible the title of Hayes to the presidency and thus
strengthen the chances of Tilden in the election of 1880. After
a hard-fought struggle in the House, Clarkson N. Potter, with
Tilden's approval, had a special committee appointed on May
20, 1878 to reinvestigate the frauds and corruption of the recent
presidential election. Potter, an ardent Tilden henchman, was
appointed chairman of the committee, and important discoveries
adverse to Hayes were counted upon with confidence.[11]

With the White House lost and his health broken, Tilden's
cup was indeed bitter. But he was yet to suffer the stigma of the
cipher dispatches. The Potter committee did its work well. It
uncovered sensational evidence of Republican corruption, which
did much to vindicate Tilden in the public mind. Early in 1877,
however, the Western Union had surrendered to Congress about
thirty thousand telegrams which had been sent by both Democratic and Republican leaders during the campaign and afterward. The Republican Senate adroitly managed to return the
Republican telegrams to Western Union, where they were dis-
creetly burned. But the Republican leaders retained some 750
Democratic telegrams. If Tilden insisted on exposures, the Republicans were quick to assure him that two could play at that
game. These Democratic telegrams were given to the *New York
Tribune*, where they were deciphered. They were published at

---

[9] Bayard MSS, Schuyler to Bayard, August 8, 1878.
[10] *Ibid.*, Bayard to Schuyler, August 8, 1878. See Barnard, *Hayes*, pp. 339-40 for
Tilden's suspicions of Bayard.
[11] *Congressional Record*, 45th Cong., 2d Sess., 3438.

the psychological moment in October 1878 and brought disgrace on Tilden's nephew, William T. Pelton, on Manton Marble, and on Smith M. Weed. The dispatches revealed that Pelton had attempted to bribe a Republican elector from Oregon and had negotiated to secure the three returning boards in dispute. Although he was penniless, Pelton had spent large sums of money which had come from Tilden's bank of deposit. He had carried on these bribery transactions from Tilden's home in Grammercy Park. Everyone asked, Was Tilden involved? On October 16, 1878 Tilden issued a vehement denial.[12] At his own request Tilden testified before a Potter subcommittee at the Fifth Avenue Hotel on February 9, 1879. For two and a half hours he was unmercifully grilled by the Republican inquisitors, Reed and Hiscock. He denied all knowledge of the cipher telegrams and emerged from the ordeal without having made any damaging admissions.[13]

There were many Democrats, however, who were of the opinion that Tilden was involved to some extent in the negotiations carried on by Colonel Pelton. Their conclusion was that his chances for the Democratic nomination in 1880 were now very slim. Eugene Casserly, ex-senator from California, who had known Tilden intimately since 1843, expressed the viewpoint of these doubting Democrats when he said that Tilden could "never . . . be so much as named for the Presidency by any sensible person."[14] Hewitt believed that, although Tilden might not have seen any of the cipher telegrams, yet he knew

---

[12] *New York Herald*, October 18, 1878. Professor Ewing believes it would have been much better for the Democrats if they had refrained from initiating any congressional investigations at this time. See Cortez A. M. Ewing, *Presidential Elections from Abraham Lincoln to Franklin D. Roosevelt*, p. 23 (Norman: University of Oklahoma Press, 1940).

[13] Mark D. Hirsch, *William C. Whitney: Modern Warwick*, pp. 117-18 (New York: Dodd, Mead and Company, 1948). This work contains an excellent account of the cipher dispatches.

[14] Bayard MSS, Eugene Casserly to Bayard, November 17, 1878.

what was going on in a general way and "could have found out
a great deal had he tried."[15] The evidence was sufficient to convince W. E. Dorsheimer, a warm Tilden supporter, that the
latter had indeed been involved.[16] Henry Watterson was deeply
concerned over the possible effects on Tilden's chances.[17]

Despite physical decrepitude and the wounds to his moral
stature resulting from the decoded telegrams, the Old Man of
Grammercy Park still held a trump card. With the definite assurance of a solid South for the first time since the Civil War,
New York's thirty-five electoral votes would be of the utmost
importance. New York in addition to a solid South meant 173
votes for the Democrats, just 12 short of victory. In 1876 Tilden
had carried New York by a plurality of thirty thousand votes.
This one fact alone might well make Tilden the available candidate in 1880—at least, so many Democrats thought before
November 1879.

John Kelly, leader of Tammany Hall from 1873 to 1885,
was to break Tilden's grip on the Empire State. Honest John
Kelly, as he was called by his enemies in derision and by his
friends with warm approval, was a member of Congress during
Buchanan's administration. An ardent Catholic, he had de-
fended his Church in the halls of Congress from the bigoted
attacks of the Know-Nothings.[18] In 1834 the Ursuline convent
at Charlestown, Massachusetts was burned and sacked. Three
years later an anti-Catholic mob marched on St. Patrick's Cathe-

---

[15] Nevins, *Hewitt*, p. 399.
[16] Flick, *Tilden*, p. 437.
[17] Tilden MSS, Henry Watterson to Tilden, November 29, 1878. Wrote Watterson:
"For the first time I am discouraged as to the outlook for the Democratic
Party. . . . I see nothing but distraction in every direction, nor any principle
of cohesion to counteract the double-course, the disease of self-seeking and
time serving which overlaps all discipline and all bounds. On the other hand,
we see the Republicans deploy like a phalanx. It is enough to make a
cat howl."
[18] *Congressional Globe*, 31st Cong., 1st Sess., 191.

dral in New York. Before they reached the church they observed Kelly and his cohorts, who were firmly entrenched in and around the old cathedral. Bishop Dubois had given instructions to Kelly and his men that they should not strike unless the church was actually attacked. The church burners had not expected opposition. They lost heart and slunk off in the direction of the Bowery.[19]

In December 1858 John Kelly resigned his seat in the Thirty-fifth Congress to become sheriff of the city and county of New York. Kelly attached himself to the Tammany Democracy in New York and was aided by that organization in securing election to Congress as well as to the offices of councilman, alderman, and sheriff. He was the first man in the history of New York City politics to be re-elected to the lucrative office of sheriff. In 1868 he received the Tammany nomination for mayor, but declined because of ill-health and sorrow over the recent death of his wife.[20] In 1868 Kelly was determined to retire from politics, and sailed for Europe with his two daughters. He returned to New York in 1871 to find the city given over to every form of official rascality and plunder. It was the reign of Boss Tweed, who defied the reformers with the much-quoted phrase, "Well, what are you going to do about it?"[21]

Kelly's resolution about retiring from New York politics was quickly broken down by such leading citizens as Tilden, Hewitt, Belmont, and Schell. These gentlemen urged him to take the lead in helping them smash the Tweed Ring. Kelly consented to the difficult task of leading a successful movement against a ring entrenched in office, with millions in stolen money at its

---

[19] J. Fairfax McLaughlin, *The Life and Times of John Kelly: Tribune of the People*, pp. 31-33. New York: American News Company, 1885.

[20] *New York Herald*, November 20, 1868.

[21] Denis T. Lynch, *Boss Tweed: The Story of a Grim Generation*, p. 370 (New York: Boni and Liveright, 1927). The author makes an excellent case for the honesty of John Kelly. See pp. 409-11.

command, and backed up by a purchased legislature.[22] Charles
O'Conor and Samuel J. Tilden made a gallant attack upon the
ring in the courts and the legislature. John Kelly carried the
war into Tammany Hall, and drove the ring politicians from its
portals. O'Conor and Tilden scotched the snake in 1871, and
Kelly killed it in 1872.[23]

Shortly before his death, while he was a prisoner in Ludlow
Street Jail, Tweed was interviewed by a newspaper reporter. He
regarded John Kelly, he said, as the most successful city politician of New York during the past thirty years. Kelly was
"always a plodder," always saving something and learning
something. He stood well in his Church and received his support
there. New York politics had always been dishonest. There had
never been a time when the Board of Aldermen could not have
been bought. "If it wasn't for John Kelly's severity, you could
buy them now."[24]

With Tweed out of the way, Kelly became the leader of a
reformed Tammany. He was the first man to suggest Tilden's
nomination for governor. Tilden was in Europe in 1874, but a
cable from Kelly was sufficient to cause him to take passage on
the first steamer for New York. He was reluctant to enter the
bitter fight for the governorship, but Kelly's persistency finally
won his acquiescence.[25] Tilden was a constant visitor at Kelly's
home during this period; and after his inauguration as governor
in January 1875 he expressed his gratitude to Honest John for
his help in both nominating and electing him.

---

[22] *New York World*, October 18, 1875. Augustus Schell, chairman of the Democratic National Committee (1872-1876), was "firmly convinced" of Kelly's
honesty. See Oliver W. Holmes, "Augustus Schell"; in *Dictionary of American
Biography*, Vol. 16, pp. 424-25.

[23] McLaughlin, *Kelly*, pp. 277-78.

[24] *New York World*, October 26, 1877.

[25] Tilden to McLaughlin. (See McLaughlin, *Kelly*, p. 286.) Tilden told McLaughlin
that, had it not been for Kelly's insistence, he would never have run for the
governorship.

During Tilden's administration as governor, he and his old friend Kelly became involved in unfortunate differences as leaders of rival wings of the Democratic party in the state. It was the old struggle for dominance between the Albany Regency and Tammany Hall. A few weeks before the St. Louis convention in 1876, Tilden visited Kelly's home. Before leaving, the governor humorously remarked:

> Now, John, you are my sponsor, or political god-father. You found me not inclined to take any office two years ago, and insisted that I should take the nomination for Governor. No matter what differences may have arisen since, remember, John, you are my sponsor.[26]

That visit and the reminiscence of a happier day in their political lives did its work well. The appearance of Kelly at the convention as an advocate of Tilden electrified that body and gave a sharp lift to Tilden's prestige.[27]

Kelly kept his pledge. Hayes came in from the rural districts of New York thirty thousand ahead of Tilden. When he reached the Harlem River, he found that Tammany Hall had given Tilden a majority of fifty-four thousand in New York City. The Empire State had been won for Tilden and the Democracy. President-elect Tilden sent a congratulatory message on that memorable election night to John Kelly. He included his warmest salutations to the invincible tribe of Saint Tammany, "the right wing of the Democratic Army."[28]

The disputed election of 1876 focused attention on the national political scene. Things were fairly quiet in New York politics for almost a year. The struggle between Kelly and Tilden was still a family affair, with each seeking to dominate Tammany from within. They were still loyal members, as were

---

[26] *Ibid.*, p. 295.
[27] *Philadelphia Times*, June 30, 1876.
[28] McLaughlin, *Kelly*, p. 296.

their adherents. In 1878, however, the feud flared up again, and the Tildenites allied themselves with the Irving Hall Democracy. This new organization had been organized in 1875 by John Morrissey, the colorful gambler and heavyweight pugilist. Morrissey had seceded from Tammany Hall when he found that he could not wrest the leadership from Kelly.[29]

By midsummer, 1878, Tilden and Kelly were both casting covetous eyes at the governorship. Lucius "Sore Eyes" Robinson was a Tilden man, and the Irving Hall Democracy—which was now the Tilden wing of the party—was intent on re-electing "Sore Eyes." Kelly recognized a war when he saw one. Henry A. Gumbleton, a Kelly man, had been removed by Robinson for taking higher fees than were permissible as clerk of New York County. Hubert O. Thompson, an ardent Tilden henchman, replaced Gumbleton. Robinson's failure to remove a Tilden man charged with similar misdoings strengthened the supposition that the political war had reached the ruthless stage.[30]

Kelly not only could recognize a fight, but he could fight as well. He accepted Gumbleton's removal as an open declaration of war, and on September 6 declared that in case the convention insisted upon the renomination of Lucius Robinson for governor, the Tammany delegation would leave in a body.[31]

The Democratic state convention was held at Syracuse on September 10 and 11, 1879. Kelly insisted upon the nomination of General H. W. Slocum. After an eight-hour struggle Robinson was nominated. When the roll call reached Cattaraugus, Schell rose from his place next to Kelly and announced that under no condition would the seventy-two followers of the Tiger support the governor. Thereupon Kelly and his braves stalked

---

[29] Hirsch, *Whitney*, pp. 149-50.
[30] DeAlva S. Alexander, *A Political History of the State of New York*, Vol. 3, p. 418 (New York: Henry Holt and Company, 1890). Lucius Robinson was elected governor of New York in 1876.
[31] *Ibid.*

out of Weiting Opera House. The rump convention nominated Robinson, 243 to 58. The Tammany bolters met at Shakespeare Hall that same evening and nominated Kelly himself for governor. The convention ended on September 12 with defeat staring both factions in the face.

The campaign was acrimonius. Kelly stumped the state, raking up Tilden's past embarrassments and cleverly thumping Robinson for his neglect of New York City issues. Montgomery Blair, a strong Tilden partisan, wrote his chief that the real question was whether or not John Kelly was to dominate the will of the Democratic party. He concluded by saying that Robinson must win.[32] The Kellyites were just as determined that Tilden should not dominate the Democratic party.

On election day, despite Tilden's best efforts, the Republicans elected the governor, attorney general, comptroller, and other officers. Kelly had accomplished his purpose. He had defeated Robinson. Cornell received 418,568 votes, Robinson 375,790, and Kelly 77,566. The combined Democratic vote would have swamped Cornell.

Professor Mark D. Hirsch refers to Kelly's bolt as a "despicable exhibition of machine politics at its worst."[33] Professor Allan Nevins characterizes Kelly as a "narrow minded martinet, suspicious and vindictive" who "displayed an arrogant hostility towards every reform element."[34] Hirsch quotes these strictures of Nevins with approval.[35] These characterizations of Kelly seem somewhat less than fair. Abram S. Hewitt denied the assertion that Kelly was a dictator. He felt that the city of New York should reward the Tammany leader with a statue rather than with caluminations.[36]

---

[32] Tilden MSS, Montgomery Blair to Tilden, September 2, 1879.
[33] Hirsch, *Whitney*, p. 153.
[34] Nevins, *Hewitt*, p. 432.
[35] Hirsch, *Whitney*, p. 148.
[36] *New York Herald*, October 31, 1875.

According to Hugh J. Hastings, a staunch Republican and editor of the *New York Commercial Advertiser*, the condition of society had improved under Kelly's leadership. Hastings remarked, with a sly dig at Tammany, that "Kelly had ruled the fierce Democracy in such a manner that life and property are comparatively safe." It required a great man indeed, thought Hastings, "to stand between the City treasury and this most dangerous mass." Dethrone Kelly, and where was the man to succeed him?[37]

After Robinson's defeat the Tilden machine leveled the charge of treachery at Kelly. Murat Halstead disagreed with those who took this position. No treachery, he insisted, could be ascribed to Kelly, who had proclaimed his purpose distinctly before the meeting of the Democratic state convention to resist the nomination of Robinson and to defeat him if that resistance was not successful.[38]

There were many who echoed the opinion of President Hayes that the defeat of Robinson foreshadowed the downfall of Tilden in the following year either at the convention or at the polls.[39] The *Richmond (Kentucky) Register* wisely reflected that, in order to be sure of New York's thirty-five votes, Tilden should be dropped and replaced by someone acceptable to Kelly. Watterson answered this counsel by retorting that "Parties do not win by sacrificing heroes to outlaws."[40]

John Kelly's unsparing denunciations of Tilden as the "old humbug of Cipher alley,"[41] together with the defeat of "Sore

---

[37] *New York Commercial Advertiser*, November 20, 1878. McGurrin asserts that in Kelly's twelve years of leadership in New York there were no scandals in the city government. See James McGurrin, *Bourke Cockran: A Free Lance in American Politics*, p. 100 (New York: Charles Scribner's Sons, 1948).

[38] *Cincinnati Commercial*, November 14, 1879.

[39] Hayes MSS, Diary, November 5, 1879.

[40] *Louisville Courier Journal*, February 4, 1880. Watterson quoted the viewpoint of the *Richmond (Kentucky) Register* before answering it.

[41] *New York World*, October 11-17, 1879.

Eyes" Robinson, turned the eyes of many politicians in the direction of Bayard as the available candidate. Montgomery Blair, a friend of Tilden, believed that many influential Southern Democrats sympathized with Kelly's attacks upon Tilden. He also believed that Kelly had acted as the "tool of the man who sold us out in 1876-7."[42] This accusation was aimed at Bayard, who appeared to be the strongest opponent that Tilden would have in the contest for the nomination in 1880.

Blair was correct in this estimate of important Southern Democrats. In 1876 the South had flocked to the banner of Tilden, and Southern leaders had been lavish with their pledges to support Bayard in 1880.[43] They could never forget that Bayard had showed effective sympathy toward the South in the dark days of Reconstruction.[44]

Tilden had carried Indiana in 1876 by a plurality of five thousand. The Hoosier State possessed fifteen electoral votes. The South's 138 in addition to New York's 35 and Indiana's 15 meant 188 votes—3 more than the Democrats needed for victory. But by 1879 the soft-money craze was abroad in Indiana, and Bayard's hard-money views made his name anathema among many important Hoosier politicians. William H. English, a wealthy banker who was later to become the Democratic vice-presidential candidate in 1880, thought he had a formula that would result in victory for Bayard. On December 3, 1879, in a long letter to the senator from Delaware, he gave a clear picture of the political situation in Indiana, which, he asserted, could be won for Bayard if the latter would consent to cooperate with Hendricks, a soft-money advocate.[45]

---

[42] Tilden MSS, Montgomery Blair to Tilden, November 19, 1879.

[43] Tansill, *Bayard*, p. 281.

[44] Bayard MSS, J. M. Leach to Bayard, October 30, 1879 and Samuel Barlow to Bayard, November 10, 1879; Marble MSS, Samuel Barlow to Manton Marble, December 30, 1879; *New Orleans Times*, November 15, 1879.

[45] Bayard MSS, W. H. English to Bayard, December 3, 1879.

English appeared to have no real understanding of Bayard's character. Bayard would not compromise his hard-money theories by consenting to run on a ticket with a soft-money advocate as his partner. He had no intention of buying the Democratic nomination by appeasing the "silverites" of the Middle West. In a letter to David A. Wells he clearly defined his position:

> As for the political field, I know not what to say excepting this—that I shall take all my wounds in front (if I am to get any) and not be struck by a stray bullet while dodging. Today I shall offer a joint resolution to put an end to the legal tender power of U. S. Treasury notes.[46]

The resolution that Bayard introduced in the Senate stunned the leaders of both parties, but the financial groups in New York and Boston were quick to realize its importance and began to circulate petitions in its favor.[47] The compliments from the big bankers poured in.[48]

From Blanton Duncan, a prominent Kentucky Democrat, came a note of warning. He reminded Bayard of the bitter feeling on the currency issues, and stressed the improbability of Greenback support. Hancock, he feared, could count on helpers who could not be won to the Bayard cause.[49] Despite this prophecy of gloom there were many Republicans who regarded Bay-

---

[46] Library of Congress, David A. Wells MSS, Bayard to David A. Wells, December 3, 1879. Although Bayard possessed considerable stock in the Colorado Silver Cliff Mining Company, he did not hesitate to fight with all his energy the silver inflationary legislation known as the Bland-Allison Act of 1878. See Bayard MSS, J. S. Moore to Bayard, February 28, 1880.

[47] Bayard MSS, J. S. Moore to Bayard, December 6, 1879.

[48] Ibid., George S. Coeprut to Bayard, December 26, 1879. Coeprut added his congratulations "to the thousands of citizens of all parties, at the good work you are doing for the country, in aiming to restore a sound financial condition." See also ibid., E. G. Spaulding to Bayard, January 30, 1880, where Spaulding informed Bayard that he had just finished reading his "able and statesman-like speech in favor of repealing the legal tender quality of the greenback currency and am very much pleased with it."

[49] Ibid., Blanton Duncan to Bayard, November 26, 1879.

ard as their most dangerous opponent.[50] In a few sentences Murat Halstead presented a clear analysis of the situation:

> Without New York the Solid South is useless for national purposes. . . . Tammany is fatally bent upon the destruction of Tilden and Tilden will cut the throat of any Tammany man that had anything to do with the Electoral Commission. . . . Mr. Bayard's strength is said to be great among the Germans but Mr. Tilden is not a German.[51]

In January of 1880 it was apparent that the crosscurrents in Democratic politics were so strong that it was very difficult to tell which presidential aspirant would finally reach the safe harbor of nomination. Charles Nordhoff, Washington correspondent of the *New York Herald,* wrote Wells that Samuel J. Randall was "inclined to push himself as Tilden's heir. They mean to slaughter Bayard."[52] Randall himself assured Chauncey F. Black that he was "really and truly indifferent to all save success of our principles being brought out in the administration of affairs."[53] Although Bayard had no intention of stepping aside in favor of Tilden's nomination, he realized that the political equation in New York politics did not offer an easy solution. There were many difficulties, and it was not long before the Tilden machine made Bayard aware of some of them.

Although there are some who insist that Tilden's thousands had no effect on Dana's political views, nevertheless the *New York Sun,* on February 24, 1880, reprinted a speech that Bayard had made at Dover, Delaware on June 27, 1861.[54] Besides

---

[50] Garfield MSS, Z. Brown to Garfield, February 27, 1880; John Sherman MSS, J. A. McDonald to John Sherman, December 17, 1879; *New York Times,* November 6, 1879.

[51] *Cincinnati Commercial,* November 20 and December 2, 1879.

[52] Wells MSS, Charles Nordhoff to David A. Wells, January 4, 1880.

[53] Library of Congress, Chauncey F. Black MSS, Samuel J. Randall to Chauncey F. Black, November 9, 1879.

[54] Flick, *Tilden,* p. 463. See footnote 8 in this chapter for Dana's debt of $45,000 to Tilden.

this speech, Dana added a choice selection of adverse editorial comment. During the course of his remarks Bayard had empha- sized that the state of Delaware had had nothing to do with the recent "secession" and "rebellion"—that is, the Civil War. He then warned of the horrors of a long and widespread civil war and expressed the opinion that, if a peaceful accommodation was impossible, the Southern states should be permitted to with- draw from the Union.[55] This was the view of General Winfield Scott, Horace Greeley, and thousands of other distinguished Americans of that day. But Bayard's enemies were out to kill him politically, and the speech was widely republished.

August Belmont, a prominent New York banker and ardent supporter of Bayard, had recently been blandly informed by an intimate friend of Tilden that the latter would support the nom- ination of Bayard if convinced that his own chances had van- ished. For a while Belmont had given some credence to this report, but after the Dover attack he was convinced that Tilden cherished a definite hostility toward Bayard. Belmont now dis- counted the possibility that Tilden would throw any votes in Bayard's direction. He was glad that now at last the mask was off. Had the Dover attack been held back a month or two longer, it would have helped Tilden and hurt Bayard. But bloody-shirt waving would not fool the people, save for a few fanatics.[56]

Belmont's letter was only one of the many consoling notes that Bayard received with reference to the *Sun's* onslaught. W. G. Whitely stated that Bayard's view was the unanimous opinion of all Democrats in civil life. Seymour and "crass old Sammy himself" held and expressed similar views. In Whitely's view the Dover speech would not cost Bayard a single vote in the North. He then went on to recount a bit of history, and in so

---

[55] *New York Sun*, February 24, 1880. According to I. C. Grubb one of Tilden's agents visited Delaware and copied Bayard's speech from the *Delaware Gazette*. See Bayard MSS, Ignatius C. Grubb to Bayard, February 24, 1880.

[56] Bayard MSS, August Belmont to Bayard, March 8, 1880.

doing was in reality sounding a warning with regard to the coming Democratic National Convention. Some Southern Democrats had recently been quite vociferous in their fears of Bayard's lack of availability in the North.[57] It was only too true that Bayard's cause was seriously handicapped by the lack of an effective political machine. Tilden's large personal fortune had provided him with one that still had a wide measure of influence in Democratic ranks.

John Hunter, one of Bayard's most active lieutenants, was keenly interested in obtaining financial assistance for his candidate. He was finally able to obtain a contribution of $5,000 from Perry Belmont. This money would be turned over to John Kelly of Tammany Hall and, according to Hunter, would ensure two sets of delegates to Cincinnati, "that is, provided we fail in the regular State Convention." These arrangements with Kelly must be kept secret; if made public, they would redouble Tilden's efforts and possibly bring Tammany into his fold.[58]

With the aid of Kelly and other anti-Tilden factions the followers of Senator Bayard had high hopes of capturing the vote of the New York delegation to the Cincinnati convention. In Pennsylvania, Bayard's advocacy of a tariff for protection as well as for revenue was gradually drawing many of the delegates to his side in spite of the efforts of Sam Randall to win the state for Tilden.[59]

Just when Bayard's political star seemed about to take off for a rapid and successful ascent, it received a severe check from out of the heart of Louisiana. On March 17 the *New Orleans Picayune* stated in an editorial that General Hancock was the only candidate who could successfully appeal to all factions within the Democratic party. He was, said the journal,

---

[57] *Ibid.*, W. G. Whitely to Bayard, February 25, 1880.
[58] *Ibid.*, John Hunter to Bayard, March 12, 1880.
[59] *Ibid.*, Lewis D. Campbell to Bayard. April 15, 1880 and Phillip Zell to Bayard, May 15, 1880.

identified with neither extremes, hard money and soft money. He was a Democrat and would stand on the financial platform to be adopted at Cincinnati. This platform would be conservative, seeking to maintain the prosperity of the country, which was in great part to be attributed to the wise policy of a Democratic Congress. Bayard, continued the *Picayune,* repelled Union voters by his Dover Green speech in June 1861, and repelled Greenback voters, not only by his extreme hard-money views, but by his advocacy of the withdrawal of the greenbacks themselves. The editorial stated that Hancock attracted Union voters by his magnificent record of battles and wounds, while he would not repel Greenback voters by taking his stand on the conservative financial platform of the Cincinnati convention.[60]

John J. Mellon, a Bayard supporter, remarked caustically that the McEnery political machine in Louisiana came out strongly for Hancock without asserting whether this support was based upon the general's record of "battles and wounds" or because his ample girth might indicate political talents.[61] No one could deny that Hancock had a brilliant record as a fighting general during the Civil War, and the South would never forget his efforts to mitigate the harshness of military rule while he was in command of the Fifth Military District, comprising the states of Louisiana and Texas. But a genius for military affairs and undoubted personal bravery did not transform Hancock into a wise statesman who was fit to become his nation's chief executive.[62] Grant had pre-eminence in both logistics and courage, but he made a miserable failure as president of the United

---

[60] *New Orleans Picayune,* March 17, 1880. The *New Orleans Times* was of the opinion that Tilden was backing Hancock against Bayard. See *New Orleans Times,* April 13, 1880.

[61] Bayard MSS, John J. Mellon to Bayard, March 17, 1880. John McEnery was the leader of the Democratic party in Louisiana.

[62] Francis A. Walker, *General Hancock,* pp. 294-306 (New York: D. Appleton and Company, 1895). See also Alvan Scott Southworth, *Life of Gen. Winfield Scott Hancock,* pp. 104-10, 136-99 (New York: American News Company, 1880).

States. The country had grown weary of the "man on horse-back" who had ridden into the White House in March 1869 because he had been heralded as the man who had saved the Union through his military valor. The times cried out for a statesman and not merely a soldier. Bayard was aware of the threat of the Hancock boom, but he was hopeful that his record in the Senate would make him the choice at Cincinnati in June.

The approach of the election of 1880 whetted political appetites. The importance of New York was a constant refrain in Southern newspapers. The *New Orleans Times,* confident that it had a success formula, advocated that the Tilden and Kelly factions forget their personal spites and jealousies and support heartily and enthusiastically the Cincinnati nominee. Then the Democratic party of New York and of the country would win the victory.[63]

After the defeat of 1879 Tilden began to express doubt as to whether he should be a candidate for the Democratic presidential nomination in 1880. He emphatically asserted that the dissension of 1879 "cannot be continued or repeated in 1880."[64] Shortly before the Robinson defeat in 1879 the Sage of Greystone had broken his silence with regard to his intentions in 1880. In an ambiguous interview with a *Washington Post* correspondent, Tilden asserted that he was not seeking the nomination nor did he contemplate doing so in the future. The Republican *New York Times* carried this interview, and accused Tilden of duplicity. The *Times* stated that people still persisted in doubting his ability to talk of politics without subterfuge. Perceptive politicians, concluded the *Times,* felt that Tilden could not even discuss his personal ambitions without more or less deliberate deceit.[65]

---

63 *New Orleans Times,* March 12, 1880.
64 Flick, *Tilden,* p. 446. Tilden's man Robinson had been badly beaten for the governorship of New York in 1879.
65 *New York Times,* October 3, 1879.

From time to time Tilden's reticence was offset by the lo-
quacity of Bigelow, who took it upon himself to explain just
what his mentor's attitude was. For Tilden to shun the canvass
of 1880, or for the party to allow him to do so, was unthinkable,
said Bigelow in a letter of February 1879.[66] This letter, written
after the publication of the cipher dispatches but before the
Kelly bolt in November 1879, seems to indicate Tilden's real
feeling. He wanted the party to insist on his nomination. Thus
vindicated, he could withdraw on the grounds of his shattered
health, and would then appoint his successor.[67]

Tilden's doubts about his availability were somewhat dis-
pelled by the encouraging letters he received. Benjamin H. Hill,
a Georgian Democrat, urged him to make a last fight for the
Democracy. The crime of 1876 should not go unpunished, and
Tilden should let the American people vindicate his name.[68] But
in spite of all this pressure Tilden must have known that his
physical infirmities would not permit him to enter the presidential race. This fact was gradually becoming known in New York
political circles. On April 5 Charles Howard, editor of the *New
York Daily Graphic,* sent Tilden a résumé of a recent *New York
Star* editorial, which asserted that the Irving Hall Democracy
had recently held a secret caucus during which five doctors had
examined Tilden. Medical men warned Tilden that the strain
of another presidential campaign would kill him. Tilden had
then appointed Henry D. Payne, an Ohio millionaire, as his
legatee. Randall, so the *Star* asserted, had been dropped because he lacked a "barrel" and Tilden refused to put up for
him.[69] William C. Whitney, an important member of the Tilden

---

[66] Bigelow to William H. Peck, February 28, 1879; in Bigelow, *Tilden,* Vol. 2,
pp. 579-80.
[67] *Indianapolis Journal,* February 25, 1880.
[68] Tilden MSS, Benjamin H. Hill to Tilden, April 12, 1880.
[69] *Ibid.,* Charles Howard to Tilden, April 5, 1880. The *New York Star* was John
Kelly's personal organ.

machine and very close to Tilden himself at this time, was Payne's son-in-law.[70] Two days after Howard's letter to Tilden, Sidney Webster assured Bayard confidentially that Tilden was finished. He was in bad health, and he had made too many political errors.[71]

In a sea of uncertainties the one certain factor was John Kelly. Tammany, he announced, would under no circumstances support Tilden for president.[72] The Tilden-dominated Democratic state committee convened on March 26 to draw up plans for the state convention. In the choice of a place it was definitely decided to keep it away from Utica, where Horatio Seymour might control it.[73] One hour later Kelly assumed the offensive by holding his own "state-committee" meeting. Three days later, on March 29, the two committees issued calls for their individual conventions to meet in Syracuse on April 20.

The regular Democratic state convention was held at the Weiting Opera House. No sooner had it assembled than William C. Whitney moved that a Committee on Resolutions be appointed with one delegate from each congressional district. All resolutions were to be referred to this committee without reading or debate. As a result the proceedings terminated in a conclusive triumph for Tilden. The convention adopted the unit rule, chose

---

[70] According to the *Cincinnati Enquirer*, May 17, 1880, Whitney became enraged at Tilden for his duplicity. The *Enquirer* charged that Tilden, in Whitney's presence, pledged himself to support Payne and then a few minutes later, after Whitney left the room, told his supporters to back Randall.

[71] Bayard MSS, Sidney Webster to Bayard, April 7, 1880.

[72] *New York Tribune*, March 17, 1880.

[73] In the Seymour papers in the New York State Library there is a large bundle of letters from correspondents all over the country, editors and politicians among them, urging Seymour to accept the Democratic presidential nomination of 1880. Seymour refused. See Mitchell, *Seymour*, p. 536. Seymour had carried New York against Grant in 1868. Both New York and Indiana were doubtful states in 1880. To win them and thus insure victory the Democrats had but to nominate Seymour and Hendricks. Thus argued the *Indianapolis Journal*, June 16, 1880.

national delegates virtually pledged to Tilden, praised the Sage, and attacked the fraudulent election of Hayes.

Across the street in Shakespeare Hall, John Kelly was holding his own convention. During the course of it he sent John B. Haskins to Weiting Opera House to propose a conference between the two groups. It was at least an attempt to secure Democratic harmony in New York. Kelly was promptly rebuffed for his trouble. Murat Halstead pointed a finger of censure at the Tildenites for their dictatorial policies.[74]

The Kelly delegates had been carefully manacled by Tilden. For the Weiting Opera House group had ruled that the New York delegation should vote as a unit and that any delegates refusing to do so would lose their seats.[75] Kelly's peace feeler having failed, the Kelly Tammanyites proceeded with their own rump convention. Tammany delegates were chosen, and Kelly vowed that he would stab Tilden as he had stabbed Robinson. Tilden, said Kelly, was elected by the votes of the people, and he had not had sufficient courage after he was elected to go forward as a brave man should go forward, and say to the people of the country: "I have been elected by the votes of the people, and you see to it that I am inaugurated."[76] Kelly insisted that, if he and his delegates were not recognized at Cincinnati, he would bolt again as he had in November 1879.[77]

John Hunter attended the Tilden convention at Syracuse. A few days before this convention opened, he wrote to Bayard that he expected to go to the national convention at Cincinnati, "unless my men are bought up, which is probable as three of them have been at Tilden's house this A.M." Hunter regretted that the regular convention (at Syracuse) would be entirely in

---

[74] *Cincinnati Commercial*, April 12, 1880.
[75] *New York Nation*, April 21, 1880. The *Nation* believed that Tilden, despite his alleged senility and decrepitude, had helped to draft this ironclad provision.
[76] Flick, *Tilden*, p. 452.
[77] *New York Times*, April 21, 1880.

Tilden's hands. He assured Bayard that there would be no chance of uniting the party at Syracuse.[78]

As soon as John Hunter returned to New York after the Syracuse convention, he told Bayard the inside story of what had happened on the floor of the Weiting Opera House. It was, he said, the most complete instance of machine rule that he had ever seen. The anti-Tilden people had certainly 40 per cent of the delegates as they came from the people, and "we thought on Monday night that we would accomplish some good." On Tuesday morning, from causes unknown to the Bayard forces, a thorough change had taken place and the Bayard men had not 15 per cent left. Hunter thought that this was brought about by Tilden's intimate friends, who assured people that he would not be a candidate and gave out the impression that he would throw his strength to Payne. This undoubtedly found favor with many and helped much. When this argument failed, other strong reasons were brought to bear.[79]

Certain Southern Democrats, fearful of Bayard's lack of a following in the North, were demanding that the Bayardites show some strength in that section. John Hunter answered that such support was already available.[80]

Barlow was fearful of Tilden's dealings with Hancock, Payne, and Randall, and he feared even more the influence wielded by Tilden's large fortune.[81] But notwithstanding all the difficulties that loomed large on the political horizon, Bayard's chances at Cincinnati were still distinctly good. On May 11 Barlow summed up the situation: "I am by no means sanguine

---

[78] Bayard MSS, John Hunter to Bayard, April 17, 1880.
[79] *Ibid.*, John Hunter to Bayard, April 22, 1880. Whitney did much maneuvering for Tilden at Syracuse. John Kelly had recommended Whitney as corporation counsel under Tilden. Kelly stressed Whitney's honesty. See Bigelow, *Tilden*, Vol. 1, pp. 375-76.
[80] Bayard MSS, John Hunter to Bayard, May 11, 1880.
[81] *Ibid.*, Barlow to Bayard, May 7, 1880.

as to your success, but your chances improve every day and if nominated you will be elected."[82]

From April until the national convention in June, rumors concerning Tilden's candidacy were retailed at a furious pace. Newspapers daily conjectured that he was either running or declining, while he maintained a sphinxlike silence. In the meantime Ohio newspapers favoring Payne were pressing his boom and discounting Thurman's candidacy.[83]

Bigelow, who certainly knew Tilden as well as, if not better than, anyone else, was convinced by May 12, 1880 that his chief had finally determined to be a candidate for the presidency.[84] A few weeks later another Tilden confidant re-echoed Bigelow's sentiments: "Mr. Tilden himself thinks he can carry New York. . . . This is no time for swapping horses. It is no time for dark horses. Expedients are always uncertain, principles never."[85]

It was a difficult decision that confronted Tilden in the spring and summer of 1880. His political machine was still well oiled, and it would continue to run until the Sage himself applied the brakes. This he was extremely reluctant to do. Burning ambition still ran through his broken body, and he clung to the hope that he would receive a unanimous nomination at Cincinnati. But in keeping with his indirect character, he was

---

[82] *Ibid.*, Barlow to Bayard, May 11, 1880.

[83] Thurman was the choice of the Ohio state convention on May 6, but the feeling prevailed that this was but a courtesy and that Payne was the real choice of the Ohio delegation. See *Cleveland Leader*, May 7, 1880 and *New York Times*, May 10, 1880.

[84] John Bigelow's Diary, May 12, 1880; in Bigelow, *Tilden*, Vol. 2, pp. 597-98.

[85] Henry Watterson in the *Louisville Courier Journal*, May 26, 1880. Alexander C. Flick feels that Tilden was the only Democrat who could have won in 1880. See Flick, *Tilden*, p. 453. There is a good deal of evidence, however, to show that leading Republicans considered Tilden to be the candidate whom they could most easily defeat. See Hayes MSS, R. B. Hayes to Guy W. Bryan, April 23, 1880. In this letter Hayes expresses his hope for Tilden's nomination and voices his fear of Bayard or Hancock. See Fish MSS, Letter Book, Hamilton Fish to W. Childs, February 25, 1880. Fish says that, if Tilden were nominated, New York could be carried with any number of candidates.

loath to come out boldly in his efforts to dominate the Cincinnati convention. Up to the very eve of the convention the Tilden delegates were in confusion and doubt.[86]

Before sailing for Europe, Jeremiah S. Black called on Tilden, and during the course of the conversation asked categorically whether he would be a candidate. He received the evasive reply: "I take no part in the matter. I hold myself perfectly free."[87] Small wonder that Whitney spoke of the situation as being muddled and went on to explain:

> One of the peculiar weaknesses of Mr. Tilden as a political leader is that he gives his whole confidence to no one, not even to those on whom he must rely for the execution of his plans. He has reserves in everything he says and he expects his supporters to guess his intention. And if we do not guess accurately he is angry. He lost the Presidential seat by just such methods. By withholding his confidence from those who represented his interest in Washington he weakened them with Democratic Senators and Congressmen who at first were willing if not anxious to submit to his lead.[88]

However successful Tilden may have been in concealing his real intentions under the cloak of ambiguous statements, his lieutenants were working arduously for his nomination. The Tilden machine's fear of Seymour had caused them to insist on Syracuse in preference to Utica as the place for the New York Democratic convention. This fear persisted; and in an effort to quell it Theodore P. Cook wrote that Seymour was fully and firmly resolved to go out of public life and remain out, but would like to take his contemporaries out with him. That was all there was to his opposition.[89]

---

[86] *New York Tribune*, June 12, 1880.

[87] Library of Congress, Jeremiah S. Black MSS, Memorandum, April 24, 1880. See also Flick, *Tilden*, p. 454.

[88] William C. Hudson, *Random Recollections of an Old Political Reporter*, pp. 106-07. New York: Cupples and Leon Company, 1911.

[89] Tilden MSS, Theodore P. Cook to Tilden, April 6, 1880.

During May, Tilden was the recipient of many letters from Randall informing him that Virginia and Arkansas were "right," and that they were doing their best to capture the Maryland delegation.[90] On May 6 Randall wrote to William H. Barnum, the chairman of the Democratic National Committee, that he thought he had a plan "by which Mr. Tilden can receive the half of Virginia's vote in Nat. Dem. Con."[91]

James Gordon Bennett, forthright editor of the *New York Herald*, announced the retirement of Seymour and urged Tilden to put his cards on the table. Seymour had declined with an emphatic negative, but "Mr. Tilden is incapable of doing the simplest thing without a mask."[92] Hewitt, although he had cooled somewhat toward Tilden, testified that in spite of his bodily infirmities Tilden's intellect was unimpaired and that he would appreciate a nomination by acclamation. If nominated, so Hewitt thought, he might even be induced to run.[93] Norvin Green, president of Western Union, assuming that Tilden was a candidate, granted him a wire from his room to the Cincinnati convention, and added that similar facilities would be given to "other prominent candidates."[94] *Harper's Weekly* and the *Indianapolis Journal* were certain that "if Tilden does not secure the nomination, he will at least dictate who shall."[95]

Meanwhile the Hancock boom, rising out of Louisiana, was moving ahead rapidly. The *New Orleans Times*, ever loyal to Bayard, sought to block the threat by airily discounting its gravity. But the threat was there.[96] Although John Hunter confided to Bayard that he had been informed that the Hancock

---

[90] See Box 34 of Tilden MSS for Randall letters.
[91] *Ibid.*, Randall to W. H. Barnum, May 6, 1880.
[92] *New York Herald*, June 17, 1880.
[93] Nevins, *Hewitt*, p. 345.
[94] Tilden MSS, Norvin Green to Tilden, June 14, 1880.
[95] *Indianapolis Journal*, February 25, 1880. See also *Harper's Weekly* 24:402, June 26, 1880.
[96] *New Orleans Times*, April 3, 1880.

movement in the South "means nothing," yet the shadow of
another "general on horseback" continued to alarm some of
Bayard's supporters.[97]

The friends of the senator from Delaware wished that the
South would come out clearly for Bayard. Sidney Webster believed that the Southern leaders had done well in repudiating
Tilden, but that their present preference was uncertain. Unless
the South came forward with a candidate soon, the chances of
Tilden's candidacy would be bright.[98] If the South would only
declare herself for Bayard, both Hunter and Webster were sure
that it would have an important bearing on New York. The
Bayardites felt that the time had come for the South to show
some appreciation of all that Bayard had done for that section.
But Southern leaders were indecisive and seemed reluctant to
climb on the Bayard band wagon.[99]

Wells was of the opinion that in Connecticut a large number
of Democrats favored Tilden because they believed he would be
able to carry New York in the fall elections.[100] But many leading New York Democrats, including John Kelly, Abram S.
Hewitt, Clarkson N. Potter, and David Dudley Field, were inclined to believe that Bayard was the logical candidate.[101]

It was next to impossible, however, to ascertain the real intentions of these vacillating New Yorkers. Perry Belmont was
afraid that W. H. Hurlbert was about to forswear his allegiance
to Bayard's banner and move over to the camp of Stephen J.

[97] Bayard MSS, John Hunter to Bayard, April 26, 1880.

[98] Ibid., Sidney Webster to Bayard, April 27, 1880. Tilden was well aware of this
Southern antipathy toward himself. Montgomery Blair informed him that "the
Southern chiefs . . . sold you out to Hayes because they said Hayes could do
more for them than you could do." Blair told Tilden that the South was sup-
porting Kelly because of Tilden's opposition to Southern claims. See Tilden
MSS, Montgomery Blair to Tilden, November 13, 1879 and June 13, 1880.

[99] Bayard MSS, Sidney Webster to Bayard, May 3, 1880.

[100] Ibid., David A. Wells to Bayard, May 20, 1880.

[101] Ibid., Marvin W. Bovee to Bayard, May 21, 1880.

Field.[102] Although Horatio Seymour had finally come out for
Bayard, Hunter had no real confidence in him. Yet New York's
factional fights were not so important as the fact that Hampton,
Lamar, Butler, and Gibson, outstanding Southern leaders, had
promised to go to Cincinnati and work for Bayard. It was essential for Bayard's success that they be held to this promise.[103]

Bayard's fight on the floor of the Senate to limit Chinese immigration to California had won for him the esteem of many
Californians.[104] Eugene Casserly wrote that his state had not forgotten Bayard's splendid fight for them, and as proof of this
fact he enclosed a clipping from the *Argonaut* of May 22, 1880.
The editorial of this date expressed the hope that the Democratic party would have enough sense to nominate Bayard, a
man who was in all respects worthy of the presidency.[105] The
sentiments expressed by the editor of the *Argonaut* were being
echoed in the hearts of thousands of Democrats from California
to Connecticut.[106]

With the Cincinnati convention but eight days off, Carson
Lake assured Tilden that Payne, because of his business interests, could defeat Garfield in Ohio.[107] Tilden's dislike of Bayard
was not lessened when R. T. Merrick informed him that the
friends of the senator from Delaware attending the Maryland
convention "cherish a personal bitterness to you."[108] And
Tilden's indecision was put to the test when A. C. McGlacklin
wired a plea not to "leave us without a principle and therefore
become a candidate. Cincinnati means defeat without you."[109]

---

102 *Ibid.*, Perry Belmont to Bayard, May 26, 1880.
103 *Ibid.*, John Hunter to Bayard, May 31, 1880.
104 *Congressional Record*, 45th Cong., 3d Sess., 1310-11.
105 Bayard MSS, Eugene Casserly to Bayard, May 22, 1880.
106 *Ibid.*, David A. Wells to Bayard, May 30, 1880; Marble MSS, David A. Wells
    to Manton Marble, June 1, 1880.
107 Tilden MSS, Carson Lake to Tilden, June 14, 1880.
108 *Ibid.*, R. T. Merrick to Tilden, June 11, 1880.
109 *Ibid.*, A. C. McGlacklin to Tilden, June 16, 1880.

Charles O'Conor, outstanding member of the New York bar, who together with Tilden and Kelly had smashed the Tweed Ring but a decade before, begged Perry Belmont to "urge every practicable effort in favor of Mr. Bayard." If nominated, thought O'Conor, Bayard's acceptance by the popular voice was to be regarded as absolutely certain. Singularly enough, this view, added O'Conor, was very frequently accompanied by remarks tending to show that Bayard's nomination was impossible. The basis of this contradictory attitude was the conception that one so good, true, and pure could not win favor with the practical politicians who were supposed to control the choice of candidates. Was this a libel on politicians as a class, or was the situation really otherwise? It was hoped by O'Conor, "for the country's sake," that whatever faults might be justly imputed to the managers of party action, these men were, at least on the Democratic side, not so perverse. Bayard was pre-eminently a fit selection. Surely it would be the part of wisdom to take him as leader in the coming struggle. As for New York, she was all for Bayard, and would pile up for him a majority hitherto unheard of.[110]

The fear of a Kelly bolt if Tilden was nominated was weakening the latter's strength, not only in the South but also in the West. A Missourian queried what course Kelly would adopt in case Tilden was the choice at Cincinnati. Daniel Magone, one of the leaders of the Tilden machine in New York, answered that he did not know and that no one else did either.[111] Apparently the Sage and his followers suspected that Honest John might be bluffing.

On June 9 the editor of the *Atlanta Constitution* confessed that he had been supporting Grant because he knew the Democrats could defeat him. New York, he asserted, was the pivotal

---

[110] Bayard MSS, Charles O'Conor to Perry Belmont, June 17, 1880.
[111] Tilden MSS, D. Magone to John Cosgrove, June 3, 1880.

state beyond all question. A renewal of the contest of 1876 was shaping up, with this difference: the Republicans would not have any returning boards, state or national, to count them in after they had been counted out at the polls. To win they must therefore carry New York, since they could not hope to carry Indiana.[112] Six days later the *Constitution* represented the voice of the solid South when it said: "It is simply folly and a waste of effort to nominate men who cannot carry New York. . . . We want no booms because we simply want a man who can secure 47 northern votes."[113]

As the time for the Cincinnati convention drew near, there were certain "ifs" that presented themselves to the minds of the politicians of that era. If Tammany did not bury the hatchet and make peace with Irving Hall, Tilden's chances were practically nil. If the South overcame its fears about Bayard's availability in the North, he stood a good chance of emerging as the nominee. If Tilden would overcome his dark thoughts about Bayard with reference to the Electoral Commission, he could easily make a president. Since New York was so crucial, perhaps the South and West might present a candidate agreeable to both Tilden and Kelly. Then there was always the possibility that the convention might go off in a great hurrah for Tilden and take its stand on the issue of the great fraud of 1876. The Sage would appreciate a courtesy nomination which would give him the right to name his heir. But there was always Kelly and the memory of his bolt which had given the Republican Cornell the governorship in 1879. These were but a few of the many political "ifs" as Democratic delegates made their way to Cincinnati in June 1880.

---

[112] *Atlanta Constitution*, June 9, 1880.
[113] *Ibid.*, June 15, 1880.

CHAPTER III

The Republican
National Convention

The Republican convention which opened in Chicago on June 2, 1880 surpassed almost all others in color, in determined purpose, in men of strong character, and in the singing and band playing that brought to the 756 delegates memories of a distant but unforgotten past.[1] The convention opened at noon on Wednesday, June 2, and did not complete its work until midnight of Tuesday, June 8. It was not only the longest Republican convention up to that time, but it was also the first in which every state was represented.[2]

The Grant forces, who had felt that Chicago afforded just the proper environment for the "Little American Ulysses," were soon disillusioned. Edwards Pierrepont was not so sure that Grant would be nominated.[3]

General Grant's lieutenants, Senator Roscoe Conkling of New York, General John A. Logan of Illinois, and Senator Don-

---

[1] Henry L. Stoddard, *As I Knew Them: Presidents and Politics from Grant to Coolidge*, p. 102 (New York: Harper and Brothers, 1927). See also Stoddard, *Presidential Sweepstakes*, p. 77.

[2] The *Indianapolis Journal*, June 2, 1880 gives data on the length of previous Republican conventions.

[3] Fish MSS, Letter Book, Edwards Pierrepont to Hamilton Fish, June 7, 1880. See *San Francisco Bulletin*, June 10, 1880 for the hostility of Chicago to the Grantites.

ald Cameron of Pennsylvania, arrived in Chicago a week before the convention opened. By means of the unit rule they had pledged their state delegations to Grant. In 1868 and again in 1872 the general had been nominated on the very first ballot. Conkling, Logan, and Cameron were in Chicago to see to it that history repeated itself.

The Blaine legions, headed by the astute William E. Chandler, were in Chicago by May 24. General Garfield, whose duty it was to give cohesion and drive to the Sherman men in their efforts to nominate "Uncle John," arrived in the early morning of the twenty-fourth and repaired to the Grant Pacific Hotel, Room 108. He contacted his fellow Ohioans, Governor William A. Dennison, Warner M. Bateman, and Charles Foster, and urged them to take an aggressive stand in favor of district representation and against the unit rule. The settlement of these principles, he declared, was more important than the fate of any candidate. A promise of cooperation on the two points was secured from the Blaine men.[4]

Both Garfield and William E. Chandler realized that 1880 would be but a facsimile of 1872 and 1868 unless they could thwart the Grant strategy, which was based on forcing the convention to adopt the unit rule. The anti-Grant forces possessed a majority in the National Committee, but its chairman, Don Cameron, was prepared to do or die for the unit rule. There were 756 delegates, and 379 votes were necessary to nominate. If the unit rule were not adopted, twenty-six bolters from Pennsylvania, eighteen from Illinois, and nineteen from New York

---

[4] Garfield MSS, Diary, May 29, 1880. Theodore Clarke Smith, in *Life and Letters of James Abram Garfield* (already cited), Vol. 2, p. 987, condemns A. K. McClure for saying that "Garfield . . . illy concealed his efforts to advance himself while ostensibly struggling for Sherman." Smith concludes that in view of "the contents of Garfield's diary and letters during the period culminating in the balloting, this theory can scarcely be considered tenable." The balloting began on June 7. Garfield's diary is blank from June 2 to July 24.

would be recognized, and would cast their votes for candidates other than Grant. Don Cameron, secretary of war under Grant, knew that these sixty-three votes were necessary if Grant was to be victorious. The unit rule would place them squarely in the Grant column. As it turned out, Grant polled 304 votes on the first ballot. If the sixty-three "scratchers" had been added, he would have been within thirteen votes of nomination, and it is very probable that these thirteen would have been forthcoming before the first ballot had been completed.[5]

With this very promising possibility as a background, the Conkling-Cameron-Logan triumvirate took their stand on the principle that the National Committee had nothing to do with the rules of the convention and could take no action concerning them. So in the deliberations preliminary to the convention itself, Chairman Cameron was determined to refuse to entertain any motion concerning the rules of the convention, including of course the unit rule. As national chairman, it was Cameron's task to call the convention to order, but it was the function of the National Committee to propose a temporary chairman. If this nominee turned out to be an anti-Grant man, a candidate favorable to the general would then be named from the floor. The specific tactics were carefully planned. In the roll call to determine the choice, Cameron would authoritatively declare that the unit rule prevailed. This action would very probably result in a majority for the Grant contender. He in turn would maintain the same attitude in subsequent roll calls relating to the credentials of delegates and to permanent organization. In short, no vote could ever be taken on the principle of unit rule without the application of that very principle itself in the vote which was to decide the issue.[6] It was a clever tactic, but Garfield and William E. Chandler also had a plan.

---

[5] Hoar, *Autobiography*, Vol. 1, p. 389.
[6] L. B. Richardson, *Chandler*, p. 250.

The National Committee met on Monday, May 31, two days prior to the scheduled opening of the convention. The committee was composed of forty-seven members. Of these, twenty-nine were anti-Grant, thus constituting a majority.[7] A motion was quickly made against unit rule, but the Stalwart Cameron refused even to recognize it, on the ground that such action was outside the province of the committee. An all-day wrangle followed. Cameron took no part in the debate, but sat in obstinate silence while his case was argued by the other Grant members of the committee. A bitter feeling was engendered in the majority members as Cameron sat in stolid gloom, refusing to make any response to overtures looking to a compromise. A strong sentiment appeared for the immediate and forceful deposition of the chairman. If this should happen, feared Murat Halstead, Grant would be beaten.[8] Cooler heads, however, prevailed; and a subcommittee headed by William E. Chandler was appointed to bring in a nomination for a temporary chairman. It chose Senator George F. Hoar, who was allegedly a neutral since he favored the nomination of Edmunds.

Realizing that Hoar's nomination would be useless if the unit rule were enforced, the anti-Grant faction made a personal appeal to Senator Conkling. William E. Chandler and Garfield intimated to Lord Roscoe that in case of necessity Cameron would be deposed and a substitute appointed. Arthur, Conkling's first lieutenant, favored conciliation. Of even greater importance was the attitude of Colonel William E. Strong of Illinois, a Grant supporter, who had been appointed sergeant at arms. For the success of the Grant plan it was necessary that Strong should recognize Cameron, and Cameron alone, as the person entitled to call the convention to order. He was now asked whom

---

[7] New Hampshire Historical Society, Chandler MSS, John W. Mason to William E. Chandler, June 29, 1880.

[8] *Ibid.*, Murat Halstead to John Sherman, May 30, 1880. This document is a telegram.

he would recognize if the committee deposed Cameron and appointed Hoar. Strong desired time for consideration, which was conceded. He then consulted ex-Senator Timothy O. Howe, an able Wisconsin lawyer. Howe advised the sergeant at arms that the committee might lawfully depose their chairman and appoint another, and that, if such action were taken, it would be his duty as sergeant at arms to recognize the new chairman and obey his lawful orders. Strong, acting on Howe's advice, promptly announced that he would recognize the chairman appointed by the National Committee.

The spirit of compromise was now made mutual and the Grant leaders reluctantly agreed that Hoar should be temporary chairman, and in order to avoid a test vote at an inopportune moment, that he should likewise serve as permanent chairman.[9] Hoar's selection as chairman implied that the principle of unit rule should not govern the convention in voting on the question of unit rule itself. This was the first of a series of victories for the anti-Grant forces, and General Grant himself was finally persuaded by the importunities of John Russell Young to write to Senator Cameron, authorizing his friends, if they saw fit, to withdraw his name from the convention. Mrs. Grant had suspected the purpose of Young's visit and had tried to thwart it. Grant did not dare let his wife know of his letter to Cameron, and he would discuss the matter with Young only during Mrs. Grant's absence.[10]

Blaine had sensed the danger inherent in the strife at Chicago, and had wired to his first lieutenant his view that it was in every way desirable to avoid an angry row and a possible smash-up in the National Committee. He expressed his willingness to smother all personal resentment for the general good of the party. He hoped that Hoar could be had for temporary

---

[9] Hoar, *Autobiography*, Vol. 1, p. 392; T. C. Smith, *Garfield*, Vol. 2, p. 1080.
[10] Badeau, *Grant*, pp. 321-22.

chairman "without contest or collision." Such self-restraint, he felt, would make him look better in the eyes of the country than would an attempt to seat one of his own supporters.[11]

Garfield made known to John Sherman the news of the important victory and assured him that the unit rule was defeated. Hoar, he was confident, would be temporary chairman without a serious contest.[12]

Sherman was informed that the feeling of the Grant men toward him was "increasingly friendly," and that they might "throw their forces" to him.[13] Desiring, if possible, to conciliate the Grant faction, Sherman asked: "Is Hoar's election as temporary Chairman acquiesced in? Does not that settle the unit rule? If so why press Cameron further? Answer."[14]

It is possible that Sherman may have had knowledge of Grant's letter to Cameron in which Grant had expressed a willingness to retire from the race if necessary for party unity.[15] At all events, Sherman was still pursuing the reasonable tactic of doing everything possible to retain the friendship of both the Grant and the Blaine factions in the hope that, when the two giants should become deadlocked, they would release their delegates to him.[16]

The first session of the convention consumed but three hours. The delegates assembled in Exposition Hall, Chicago, at twelve noon, on Wednesday, June 2. The three hours of the opening

---

[11] Chandler MSS, James G. Blaine to William E. Chandler, June 1, 1880.

[12] John Sherman MSS, James A. Garfield to John Sherman, June 1, 1880.

[13] *Ibid.*, Warner M. Bateman to John Sherman, June 1, 1880.

[14] *Ibid.*, John Sherman to Warner M. Bateman, June 1, 1880.

[15] William Tecumseh Sherman was a close friend of John Russell Young, and Young may have informed General Sherman of the Grant letter to Cameron. If this is true, the general could easily have informed his brother John of Grant's attitude. See William T. Sherman MSS, Letter Book, Young to William T. Sherman, February 14, 1880. This letter indicates the intimacy between General Sherman and Young.

[16] John Sherman MSS, W. Dennison to John Sherman, June 1, 1880. Dennison was governor of Ohio during the Civil War.

day were devoted mainly to the formation of committees. After the opening prayer Cameron told the convention:

> Our country can . . . no longer be satisfied with . . . isolation . . . we must place in position men whose familiarity with other nations will enable them to direct our affairs so that we will take the lead in commerce, as we have in agriculture and manufactures.

Grant's recent world tour was supposed to have given him this knowledge of "other nations" to which Cameron alluded.[17]

Having thus fired the opening gun for his old chieftain, the chairman told the eager Half-Breeds what they had been waiting to hear: "I have been instructed by the Republican National Committee to place in nomination as temporary chairman the Honorable George F. Hoar of Massachusetts." After Hoar's nomination had been unanimously agreed upon, he made a short speech in which he enumerated the many benefits the Republican party had conferred upon the country. The rest of the time was given over to the formation of the committees on credentials, rules, permanent organization, and resolutions. William E. Chandler was elected chairman of the Committee on Credentials, while Garfield was chosen to head the Committee on Rules. All this was accomplished by three o'clock in the afternoon, when Roscoe Conkling, bloody but unbowed, moved an adjournment until eleven o'clock the following morning.[18]

Thus the first day of what was to prove one of the most dramatic and historic conventions in all American history ended in a triumph for the Half-Breeds. But the Stalwarts let it be known that they had only begun to fight. Conkling gave notice to Garfield that he would fight for the unit rule to the bitter end, despite his respect for Garfield as a possible dark horse.[19]

---

17 *Proceedings of the Republican National Convention Held in Chicago, Illinois, June 2-8, 1880,* p. 5. Chicago: John B. Jeffery Company, 1881.
18 *Ibid.*
19 John Sherman MSS, W. Dennison to John Sherman, June 2, 1880.

On the next day, Thursday, June 3, the convention reassembled at the appointed hour of eleven o'clock. It was a scorching-hot day, and the ten thousand and some people who jammed the barnlike Exposition Hall did not add to the comfort of the political gladiators. The bargain made on May 31 was promptly carried out when Henry R. Pierson of New York, the chairman of the Committee on Permanent Organization, stated that he had the honor of presenting to the convention "the Hon. George F. Hoar, of Massachusetts, as the Permanent President of the Convention."[20] Nothing of importance could be accomplished until the Committee on Credentials and the Committee on Rules were ready to report. When Conkling found that they were not yet ready, he sensibly moved an adjournment until six o'clock that evening. It was about eleven-thirty A.M. Eugene Hale, a Blaine Half-Breed from Maine, successfully opposed the motion of Conkling, asserting that the convention was ready to go to work. Conkling replied sarcastically, and pointed out that the only work which would be accomplished between then and four or five o'clock would be to sit there "idle on uncushioned seats—fortunately with backs, while a vast number of other persons sit in the galleries on benches without either cushions or backs."[21]

Senator Conkling was right on the question at issue, for until the Committee on Credentials and the Committee on Rules had determined whether or not the unit rule was to prevail and had set up the rules which would govern the conduct and procedure of the convention, nothing of any consequence could be transacted. Nevertheless the anti-Grant faction won out on the question of adjournment. The Stalwarts had to sit it out under the hot roof until seven-thirty that evening.

Friday, June 4, according to Wharton Barker's account, was to present Garfield, Barker, Henry C. Lea, and the whole Phila-

---

[20] *Proceedings, Republican Convention, 1880*, p. 22.
[21] *Ibid.*, pp. 17-18.

delphia Committee for Garfield with the opportunity for which they had been anxiously waiting. Barker relates that the convention reassembled at ten o'clock in the morning. The prayer had no sooner been offered when Conkling leaped to his feet and resolved that it was the sense of the convention that every member of it was bound in honor to support its nominee, whoever that nominee might be, and that no man might hold a seat who was not ready to so agree.[22]

Thomas C. Platt, senator from New York and close friend of Conkling, asserted that this was aimed at certain Hayes delegates who had openly threatened to bolt Grant in case he were nominated.[23] Eugene Hale, the Blaine Half-Breed from Maine, was in substantial agreement with Senator Conkling, but insisted that a Republican convention did not need to be instructed that the first and underlying duty of all members, after the convention had nominated its candidate, was to elect him over a Democratic candidate.[24]

The motion for a call of the roll was then agreed upon. The result was 716 yeas to 3 nays. Conkling rose once more and resolved that the delegates who had voted that they would not abide by the action of the convention did not deserve, and had forfeited, their votes in this convention.[25]

The protesting votes had come from three "eccentric"[26] West Virginia delegates. Wharton Barker, continuing his account, now claims that he himself stepped into the picture. Garfield had been carefully instructed by Barker to be ready to rise and speak at a moment's notice on a signal from the platform. His

---

[22] *Ibid.*, p. 34.
[23] Louis J. Lang, editor, *The Autobiography of Thomas Collier Platt*, p. 102 (New York: B. W. Dodge and Company, 1910). See also Schurz MSS, L. Q. C. Lamar to Carl Schurz, February 23, 1880. Schurz and his followers were ready to support Bayard in case of Grant's nomination.
[24] *Proceedings, Republican Convention, 1880*, p. 34.
[25] *Ibid.*, p. 36.
[26] T. C. Smith, *Garfield*, Vol. 2, p. 971. "Eccentric" is Professor Smith's own word.

managers were anxious to have him miss no chance of breaking into the discussion at any moment opportune for his interests.[27]

Such a moment came when Conkling sat down after moving that the three West Virginia delegates should be deprived of their seats. The convention broke into an uproar. The Grant men were applauding deliriously. The Sherman and Blaine partisans were hissing.

Amid the bedlam Barker insists that he signaled to Garfield to speak, but the latter, in the tumult, missed the cue. There followed a quick byplay calculated to attract Garfield's attention. Former Vice-President Hamlin shouldered his way to the platform and called out loudly, "I would give $5000 to be a delegate to this Convention so that I might reply to Conkling and speak against his resolution." Wayne MacVeagh, for Hoar's benefit, remarked in almost stentorian tones that Barker had said that Garfield wished to answer Conkling. Hoar, gladly picking up the hint, looked toward Garfield's place in the Ohio delegation; but all was quiet there. As Hoar turned to MacVeagh with a puzzled expression while the latter pleaded with him to look again, Garfield, finally catching Barker's nod, rose slowly, screwing himself, as it were, to his feet. He was obviously steeling himself painfully for an effort which he knew would be his making or undoing as a candidate. He was recognized by Hoar and began to speak.[28]

---

[27] Wharton Barker, "The Secret History of Garfield's Nomination," *Pearson's Magazine* 35:440, May 1916. See also Library of Congress, John C. Spooner MSS, Wharton Barker to John C. Spooner, June 16, 1893. In this letter Barker states: "I think we talked at Chicago during the Rep. Convention of 1880 when I was making combinations that led to the nomination of Gen. Garfield for President. The Wisconsin men with whom I negotiated were Gov. Pound and Mr. Payne and I cannot forget the action of the Wisconsin delegation; I was the director of the Garfield campaign at the Convention." This letter to Spooner was written thirteen years after the event, whereas the article referred to above, originally composed in 1912, was penned thirty-two years after the 1880 convention.

[28] Barker, "Garfield's Nomination," p. 441.

Besides being a talented orator Garfield was a skilled debater. He said that he regretted the dissenters' decision to risk the harmony of the convention, but he respected their right to vote against the resolution while supporting—as they declared they would support—the nominee of the convention. Not by any vote of his would they be deprived of their seats or their freedom of action. He trusted that Conkling would withdraw the resolution.[29]

This speech was to make him the man of the hour. At its end Conkling was forced to withdraw his resolution and, even before Garfield concluded his speech, Conkling wrote him the following note: "New York requests that Ohio's real candidate and dark horse come forward. We want him in our seats while we prepare our ballots."[30]

A few moments later—if Barker's testimony is to be relied upon—Garfield and Barker met in the lobby. "I did the best I could upon such short notice," confided the general to his friend; "I do not believe Conkling will want to tackle me again." Barker was feeling very content and very confident. "Nothing," he assured Garfield, "but a blunder on your part can now prevent you from receiving the nomination for President from this Convention."[31]

With this preliminary skirmish over, the convention took up the seemingly interminable task of settling the question of unit rule. Garfield, as chairman of the Committee on Rules, presented the majority report. Before he was halfway through, Conkling realized that the Half-Breeds had scored another triumph. For the eighth rule of the report stated that, if the vote of any state were challenged, "the President of the Convention shall direct the roll of members . . . to be called, and the result

---

[29] *Proceedings, Republican Convention, 1880*, pp. 40-41. This is essentially Barker's account. The proceedings of the convention merely give Garfield's speech.
[30] Garfield MSS, R. C. to Garfield, June 1880.
[31] Barker, "Garfield's Nomination," p. 441.

shall be recorded in accordance with the votes individually given."[32] The majority report of the Committee on Credentials was then read by the secretary of that committee, Samuel Fessenden. It was a lengthy report, and in its essence it represented another triumph for the anti-Grant forces. It boldly asserted that Republican traditions gave the lie to the unit rule and that the justice and equity of recognizing, securing, and protecting congressional district representation was also demonstrated by the actual precedents of the Republican party since its organization in 1856.[33]

The minority reports of both the Committee on Rules and the Committee on Credentials presented the case for the unit rule. Green R. Raum of Illinois, a Logan Stalwart, was not easily answered when he reminded the delegates that in 1860, when Lincoln was presented by the Republicans of Illinois, the delegates were selected by a state convention and the following resolution was adopted:

> Resolved, that Abraham Lincoln is the choice of the Republican party of Illinois for the Presidency, and the delegates from this State are instructed to use all honorable means to secure his nomination by the Chicago Convention, and vote as a unit for him.[34]

Raum went on to show how the same procedure was used in Illinois in 1864, 1868, 1872, and finally in 1876.[35] The arguments, pro and con, continued all that day and night, and into the early hours of the next day. Finally, in desperation, the committee reports were neatly filed away, and the 756 delegates were asked to vote on eleven distinct cases involving contested seats. The important cases turned on the right of a state convention to override the decision of a district convention and to send

---

[32] *Proceedings, Republican Convention, 1880*, p. 43.
[33] *Ibid.*, p. 49.
[34] *Ibid.*, p. 106.
[35] *Ibid.*, pp. 106-07.

as delegates men elected by themselves without regard to the elections of the district groups. The decision in these contested cases was the final test on unit rule itself, and in all of them the majority reports of the Committee on Rules and the Committee on Credentials were sustained. The closest vote came in the contest over the First District of Illinois. The result there was 384 to 356.[36] Murat Halstead felt that this was the crucial point and that the defeat of Grant was now assured.[37]

Friday, June 4, had been an important as well as a long day. The convention had reopened at ten o'clock in the morning, and when the gavel finally announced the end of the session, it was twenty minutes past two o'clock on Saturday morning. During those sixteen hours the unit rule had been buried, and General Garfield had risen to a political prominence far above that of the dark-horse variety.

At eleven o'clock on Saturday morning, June 5, the tired delegates resumed their labors. The Half-Breeds were sure that the prolongation of the convention into another week was sought for by Logan; for Logan, so the Half-Breeds claimed, was convinced that the Southern delegates would be too poor to sustain the enormous expense of remaining at Chicago, especially because a large number of railroad tickets would expire.[38]

Impelled by these fears, Willard Warner of Alabama made a speech from the floor in which he referred to the fact that many of the delegates were uneasy about their return tickets, and he urged the convention to pass a resolution asking the chairman and secretary to communicate with the railroads, requesting that the validity of the tickets might be extended at least three days beyond the end of the convention.[39] Action was

---

[36] Ibid.
[37] Cincinnati Commercial, June 5, 1880. See Hayes MSS, Diary, June 5, 1880. Hayes expresses the same idea as Halstead.
[38] John Sherman MSS, Moulton to J. Sherman, June 4, 1880.
[39] Proceedings, Republican Convention, 1880, p. 127.

immediately taken, and at the opening of the next session it was announced that the railroads had graciously complied with the wishes of the chairman.[40]

At this time Garfield moved that the Committee on Resolutions be ordered to report. The motion was agreed to, and Edwards Pierrepont, a Grant Stalwart and chairman of the committee, assured the convention that the committee had endeavored to present resolutions which would preserve the harmony of the convention and which would not awaken angry debate or cause long delay.[41]

This was an apt introduction to a platform that was to ignore civil-service reform. Perhaps it was calculated to prepare the convention for just such an omission. The platform contained the usual Republican claims of having "transformed 4,000,000 human beings from the likeness of things to the rank of citizens," and of having made a "sovereign nation" out of "confederate States." After having given President Hayes his mead of praise, a plank was added which charged the Democratic party with endeavoring to "obliterate the sacred memories of the war, and to overcome its inestimably valuable results of nationality, personal freedom and individual equality." The tariff plank, in an effort to win the vote of both capital and labor, affirmed the "belief, avowed in 1876, that the duties levied for the purpose of revenue should so discriminate as to favor American Labor." Instead of forbidding federal or state aid to Catholic schools, which would have lost the party more Catholic votes than it could afford, a plank was inserted opposing the use of public funds for sectarian schools in general:

> The Constitution wisely forbids Congress to make any law respecting the establishment of religion, but it is idle to hope that the Nation can be protected against the influence of secret sectarianism

---

[40] *Ibid.,* p. 195.
[41] *Ibid.,* p. 160.

while each state is exposed to its domination. We, therefore, recommend that the Constitution be so amended as to lay the same prohibition upon the Legislature of each state, and to forbid the appropriation of public funds to the support of sectarian schools.[42]

When Charles W. Clisbee, the secretary of the Committee on Resolutions, finished reading the platform, Barker of Massachusetts proposed an additional plank asserting that the "reform of the civil service shall be thorough, radical and complete."[43] Webster Flanagan, delegate at large from Texas and an ardent Grant supporter, then arose and made a speech on the subject of civil service which was marked by an honesty somewhat unusual at political conventions:

> Texas has had quite enough of the civil service. During the last four years, Sir, out of 1,400 officers appointed by the President of the United States, 140 represented the Republican party. We are not here, Sir, for the purpose of providing officers for the Democracy. There is one plank in the Democratic party that I have ever admired, and that is, "To the victors belong the spoils." After we have won the race as we will, we will give those who are entitled to positions office. What are we up here for? I mean that members of the Republican party are entitled to office, and if we are victorious we will have office. I therefore move to lay the amendment on the table.[44]

These remarks drew a good many laughs from the members of the convention. A plank on civil-service reform, albeit a somewhat watered-down one, was finally adopted. This plank, by stating "that fitness, ascertained by proper practical tests, shall admit to the public service," was vague enough to satisfy both spoilers and reformers.[45]

It was about ten o'clock, Saturday night, June 5, when the weary delegates finally adopted the platform together with the amendment on civil service. Nominations for the presidency

---

42 *Ibid.*, pp. 61-62.

43 *Ibid.*, p. 163.

44 *Ibid.*, pp. 164-65.

45 *Ibid.*, p. 169.

were next in order. Blaine was the first candidate presented to the 756 delegates for their "sober" consideration.[46] The crowd, remembering Ingersoll's famous Plumed Knight speech of four years ago, was in hopes of hearing the famous orator again. George A. Hook, a wealthy Chicago liquor dealer, told William E. Chandler that a nominating speech by Ingersoll would assure the prize for Blaine.[47]

Henry Ward Beecher, one of the foremost orators of that day, had styled Ingersoll "the most brilliant speaker of the English tongue of all men on this globe."[48] But Chandler had weighed every aspect of the situation most carefully and had decided to follow the advice of Charles A. Stott, who had declared that Ingersoll's avowed atheism would compromise any beneficial efforts that his rare eloquence might produce.[49]

Ingersoll's role at Chicago was therefore reduced to waving a red shawl in a gesture of ballyhoo, while the important task of presenting the candidate was entrusted to an insignificant millionaire from Detroit, James F. Joy. It would be difficult to imagine a duller and flatter performance than that of this speaker. He began by regretting that he had been chosen to make the nomination. He promised to be brief and assured the convention that his words would benefit the candidate but little. After a sketchy and inadequate outline of Blaine's political career, Joy insisted that Michigan would vote Republican even if Blaine were not nominated. He terminated his dismal effort by apologizing for having "been longer than I intended."[50]

---

[46] A few minutes before the nominations began, Chairman George F. Hoar introduced a resolution banning all intoxicating liquors from the convention hall. See *ibid.*, p. 169.

[47] Chandler MSS, George A. Hook to William E. Chandler, June 3, 1880.

[48] Library of Congress, Robert G. Ingersoll MSS. There is a typed copy of a speech by Beecher dated October 31, 1880 in the Ingersoll papers which contains the above quotation.

[49] Chandler MSS, Charles A. Stott to William E. Chandler, May 25, 1880.

[50] *Proceedings, Republican Convention, 1880,* pp. 175-77.

The name of Senator William Windom was then presented to the convention in a perfunctory speech by E. F. Drake, a delegate from Minnesota. This speaker consumed about three minutes and stressed Senator Windom's twenty years of service in Congress.

The state of New York was next on the roll call, and General Logan from Grant's own state of Illinois, the commander of the GAR, opened a scene that was to become famous in American political history. Logan was brief and to the point: "In the name of our loyal citizens, soldiers and sailors—in the name of loyality, of liberty, of humanity and justice I nominate Ulysses S. Grant for President."[51] Brief as were these words, the cheering that followed them lasted long enough to give Conkling the opportunity he desired. When the cheering died down, he was found standing on a reporters' table instead of on the speaker's platform. Few men had greater dramatic instinct. He knew the value of waiting for absolute silence. He was in magnificent form, and in a voice that any orator might well envy, he quoted the opening lines of Miles O'Reilly's famous verse:

> If asked what state he hails from
> Our sole reply shall be
> He hails from Appomattox
> And its famous apple tree!

The enthusiasm aroused by these few lines showed where the heart of the convention was. But in Conkling's speech no olive branch was held out to the Half-Breeds. He was not content with focusing the attention of the vast assembly on the sterling qualities of General Grant, but insisted on telling the anti-Grant faction just what he thought of them. Conciliation might have won for Grant, but Senator Conkling never asked for and never gave quarter. Having begun what was to prove the greatest

---

[51] Stoddard, *Presidential Sweepstakes*, pp. 80-81.

speech of his career, and one which ranks with the classics in American political history, Conkling immediately struck at the opponents of the unit rule.

> In obedience to the instructions which I should never dare to disregard, I rise to propose a nomination with which the country and the Republican party can grandly win. . . . New York is for Ulysses S. Grant. Never defeated—in peace or war—his name is the most illustrious borne by living man.[52]

Platt tells us that at this last sentence "There was an outburst of mad enthusiasm . . . that shook the convention hall."[53] Conkling's diction was perfect, and the convention caught his every word. As soon as the uproar subsided, he broke a lance on the Plumed Knight, and explained that with Grant as the leader of the party there would be no "defensive" campaign. There would be nothing to explain away. There would be no apologies to make. The shafts and arrows had all been aimed at him and they lay, broken and harmless, at his feet.[54]

Conkling then attempted to refute the argument founded on the idea that American tradition looked askance at a third term. In precise and clearly enunciated phrases he declared that the only argument against the nomination of Grant was one that would dumfound Solomon. Having tried Grant twice and found him faithful, we must not, even after an interval of years, trust him again. What man, asked the orator, do you reject because by his works you have known him, and found him faithful and fit? To all opposed to Grant, Conkling said: "Show me a better man! Name one, and I am answered!"[55]

Conkling resumed the offensive, and in stentorian tones proclaimed that nobody was really disquieted about a third term

---

[52] *Proceedings, Republican Convention, 1880*, pp. 179-80.
[53] Platt, *Autobiography*, p. 106.
[54] *Proceedings, Republican Convention, 1880*, p. 181.
[55] *Ibid.*

except those who hopelessly longed for a first term. Grant, without effort or intrigue on his part, was the only candidate whose friends had never threatened to bolt unless the convention did as they said.[56]

Even in his peroration Conkling turned his venomous sarcasm in the direction of the Curtis-Schurz faction. He took the stand that Grant and his friends held that the rightful rule of the majority was the very essence of their faith against not only the common enemy but against the "charlatans, joyhawkers, tramps and guerrillas who deploy between the lines and forage, now on one side and then on the other."[57]

Conkling had succeeded in making it crystal-clear to his opponents that in the event of a Grant victory they had better be prepared to plan careers in nongovernmental fields. "To the victors belong the spoils" was going to be applied within the Republican party itself. In his conclusion Conkling made the following stirring appeal:

> Gentlemen, we have only to listen above the din and look beyond the dust of an hour, to behold the Republican party advancing, with its ensigns resplendent with illustrious achievement, marching to certain and lasting victory, with its greatest Marshall at its head.[58]

As Conkling retired to his seat ten thousand voices filled Exposition Hall with deafening and sustained applause for Grant. For at least thirty, and possibly forty-five, minutes, the convention was a bedlam of hurrahs, aisle marching, and general confusion.[59] Even the old fife-and-drum corps sounded its

---

[56] *Ibid.*, p. 182.
[57] *Ibid.*
[58] *Ibid.*
[59] John Sherman MSS, unsigned telegram to John Sherman, June 5, 1880. This telegram sent to John Sherman mentions the fact that the cheering for Grant lasted about a half hour. It is unsigned but was probably sent by Warner M. Bateman.

shrill note. If the balloting had begun at that moment, Grant would probably have won on the first ballot as he had in 1872 and 1868. The *Chicago Inter-Ocean* in commenting on the speech said: "The play of sarcasm, the flash of scorn, the saber-cuts of severity, and all the pageantry of eloquence were used to help Grant. The address had the warmth, the eulogy, the finish of a poem, the force and fire of a philippic." Grant, the newspaper continued, "was in every line of it. His spirit breathed in every sentence, his personality lived and moved in the smooth insistence of the magic words, and stood revealed in the climax of the peroration."[60]

But George S. Boutwell, secretary of the treasury under Grant, while praising Conkling's great effort, made an important distinction. Boutwell asserted that whatever Conkling said in support of Grant's cause was of the highest order of dramatic eloquence, but that, when he dealt with his opponents, his speech intensified the opposition to General Grant.[61]

It was almost midnight when the tumult and shouting for the hero of Appomattox died down. Ohio was next on the roll call of the states, and according to Barker this signified another golden opportunity for Garfield. Garfield had known for some time that he was to present the name of John Sherman to the convention, yet on June 2 he wrote to his wife that he had not yet made the first step in preparing the nominating speech and that he foresaw no opportunity for preparing it. It was, he confided to his spouse, a "frightful mistake" that he had not written it before he came to Chicago. The address, he feared, would fall far below what was expected of him.[62]

---

[60] Platt, *Autobiography*, p. 111.
[61] George S. Boutwell, *Reminiscences of Sixty Years in Public Affairs*, Vol. 2, p. 268. New York: McClure, Phillips and Company, 1902.
[62] Garfield MSS, James Garfield to Mrs. Garfield, June 2, 1880. Throughout his political career Garfield was known as a man who prepared his speeches very carefully.

On June 5, the very day he was to make his speech nominating Sherman, he was greeted by the convention with much enthusiasm.[63] If we can believe Barker, he was a willing accomplice in the arrangements for this staged applause. Barker tells us that at his suggestion Garfield had agreed to make a late entrance at each session, so as to "give him a clear field against Conkling, who upon entering was sure to be greeted with applause."[64] Barker was determined that the cheers for Garfield should attract the attention of everyone in the hall, and for this purpose had arranged claques in various parts of the audience. "Whenever," he blandly said later, "Garfield entered the hall, arose to speak, or moved about, he was greeted with prolonged applause." Garfield was immensely popular with the galleries, which were quick to join in the applause begun by the two claques which Barker claims to have stationed there.[65]

The political position of Garfield at this time is somewhat difficult to define. It is quite possible that Garfield himself could not have defined his position at this time. Apparently he did not attempt any explanation. His diary is blank for these crucial convention days. Historians will not easily come by the truth in this matter. They will have to examine the testimony of witnesses. The witnesses themselves will have to be ruthlessly gone over for any evidence of bias. This we do know: not only had Garfield previously written a letter advocating the nomination of Sherman, but he had willingly accepted the responsibility of being a delegate at large for him. He had even promised to deliver the nominating speech.[66] Furthermore, Garfield, at the time of his campaign for the senatorship, had made a promise that he would support Sherman's candidacy at Chicago if Sherman

---

[63] John Sherman MSS, Warner M. Bateman (?) to John Sherman, June 5, 1880. This is an unsigned telegram, probably sent by Bateman.

[64] Barker, "Garfield's Nomination," p. 440.

[65] *Ibid.*

[66] Garfield MSS, B. A. Hinsdale to Garfield, April 23, 1880.

would back his efforts to reach the Senate.[67] Sherman had supported Garfield in his campaign, the senatorship had been won, and the importance of the Sherman group's contribution to the happy result had been acknowledged.[68] Sherman felt understandably confident that the debt of gratitude which Garfield owed him would be repaid.

Now came the time for Garfield to make his nomination speech for Sherman. When it was all over the Sherman supporters felt it was very unsatisfactory. At the end of his routine introductory paragraph, which observed all the dreary amenities of convention oratory, the general asked a rhetorical question: "What do we want?" With rather suspicious alacrity a voice cried out, "We want Garfield."[69]

The core of the speech lay in Garfield's appeal for party harmony as a means to victory. How, he declaimed, could victory be achieved? Surely not by assailing our Republican brethren. This was his retort to Conkling. The latter had struck out at those whom he believed to be hypocritical and insincere. Garfield strove to pour oil on, and to bind up the wounds of these injured politicians. He sought to restore the shaken confidence of the Half-Breeds, whom Senator Conkling had verbally battered. He solemnly asked God to forbid that he should say one word against, or cast one shadow upon, any name on the roll of "our heroes." "The coming fight," he declared, "is our Thermopylae. . . . If our Spartan hosts are united, we can

---

[67] Garfield MSS, Diary, November 23, 1879.

[68] John Sherman MSS, J. W. Tyler to Garfield, January 14, 1880. Garfield either forwarded this letter to Sherman, or Tyler sent a copy of it to Sherman. This letter was a reply to one from Garfield expressing his thanks for the efforts of Sherman's friends in helping him toward the senatorship. "Garfield accepted the aid of Sherman in the matter of the Senatorship, promising to 'do what he could for him' in the contest for the Presidential nomination" (Robert G. Caldwell, *James A. Garfield*, p. 279 [New York: Dodd, Mead and Company, 1931]).

[69] *Proceedings, Republican Convention, 1880*, p. 184.

withstand all the Persians that the Xerxes of Democracy can bring against us." But in order to win victory there was need of the vote of every Republican, of every Grant Republican, and of every anti-Grant Republican, in America. Every Blaine man and every anti-Blaine man would be needed in the campaign. In short, the vote of every follower of every candidate was required in order to make victory certain.[70]

The Sherman supporters were by this time silently praying that Garfield would at least mention Sherman's name. Ohio's senator-elect talked for fifteen minutes. His address was seventeen paragraphs in length. Not until the sixteenth paragraph did he provide a hint as to whom he was nominating. In the last sentence of the last paragraph Sherman's name was finally mentioned. The friends of Sherman were understandably and audibly disappointed at Garfield's affirmation that he was presenting Sherman for nomination "not as a better Republican or a better man than thousands of others . . . , but . . . for deliberate and favorable consideration."[71]

Sherman's friends were sick at heart. Joseph H. Geiger was disgusted, and reported to the secretary of the treasury what he regarded as Garfield's treason. The general, in Geiger's opinion, was seeking the nomination himself. He had been of no service whatever to Sherman at Chicago.[72] It was believed by W. P. Nixon that Charles Foster, governor of Ohio and delegate at large along with Garfield, was conspiring to bring Garfield out as a candidate and to transfer to him the Sherman forces, and he felt that Garfield had full knowledge of this fact.[73] This surmise with respect to Foster had been voiced in the *Cincinnati Commercial* by Murat Halstead. He thought that Foster was actually managing the Garfield boom with the hope of succeed-

---

70 *Ibid.*, p. 185.
71 *Ibid.*, p. 186.
72 John Sherman MSS, Joseph H. Geiger to John Sherman, June 6, 1880.
73 *Ibid.*, W. P. Nixon to John Sherman, June 6, 1880.

ing the latter in the senatorship, or, in the event of Garfield's defeat, of being helped by the general for the second place on the ticket.[74] After Garfield's nomination Halstead wired to Foster: "Tell Garfield I forgive him."[75]

It was close to midnight when Garfield finished the delivery of his unprepared speech in which he nominated Sherman. The roll call of the states continued, and on the call of the state of Vermont, Frederick Billings arose and in a short speech nominated George F. Edmunds.[76]

Edmunds had not sought the office, and had actually stated that Grant was his first choice. The fact that his name was introduced to the convention represented no duplicity on his part. He had done no maneuvering. He simply was not in a position to prevent others from nominating him. He was for General Grant, and he meant what he said. Grant never forgot Edmunds' loyalty, and in the crucial hour of the convention wrote that "my preference is most unquestionably for Edmunds above all others named."[77] There remained but one more name to be put in nomination—Elihu B. Washburne of Illinois. John B. Cassoday, chairman of the Wisconsin delegation, did the honors for this candidate. He eulogized him as the man "who, at the breaking out of the War sought out an obscure individual in Galena, led him to Springfield, up to the mountain of his glory, and stands by his side, one of his chief admirers and friends today."[78] This description of Washburne's position was not quite exact. It is true that he had been the maker of Grant, but by 1877 he was secretly in opposition to him even though on the

---

[74] Garfield MSS, A. D. Rogers to Foster, June 5, 1880.

[75] *Ibid.*, Halstead to Foster, June 5, 1880.

[76] *Proceedings, Republican Convention, 1880,* p. 190. George F. Hoar, Garfield's friend, thinks that Garfield did a good job in behalf of Sherman. See Hoar, *Autobiography,* Vol. 1, pp. 394-95.

[77] Library of Congress, Roscoe Conkling MSS, U. S. Grant to Fred Grant, June 8, 1880.

[78] *Proceedings, Republican Convention, 1880,* p. 193.

surface he continued to appear loyal.[79] Grant had evidence of Washburne's disloyalty, and never forgave him for it.[80]

Augustus Brandegee of Connecticut, in seconding the nomination, made a powerful appeal which laid great stress on Washburne's aid to the Germans while he had been our minister to France during the Franco-Prussian War. Brandegee reminded the delegates that in the city of New York alone there were one hundred and fifty thousand Germans. There were, he continued, sons and daughters of the Fatherland in every "Northern Republican and doubtful State." German-American voters could never forget that Washburne had collected some thirty thousand Germans within the black and scarred walls of Paris "with the Commune howling like tigers to lap their blood." And beneath the flag of his country every one of them had been safe. There was not a German that would not take up his name. He would carry four fifths of the whole German vote of the United States.[81]

At this point in Brandegee's address Roscoe Conkling shook his head vigorously. Perhaps he was trying to indicate to the convention that his New York machine would kill any enemy of Grant, Washburne included. Brandegee, noticing Conkling's vehement dissent, gave an answer that was to do serious harm to Grant's cause:

> The gentleman from New York shakes his head. He shakes his head magnificently. No man can shake it like him, nor shake such rhetoric and wisdom out of it. But let me tell the gentleman from New York he cannot sit down at the ear of every voter and give the argument that he has given tonight against the tradition of our

---

[79] Washburne MSS, W. H. French to E. B. Washburne, 1879. No month or day is given in the original.

[80] Badeau, *Grant*, p. 322. After the nomination of Garfield, Colonel Frederick Grant, son of the general, was reported to have said that "Mr. Washburne was a . . . liar and fraud." See *Chicago Tribune*, June 12, 1880.

[81] *Proceedings, Republican Convention, 1880*, p. 194.

fathers. He may, by the magic of his eloquence, take this Convention and the galleries off their feet, in his fervor; but even his great abilities, even his unmatched eloquence cannot go down to the fireside of every voter and persuade them that all the traditions of the fathers with reference to a third term are but humbug and masquerade. Does he not know that his candidate would be on the defensive, that even the magic name of Grant can hardly carry him in this Convention. Does he not know—no one knows so well as he—that the name of Grant would carry this Convention through by storm if there were not an invincible argument against his nomination?[82]

This was a good speech, and no one realized it more than Conkling. The time element was of high importance. If only he could have been the last speaker! And if only the balloting could have taken place immediately after the great demonstration for General Grant! These and other thoughts must have been running through the mind of Roscoe Conkling as the convention prepared to adjourn. It was Saturday night, and it was after midnight. On Monday morning, at ten o'clock, the balloting would finally begin.

The convention was now four days old, and Sunday provided a welcome respite for the tired delegates. It provided time also for the politicians to agree on a candidate if that was possible. On Thursday, June 3, H. E. Cuney had told William E. Chandler that he wanted some money and must have it if he was expected to do anything. Before leaving Washington he had been instructed, he said, to see Chandler about all money matters. He declared he was doing all he could to keep the Grant Negro delegates from bolting to Sherman or to some other dark horse, and this required some funds. There were, he was sure, some Grant men he could control on the first ballot if he had the means.[83]

---

[82] *Ibid.* Brandegee was a delegate at large from New London, Connecticut.
[83] Chandler MSS, H. E. Cuney to William E. Chandler, June 3, 1880.

It was patent to the politicians that a "break" would come, for Blaine's boom was collapsing.[84] The wise ones were saying that "Grant should be taken out of the race before he goes over the wheel."[85] There were indications that the convention was preparing for a sudden shift.

As the balloting began on Monday morning at ten o'clock, a great storm was raging and the telegraph wires throughout the North were down. The managers in Chicago were thus left to their own devices.

There was a great deal of guessing as to what Senator Conkling would do about the bolters in the New York delegation. Despite the convention's smashing of the unit rule, Conkling still believed that the New York delegation was pledged to vote as a unit for Grant. As chairman of New York's delegation he knew that, if he cast the state's entire vote for Grant, it was certain that somebody would ask for and be granted a roll call. He quieted all rumors when he told the convention that he thought it best to have the New York delegates vote individually. At this announcement a few hearts beat more rapidly, and a few throats tightened. For now the rebels must announce their dissent publicly, and this would not be an easy task with the blue-gray eyes of Conkling, unspeakably cold, such a short distance away.[86]

John Birdsall of Queens County was the first Blaine man. He had declared on the floor of the state Senate that he would vote for Blaine. He kept his promise. But he did it in a low voice and he sat down in a hurry with his face flaming as though from shame. There were hisses from the Conkling machine. But courage gradually took hold of the other "scratchers," and by the time William H. Robertson cast his vote, loudly, boldly, and without hesitation, there were a few cheers.[87]

---

[84] John Sherman MSS, W. Dennison to John Sherman, June 1, 1880.
[85] *Cincinnati Commercial*, June 5, 1880.
[86] Chidsey, *Conkling*, p. 290.
[87] *Proceedings, Republican Convention, 1880*, pp. 199-200.

Fifty-one of the New York votes went to Grant on that ballot, seventeen went to Blaine, and two to Sherman. On the first ballot Grant led with 304 votes, closely followed by Blaine with 284. The combined votes of Sherman (93), Edmunds (34), Washburne (30), and Windom (10) represented only 21 per cent of the entire convention. It was apparent that the struggle was between Grant and Blaine and that, as long as their forces remained intact, only Sherman votes could give either of them the majority (379) necessary for the nomination. There was no essential change in the above tabulation during the twenty-eight ballots taken on Monday and the five more on Tuesday morning. Grant's strength fluctuated between 302 and 309, and Blaine's between 275 and 285. On the thirtieth ballot John Sherman's votes rose to 120 by reason of the accession of 21 Edmunds delegates from Massachusetts, and Sherman's supporters jubilantly predicted that the Half-Breeds would stampede to their candidate. But it was a false alarm. Sherman's count quickly declined again to the proportions of a makeweight. The stampede was soon to come, but it would not be for Sherman.[88] On the second ballot W. A. M. Grier of Hazelton, Pennsylvania, had cast a vote for James A. Garfield, and on almost every succeeding ballot the senator-elect from Ohio had received one or two votes in an effort to keep his name before the convention. Barker insists that he, along with Streight of Indiana, Sheldon of Ohio, and Governor Pound of Wisconsin, were patiently waiting for the psychological moment to put Garfield in the running. That moment finally arrived. On the thirty-fourth ballot Pound threw Wisconsin's sixteen votes to Garfield. On the thirty-fifth, Streight swung Indiana's twenty-seven to Garfield, which, with scattered votes from Maryland, Mississippi, and North Carolina,

---

[88] Perhaps the hardest blow of all for Sherman during the convention was the fact that ten Ohio delegates refused to vote for him. See Jeannette P. Nichols, "John Sherman"; in *Dictionary of American Biography*, Vol. 17, pp. 84-88.

gave him a total of fifty. On the thirty-sixth, the anti-Grant delegates from state after state flocked to the Garfield banner, and
nominated him with 399 votes. Conkling moved a resolution to
make the choice unanimous. The resolution was seconded by
Hale of Maine and Foster of Ohio. As though a little frightened
by what it had done, the convention instantly completed the
ticket by the nomination of Arthur of New York for vice-
president.[89] As Whitelaw Reid, a staunch partisan of the Blaine
Half-Breeds, phrased it: "Even the Grant people can join the
jubilee for they have named the Vice-President which was a
good deal for a minority to accomplish."[90]

As Reid penned these words of consolation for Stalwart con-
sumption, Colonel William M. Grosvenor, a prominent Missouri
politician, was informing Carl Schurz that Arthur was a necessity and that "Conkling and Co. were half ready to knife the
candidate." He asked Schurz to secure for him all the documents bearing upon the Crédit Mobilier and DeGolyer cases and
to send them to him as soon as possible.[91] It would take a lot of
explaining to free Garfield's name from the shadow of political
scandal, and his henchmen were losing no time in their efforts
to anticipate the coming attacks of the Democrats.

The Grant phalanx, 306 strong, held their line unbroken
until all went down together "facing the foe," as one veteran
proudly reported.[92] A medal was struck by Chauncy I. Filley of
St. Louis to commemorate the fidelity of the 306, and as many
of them as could do so agreed to meet for an annual dinner in
New York City. Grant's son wrote his hearty thanks to Roscoe

---

[89] *Proceedings, Republican Convention, 1880,* pp. 198, 259, 267, 269, 270. Colonel
Abel D. Streight was a wealthy lumberman from Indiana. He was not a delegate to the convention.
[90] *New York Tribune,* June 9, 1880. Whitelaw Reid, a close friend of Blaine's, was
the editor of the *Tribune* at this time.
[91] Schurz MSS, William M. Grosvenor to Carl Schurz, June 9, 1880.
[92] Stoddard, *Presidential Sweepstakes,* p. 83.

Conkling, and expressed the opinion that the Republican party would regret before November that they had not followed Conkling's advice.[93] Blaine himself thought that Garfield would probably lose the election, but declared that he himself would prefer to see the party lose with Garfield than win with Grant. It was Blaine's prediction that the Stalwarts would not vote for Garfield and that Sherman would never forgive him for the apparent treachery at the convention.[94]

On the day following the close of the convention E. B. Martindale, in an editorial which followed the pattern set by the majority of American newspapers, observed that the nomination of Garfield, like that of Lincoln, was a surprise. Such a thing had seemed impossible until the last hour and the last ballot. The spontaneity in Garfield's case was not imaginary but real, a clear case of the office seeking the man.[95]

Wharton Barker had a different story. Barker claims to have been the chief architect of the coup. He had arranged, so he claims, with W. A. M. Grier of Pennsylvania to vote for Garfield on the first and all subsequent ballots in order to keep his name before the convention.[96]

When Wisconsin had broken for Garfield and when Indiana immediately followed suit, many, like Martindale, had pronounced it "a clear case of the office seeking the man." But Barker insists that he arranged to have Governor Pound of Wisconsin and Colonel Streight of Indiana decide when the time had come for the break to Garfield and that he had arranged for their cooperation weeks before the convention.[97]

---

[93] Conkling MSS, Fred Grant to Roscoe Conkling, June 8, 1880.

[94] Blaine to M. P. Curran. See M. P. Curran, *Life of Patrick Collins*, p. 82 (Norwood: Norwood Press, 1906). Curran was a newspaper reporter.

[95] *Indianapolis Journal*, June 9, 1880.

[96] Barker, "Garfield's Nomination," p. 440. See also Garfield MSS, Diary, February 18, 1880 for the story of W. Barker's visit and proposal to Garfield.

[97] Barker, "Garfield's Nomination," p. 440.

Part of Barker's plan, he tells us, had been to get the Sherman vote for Garfield.[98] By Saturday, June 5, every part of his program had been taken care of except that which pertained to the transfer of the Sherman vote to Garfield. Feeling that President Hayes was the man who could swing Sherman, Barker started for the East, and wired Hayes first from Chicago and again from Harrisburg.[99] No evidence exists which would prove that Hayes joined hands with Barker. When Barker reached Philadelphia he wired Carl Schurz that Garfield could be nominated if Sherman were out of the way. He urged Schurz to do everything possible to block Grant.[100]

Schurz's reaction to this appeal, as in the case of Hayes, is not discoverable in the documents; but before the thirty-sixth ballot, which nominated Garfield, was taken, Barker asserts that he was satisfied that the major part of the Sherman delegates would follow a break from Blaine to Garfield and so advised Colonel Streight, the commander of the Garfield forces. In consultation with Pound, Streight concluded that the time for the break had come. Pound swung Wisconsin's sixteen votes for Garfield, and on the thirty-fifth ballot Streight delivered Indiana's twenty-seven. On the next ballot came the stampede and the nomination.[101]

It was definitely the last scene of the last act when the Wisconsin delegation came over to the Garfield column. At this moment the senator-elect from Ohio rose to protest the use of his name. The chairman, Senator George F. Hoar, describes the incident in his *Autobiography*:

> Mr. Garfield of Ohio: Mr. President . . .
> The President: For what purpose does the gentleman rise?

98 *Ibid.*
99 *Ibid.*
100 Schurz MSS, Wharton Barker to Carl Schurz, June 8, 1880.
101 Barker, "Garfield's Nomination," p. 442.

MR. GARFIELD: I rise to a question of order.

THE PRESIDENT: The gentleman from Ohio rises to a question of order.

MR. GARFIELD: I challenge the correctness of the announcement. The announcement contains votes for me. No man has the right without the consent of the person voted for to announce that person's name and vote for him in this Convention.

THE PRESIDENT: The gentleman from Ohio is not stating a question of order. He will resume his seat.[102]

Garfield "reluctantly" resumed his seat. Hoar asserts that the above report is absolutely correct, "except that where there is a period at the end of Mr. Garfield's last sentence there should be a dash, indicating that the sentence was not finished."[103] Hoar interrupted Garfield in the middle of his sentence, since he was terribly afraid that he would say something that would make his nomination, or his acceptance, impossible.[104]

Garfield afterwards said to a newspaper reporter: "If Senator Hoar had permitted, I would have forbidden anybody to vote for me. But he took me off my feet before I had said what I intended."[105] Naturally there were those who accepted this explanation as quite reasonable. Others thought differently. They felt that Garfield could have used his powerful voice in decisively stemming the tide that began to move toward him. In a few minutes that tide carried Garfield to victory. James Ford Rhodes, a contemporary of Garfield's, was among those who thought that he was less than truthful.[106] The *New Orleans Times*,

---

[102] Hoar, *Autobiography*, Vol. 1, pp. 396-97.

[103] *Ibid.*, p. 397.

[104] *Ibid.*

[105] Rhodes, *United States*, Vol. 8, p. 126.

[106] *Ibid.* Says Rhodes: "Nobody can doubt that Garfield, with his magnificent presence and stentorian voice, could have commanded the attention of the convention and by declining emphatically to be a candidate under any circumstances, have turned the tide which was setting in his favor. . . . But apparently the thought of his trust was overpowered by the conviction that the prize was his without the usual hard preliminary work."

in a forthright editorial, satirized what it termed Garfield's "attitudinizing."[107]

Garfield won the nomination on the sixth and last day of the convention. On the fifth day, Monday, June 7, Grier, who had been voting for Garfield for some twenty-five ballots, asked his favorite whether he would support a protective tariff.[108] Garfield's answer cannot be found in the documents.

If we accept Barker's account, Pound, acting for Elisha W. Keyes, gave the word to the Wisconsin delegation to vote for Garfield, but it is not certain who was the first in the delegation to suggest that its votes be cast for Garfield. John B. Cassoday, chairman of the Wisconsin delegation, has some support for the honor. As early as May 3, 1880 Cassoday informed Elisha W. Keyes that, since the Wisconsin delegation was unpledged, it might be possible for them to determine the ticket.[109] The *Mil-*

---

[107] *New Orleans Times*, June 17, 1880. The editorial states that Garfield rose "to protest after he had been voted for some thirty-four times, that his name ought not to be used because he had not been put in nomination. He did not rise to say that he was for his friend Sherman and would not allow his name to be used. He made a point of order which he knew the President would rule against him and thereby indicate to the Convention that he might be voted for. He knew this for he had been chairman of the Committee on Rules. The ruse succeeded. In a few minutes the struggle was over. The hero of the most masterly piece of attitudinizing in the history of politics reaped the reward of his strategy." See also *San Francisco Bulletin*, June 10, 1880. This paper suspects Garfield of "acting."

[108] Garfield MSS, W. A. M. Grier to Garfield, June 7, 1880. Different from but not necessarily contradictory to W. Barker's account is that of Andrew Jackson Turner, a Wisconsin delegate to the convention. Recalling the sudden swing to Garfield, he says: "It is absolutely certain that no delegate outside of our own delegation suspected that anything of the sort was about to happen. They could not have done so, for we didn't know ourselves what we were going to do until a moment before." See Henry C. Campbell, *Wisconsin in Three Centuries, 1634-1905*, Vol. 4, pp. 285-90 (New York: Century History Company, 1906). A. J. Turner, father of the historian Frederick Jackson Turner, published the *Portage (Wisconsin) State Register*.

[109] Cassoday to Keyes, May 3, 1880. Quoted from Keyes MSS as found on p. 56 of Dorothy Ganfield, *The Federal Influence of Wisconsin 1880-1907* (unpublished dissertation, University of Wisconsin, 1928).

waukee Sentinel felt that the switch to Garfield "was probably done at the suggestion of Jeremiah M. Rusk, later Governor of the State and Secretary of Agriculture."[110] Andrew Jackson Turner admits that he "stuffed the hat" when approached by Senator Dickinson of the New York delegation just after the Wisconsin vote for Garfield. Dickinson asked Turner if there was "a concerted movement looking to the nomination of General Garfield." Turner "deceived" his friend Dickinson by replying "in the most confidential and positive manner possible, that there was, and that General Garfield's nomination was certain to be made." Just after this chat Turner recorded that the "twenty Blaine men from New York immediately came into our camp."[111] The stampede to Garfield could not be stopped.

While the excitement of the Chicago convention mounted and mounted, General Grant sat quietly on the porch of his home in Galena, Illinois. A message from Grant reached Conkling during one of the bitter sessions of the convention. The substance of General Grant's communication was to this effect:

> The personal feelings of partisans of the leading candidates had grown to be so bitter, that it might become advisable for the good of the Republican Party to select as their candidate some one whose name had not yet been prominently before the convention, and that he therefore wrote to say to those who represented his interests in the convention, that it would be quite satisfactory to him if they would confer with those who represented the interests of Mr. Blaine and decided to have both his name and Mr. Blaine's withdrawn from before the convention.[112]

---

[110] *Milwaukee Sentinel,* October 23, 1896, as found on p. 57 of Ganfield, *Wisconsin.*

[111] Campbell, *Wisconsin,* Vol. 4, pp. 285-90. This is A. J. Turner's own account of the convention. See Herman Julius Deutsch, *Political Forces in Wisconsin 1871-1881,* pp. 268-71 (unpublished dissertation, University of Wisconsin, 1929).

[112] Frederick D. Grant to George S. Boutwell, May 30, 1897. See Boutwell, *Reminiscences,* Vol. 2, pp. 271-72. General Grant's son, who had been commissioned by his father to inform Conkling of the general's attitude, is here giving Boutwell the substance of what he told Conkling.

It is quite possible that Conkling might have swung New York to Blaine had it not been for this letter. For on June 9, the morning after the convention, Senator Conkling told Charles Emory Smith that "he would have far rather had Blaine nominated than Garfield," whom he described as an "angleworm."[113] Blaine, in answer to a query from Senator Blair of New Hampshire, asserted that in the event of Grant's and his own failure he favored Conkling. This information was conveyed to the gentleman from New York.[114]

During the crucial thirty-sixth ballot, just after Maine had cast her fourteen votes for Garfield, Senator John P. Jones of Nevada, a Grant Stalwart, rushed to Conkling's side and said: "Now is your chance to do the great act; throw the vote of New York for Blaine." Conkling replied, "There isn't time to poll the delegation." Jones knew this only too well, and snapped back, "Cast the vote and poll the delegation afterwards."[115] Conkling, no doubt, felt that this would be disloyal to the country's greatest marshal, and "in obedience to instruction," which he had earlier averred "he would never disobey," he cast the fifty New York Stalwart votes for Grant. The New York bolters, headed by Robertson, moved into the Garfield column.[116]

Certainly there was never a more exciting day in all Republican convention history than June 8, 1880. On that day Garfield was nominated at 2:30 P.M., Chicago time. Blaine, just three minutes before, had wired him that the vote of Maine had that minute been cast for him and that he hoped it would aid in securing his nomination and assuring victory for the Republican party.[117]

---

[113] Charles Emory Smith, "How Conkling Missed Nominating Blaine." *Saturday Evening Post* 173:2-3, June 8, 1901.
[114] *Ibid.*
[115] *Ibid.*
[116] *Proceedings, Republican Convention, 1880*, p. 271.
[117] Garfield MSS, Blaine to Garfield, June 8, 1880.

In a telegram marked 2:48 P.M., Chicago time, John Sherman advised Dennison that, whenever the vote of Ohio would be likely to assure the nomination of Garfield, he would appeal to every delegate to vote for him. He urged that Ohio be solid, and that the same appeal be made in his name to North Carolina and every delegate who had voted for him.[118]

After a careful study of this and of other evidence it seems clear that General Charles H. T. Collis was correct when he stated that Garfield "was nominated before any message from Blaine or Sherman was received."[119]

The nomination of Arthur for the vice-presidency was the work of Garfield's Ohio supporters.[120] It was their way of asking the irate Senator Conkling to support the ticket in the all-important Empire State. But John Sherman thought that the nomination of Arthur was "a ridiculous burlesque," for he had "never held an office except the one he was removed from." Sherman had a doubt about Garfield's role at the convention and asked Warner M. Bateman for his "frank and free opinion on the subject."[121]

After Garfield's assassination Senator Justin S. Morrill of Vermont told Sherman the following confidential story. Morrill claimed he had never narrated the tale before, "lest it might do harm." A few days before the convention Morrill in a conversation with Garfield asked who was to be the dark horse. Garfield answered: "At all events John Sherman would not be in his way as two-thirds of the delegates would be for him [Garfield]

---

[118] John Sherman MSS, John Sherman to Dennison, June 8, 1880. According to Garfield's diary Sherman had told Garfield that he would swing the Ohio delegation to him when his own (Sherman's) nomination was hopeless. See Garfield MSS, Diary, February 18, 1880.

[119] *New York Herald*, June 20, 1880. Collis was present at the convention.

[120] Chandler MSS, Warner M. Bateman to William E. Chandler, June 14, 1880. Bateman tells Chandler that Arthur's nomination was the "hasty work of my friend Gov. Dennison."

[121] John Sherman MSS, John Sherman to Warner M. Bateman, June 9, 1880.

whenever the time comes." Morrill further said: "The Convention clearly showed that Garfield was even then contemplating and working for his own nomination."[122]

The Democratic press lost no time in training its heaviest guns on Arthur. Six days after his nomination the *Louisville Courier Journal* ran a picture of Arthur with the caption: "Nominated at Chicago for the Vice-Presidency. Suspended by President Hayes from the New York Collectorship, that the office might be honestly administered."[123] The *Concord (New Hampshire) People and Patriot* expressed its conviction that Arthur represented the New York machine. He had been "kicked out of the Custom House by Hayes and Sherman for inefficiency and general corruption."[124] The same journal was even less sympathetic toward the head of the ticket. Garfield, in its opinion, was "a clever trickster in politics" and belonged to "that illustrious and fragrant band of office seekers and office holders known as 'Christian statesmen.'" He had made a "hypocritical pretense" of supporting Sherman.[125] The *New Orleans Times* felt that the nomination of Arthur was in reality "a slap at Hayes and civil service reform."[126]

The reason for choosing Arthur was clear: without Conkling the Empire State would be lost. Since New York was vital, Arthur was nominated with the hope that Conkling would put his shoulder to the wheel for the Grand Old Party.

The general tendency of the Republican press was one of a discreet silence with regard to the vice-presidential nominee. The Stalwart *New York Times* was one of the few to break this pattern when, on June 9, it asserted that it had had frequent

---

[122] John Sherman MSS, Memorandum starting, "In a conversation this day with Senator Morrill of Vt.," February 12, 1883.

[123] *Louisville Courier Journal*, June 14, 1880.

[124] *Concord People and Patriot*, June 9, 1880.

[125] *Ibid.*

[126] *New Orleans Times*, June 9, 1880.

occasion to affirm the integrity and ability of General Arthur
as a public servant.[127]

Garfield acquiesced in Arthur's nomination, but he would
have much preferred the New York banker, Levi P. Morton.
This preference is revealed in a letter from William E. Curtis
to Morton, in which Garfield is reported by Curtis as speaking
of Morton in the highest terms. Garfield expressed regret that
the New Yorker's name had not been placed on the ticket, for
he felt certain that this would have removed New York from the
doubtful list.[128]

President Hayes, like General Garfield, was none too confident about the outcome of the coming election. Victory for the
Republicans was by no means assured. Shortly after the convention he recorded in his diary: "But now how to win. The
contest will be close and fierce. We may be beaten. . . . We must
neglect no element of success."[129]

Garfield proclaimed again and again that he "did not desire
the nomination,"[130] but there remained a considerable number
of politicians who wrote him down as a "pretender."[131] They felt
that if he had, like Roscoe Conkling, declared himself out of
the race, he could have won the nomination for John Sherman.
Hayes thought that Garfield could not have been nominated if

---

[127] *New York Times*, June 9, 1880. Gaillard Hunt is of the opinion that on June 8
the tired convention would have turned to the first dark horse who could
muster fifty votes. Hunt thinks Washburne would have been this man were it
not for the fact that he was known to be a loyal Grant man. See Gaillard
Hunt, *Israel, Elihu, and Cadwallader Washburn: A Chapter in American
Biography*, p. 281 (New York: The Macmillan Company, 1925). Garfield
believed that Washburne was guilty of political perfidy toward Grant. See
Garfield MSS, Diary, May 15, 1880.

[128] New York Public Library, Levi P. Morton MSS, William E. Curtis to Levi P.
Morton, July 20, 1880. Morton refused the nomination upon the advice of
Conkling. See Chidsey, *Conkling*, p. 293.

[129] Hayes MSS, Diary, June 11, 1880.

[130] Jeremiah S. Black MSS, Garfield to Jeremiah S. Black, July 20, 1880.

[131] *Louisville Courier Journal*, June 11, 1880.

he had gone into a contest for the nomination.[132] It is quite conceivable that Garfield was convinced that it was possible for him to remain loyal to Sherman in spite of the circumstances in which he found himself.[133]

While the American press was by no means in agreement as to the honesty of Garfield, an almost complete unanimity was reached on the third-term issue. Both Republican and Democratic papers were quite sure that if Grant, who was a popular

---

[132] Hayes MSS, R. B. Hayes to George W. Jones, June 11, 1880. The lesson of Garfield's nomination was not lost on Republican politicians. Three conventions later William McKinley, another Ohioan, came to Minneapolis to nominate Benjamin Harrison. Louis T. Michener, one of Harrison's political managers, remembering Garfield's tactics, suspected McKinley's loyalty. Michener set a watch on McKinley and discovered that he was busying himself attending anti-Harrison meetings. In the few days preceding the opening of the convention Michener kept a sharp eye on Convention Hall. His sleuthing was rewarded when he found several huge wooden boxes in the attic of the building. They had been sent from Cleveland by Mark Hanna. Michener's suspicions were confirmed when he discovered that the boxes contained McKinley pennants as well as horns and other noisemaking instruments. He quickly adopted a plan guaranteed to prevent McKinley from "Garfielding" the convention. McKinley was elected chairman by acclamation, "had his half hour of boisterous admiration, and then became the hum-drum presiding officer of the Convention, receiving but little applause at any time, and so acting and ruling so as to create discontent often. . . . This makes it impossible for McKinley to Garfield the Convention" (Library of Congress, Louis T. Michener MSS, 1892, no. AC. 4161A, pp. 7-8. This is a typewritten memorandum giving a full account of the Republican convention of 1892).

[133] George C. Tichenor, in a letter to John Sherman dated June 26, 1880 (in John Sherman MSS) related the following story. It concerns a certain Mrs. Dora who was seeking employment in the Chicago post office. She felt that the Republican party owed her a lucrative position as a reward for her labors in behalf of Garfield. After careful investigation Tichenor found that she "was in communication with Foster and Nichol during the convention and was paid by them for her services; and that she visited several of the Southern delegates, amongst others Peter of Virginia. . . . She says also that Foster told her that Garfield was to be the nominee *before the day of his nomination* . . . she . . . had been cautioned against giving anything away. I have felt all along that Gen. Garfield acted fairly but that impression cannot be maintained if Foster is accepted as his chosen lieutenant, for the opinion is very general that Foster betrayed you in a shameful manner and the Republicans of this country are too decent to respect an ingrate and a traitor."

hero, could not achieve the third-term nomination, "it is not supposable that anyone else will even be thought of in that connection while the present order of constitutional government in the country shall continue."[134] Grant came awfully close to the prize, and it is quite conceivable that, in spite of tradition and interparty factions, he could have been nominated. Conkling was an astute manager, and if Grant had listened to him rather than to Mrs. Grant, the general's return might well have been the decisive factor at the convention that Conkling intended it to be. As it turned out, Mrs. Grant insisted on an early return with the result that Grant's triumphal receptions in the states were poorly timed. It seems highly probable that if his return had been properly synchronized with the opening of the convention, Grant might well have ridden to victory on the first ballot.

---

[134] *New Orleans Times,* June 15, 1880.

CHAPTER IV

The Democratic
National Convention

Ambition still lived on in the broken body of the Sage of Greystone, and in the weeks preceding the meeting of the Democratic convention at Cincinnati, Tilden's supporters cherished a hope that he would run. It was apparent that in spite of his physical weakness, he ardently desired the nomination at Cincinnati. But in keeping with his indecisive character he took refuge in ambiguity, and up to the very eve of the Cincinnati convention the delegates were in confusion and doubt.[1] As late as May 22 Smith M. Weed, his lieutenant, declared that Tilden was out of the race,[2] but five days later the *New York Star* stated that Tilden had once again changed front and would now be a candidate.[3] It was not surprising that on May 17 the Young Men's Democratic Club—their patience no doubt exhausted—tabled a resolution supporting Tilden.[4]

Tilden's silence gave encouragement to the other candidates. Then, just as Weed and Daniel Manning were about to entrain for Cincinnati, he told them that he would not accept unless the nomination were unanimous. He added that, since unanimity

---

[1] *New York Tribune*, June 12, 1880.
[2] *New York Star*, May 23, 1880.
[3] *Ibid.*, May 27, 1880.
[4] *New York Tribune*, May 18, 1880.

seemed most unlikely, his first choice was Payne, and his second Randall. But while Tilden was busy adopting this "withdrawing" attitude, he was at the same time taking steps to advance his own candidacy. A telegram was sent to Payne, asking him to accept second place on the Tilden ticket, to which request Payne gave his consent.[5]

Thoroughly in character, Tilden handed Manning, his staunch supporter and the banker-publisher of the *Albany Argus*, a letter which hinted that his health might not permit him to accept the nomination even if it should be offered. This letter, dated June 18 and addressed to the New York delegation, was to be held in reserve and read to the convention.[6] Manning did not divulge its contents until rumor reached Cincinnati that Tilden's brother Henry was on his way with a copy of the letter. Manning then felt constrained to anticipate his arrival and disclose the original to the New York delegation to avoid being accused of deception.[7] The delegates were anxious to get a look at the letter in the hope that it might clarify a situation that was "so muddled that it could not be straightened out."[8] Before Manning decided to read the letter he had been insisting that Tilden wanted the nomination. Whitney felt that Manning had completely misread Tilden's intentions. Whitney's interpretation of the Sage's Delphic utterances was that Tilden desired Payne's nomination.[9] Tilden, as the delegates should have expected, stated his position in terms that few really understood. The letter was long and inconclusive, containing much irrelevant material. After rehearsing the many benefits he had

---

[5] Flick, *Tilden*, p. 457.

[6] Hudson, *Recollections*, p. 109.

[7] Roscoe C. E. Brown, *History of the State of New York*, Vol. 3, pp. 248-49 (Syracuse: Syracuse Press, 1922) and Alexander, *New York*, Vol. 3, p. 455 support this view.

[8] Hudson, *Recollections*, p. 106.

[9] *Ibid.*, p. 108. This and the preceding footnote cover part of an interview granted by Whitney to Hudson a few days before the Cincinnati convention.

conferred upon the country, including his smashing of the Tweed and Canal rings, he went on to describe how he had been deprived of the presidency by the perfidious Electoral Commission. He had worn himself out working for the welfare of others. Since he had faithfully borne his full share of labor and care in the public service, "wearing the marks of its burdens," he declared that he desired nothing so much as an honorable discharge and to "lay down the honors and toils of even *quasi* party leadership." He sought the repose of private life.[10]

To those who might assert that he was withdrawing rather than face certain defeat in the coming election he stated that he renounced renomination for the presidency with no doubt in his mind as to the vote of the state of New York or of the United States. He believed that it was a renunciation of re-election to the presidency.[11]

What meaning was Tilden trying to convey to his bewildered delegates? Some felt that the letter was a subtle bid for the nomination; others that it was really an absolute refusal. Tilden reminded his audience that four years previously he had told the convention that, if he were summoned by the suffrages of his countrymen to attempt this work, he would endeavor "with God's help" to be the efficient instrument of their will.[12] But now he feared that the responsibility of the presidential office was beyond his strength. Thomas F. Bayard, whom Tilden considered his only serious rival for the nomination, had been dealt with when Tilden let it be known that he could never forgive

---

[10] The script of the Tilden letter is included among the Manton Marble MSS under date of June 18, 1880, Vol. 53, no. 248. The letter as found in the Marble collection states that Tilden is incapacitated, while the script intended to be read at the convention merely states that the Sage fears that the presidency is "beyond my strength." See *Official Proceedings of the Democratic National Convention, Held in Cincinnati, Ohio, June 22-24, 1880*, p. 107 (Dayton: Daily Journal Press, 1882).

[11] *Proceedings, Democratic Convention, 1880*, p. 106.

[12] *Ibid.*

him for his cooperation with the Electoral Commission scheme.[13] Although Tilden disclaimed any responsibility for the commission, it is interesting to note that President Hayes told Colonel Thomas C. Donaldson that, while he was opposed to the Electoral Commission bill, Tilden was in favor of it until Judge Davis went to the Senate. He then became opposed to it.[14] About the same time that Bayard was being advised that his nomination was assured if Tilden should not stop him, Tilden's henchmen were asserting that they would see to it that Bayard did not get a two-thirds vote.[15]

When Manning presented Tilden's artful letter to the New York delegation at Cincinnati on June 21, a majority of the members decided to interpret it as a withdrawal from the presidential race. But there were many keen political observers who considered it to be a subtle bid for the nomination. As soon as Bradley T. Johnson read the letter, he was convinced that it was merely a trick on Tilden's part to promote his own interests and secure the nomination.[16]

If the Tilden newspapers are a reflection of his intentions, then the letter must be considered an outright appeal for the nomination. The very day the letter was published, Dana wrote in the *New York Sun* that the Democrats would be deprived of their most important issue if Tilden was not nominated. Nothing short of his death should prevent Tilden's final inauguration,

---

[13] *Ibid.*, p. 107 and *New York Sun*, August 5, 1878.

[14] Donaldson MSS, Memoirs, December 17, 1879. Donaldson is recording a conversation he had with Hayes. In 1880 Hayes offered to make his friend Colonel Donaldson the governor of Idaho. Donaldson declined. Donaldson's *Public Domain* is still a standard reference work for national public lands.

[15] Bayard MSS, W. R. Chandlinn to Bayard, June 21, 1880 and William C. Whitney in Hudson, *Recollections*, pp. 108-09.

[16] Bayard MSS, Bradley T. Johnson to Bayard, June 21, 1880. He goes on to urge that Bayard's nomination be pressed on the issue of the Electoral Commission. Bayard should meet Tilden on the issue on which he was perfectly right and Tilden perfectly wrong: "Let us make an issue of an honest man against rogues."

since he had been elected by the American people.[17] Not to be outdone, Henry Watterson, like Dana financially in debt to Tilden, warned the delegates that refusal to renominate Tilden would be a confession that he was not elected in 1876.[18]

Tilden's opponents agreed with his friends, and John Kelly declared that the letter was a bid for the nomination.[19] The *St. Louis Globe Democrat*, a Grant paper, asserted that Tilden's elaborate self-praise was received by his friends as evidence of sinister intentions. They recognized in his manner his usual political practices.[20]

James Gordon Bennett declared that the letter was a "dextrous plea for renomination," while the *San Francisco Bulletin* was sure that Tilden's real meaning was, "I can't serve, but if I am not nominated the true issue of the campaign will be left out."[21] Murat Halstead wrote in his paper, the *Cincinnati Commercial*, that it would remain a problem for all time whether or not Tilden's letter was really intended as an abdication of his claims to the nomination.[22]

The Bayard supporters in Cincinnati were jubilant over the fact that the New York delegation had decided to take Tilden at his word. They soon realized, however, that Tilden was not the only one in the presidential race who would push Bayard hard

---

[17] *New York Sun*, June 21, 1880. At this time Dana was heading his editorial page with the House resolution of March 3, 1877. This resolution concluded with the words, "Tilden . . . was thereby duly elected President of the United States." See the *New York Sun* for May 8, 1880 and also the *Congressional Record*, 44th Cong., 2d Sess., 226.

[18] *Louisville Courier Journal*, June 22, 1880.

[19] *St. Louis Globe Democrat*, June 26, 1880.

[20] *Ibid.*

[21] *San Francisco Bulletin*, June 21, 1880. The quotation from the *New York Herald* written by Bennett is included in this issue of the *Bulletin*.

[22] *Cincinnati Commercial*, June 25, 1880. Halstead had told Tilden's friend George Hoadly that, if Grant were nominated, he would sell the *Commercial* to Horace White to be used by him to support Tilden. See letter of February 17, 1880, from Hoadly to Tilden in the Tilden MSS.

for honors. Hancock, Hendricks, Thurman, Payne, and Field were very much in the public eye, and Hancock was gaining strength every day. On June 21, the day before the convention opened, the Bayardites considered the outcome to be very much in doubt. George Bates sent a long telegram to Bayard in which he tried to give the senator from Delaware an over-all picture of the situation at Cincinnati on the eve of the convention. Bates found that Bayard's strength was "good and largely diffused," but that the situation as a whole was risky and chaotic.[23]

The old phobia about the Dixie delegates, which had been haunting the Bayard adherents for some time, cropped up again at Cincinnati. Later that same afternoon Bates dispatched another long and detailed telegram to Bayard reporting that, while the Bayard supporters could feel a growing strength, "the condition of New York and uncertainty as to its future attitude, coupled with the extreme sensitiveness of the South to the judgment of the New York men made the situation extremely delicate." The telegram also assured Bayard that "every honorable effort" was being made for the cause and that the canvass was being conducted as he would wish it.[24]

---

[23] Bayard MSS, George H. Bates to Bayard, June 21, 1880. The general comment is followed by specific details: "Tilden and Seymour are both out. The New York delegation is broken and can't be delivered to Payne who is supported by most of Tilden's forces. Part of them have gone to Randall who is fighting for himself and renders Pennsylvania delegation unsettled. He is very cordial to us and says no antagonism between us. When he is out of the way he joins us. The Field boom has been active but today much less so, and its methods have disgusted many. Thurman develops no strength. Our friends outside of the state are getting to work, Stockton and McPherson doing all they can, also Saltonstall."

[24] *Ibid.*, George H. Bates to Bayard, June 21, 1880. Again the specific details are given: "Lamar arrived yesterday. Old hands admit that no convention was so chaotic and so hard to form any reliable opinion about. If we can show a fair strength North, the South will come to us with great force. Randall is wavering whether he will not get out of the way. The only thing we have to meet is the Dover speech and its supposed effect upon availability. . . . Since last night's Tilden break, Kentucky comes to us nearly solid. Pennsylvania now hopeful but I cannot safely ascertain how to estimate votes in detail."

This uncertainty continued when the convention was called to order on June 22 in Cincinnati at 12:38 P.M. by William H. Barnum, chairman of the Democratic National Committee. After the opening prayer, which begged God "to illumine the minds of this Assembly," Judge George Hoadly, a Tilden intimate, was unanimously chosen temporary chairman.[25] In a brief address Hoadly reminded the Democrats of their recent good fortune in that since June 8 it had been certain that the "usurper" would not be immediately followed by the "monarch."[26] Yet he warned them that the real danger was in the Republican party, where the possibility of the third term existed.[27] In an obvious attempt to answer John Kelly's cutting editorials about the Old Humbug of Cipher Alley, Hoadly asserted that Tilden and Hendricks were "two of the foremost statesmen of the Nation," and that they were worthy of the "most enthusiastic political devotion."[28] Turning from Kelly, Hoadly hurled a sharp shaft in the direction of Senators Bayard and Thurman by declaring that, if the Democrats were again successful in the coming election, "no cunning device of dishonest arbitration would rob them of the fruits of their triumph."[29]

The first rift in the harmony of the convention came during the appointment of the three important committees on organization, credentials, and resolutions. On the call of the state of New York, John Kelly rose and attempted to address the chair. Hoadly, following out the Tilden nonconciliation policy, refused to recognize Kelly. John B. Haskins, Kelly's lieutenant, leaped to his feet in an attempt to address the convention. The chairman meted out the same treatment to Haskins and called upon the sergeant at arms, who compelled Haskins to take his

---

[25] *Proceedings, Democratic Convention, 1880*, p. 2.
[26] *Ibid.*, p. 6. Garfield had been nominated on June 8.
[27] *Ibid.*
[28] *Ibid.*, p. 5.
[29] *Ibid.*

seat.[30] Whatever the sergeant at arms may have done in the case of Haskins, it is not recorded that Kelly was "compelled" to take his seat. If that had been attempted, it is quite likely that the convention would have been without a sergeant at arms, for Kelly possessed a powerful physique and a record in "free-for-alls" which did not invite challenge. With the Tammany Tiger thus held at bay by a chairman who was partial to Tilden's Irving Hall, the committees were finally formed. The convention then adjourned until 10:00 A.M. the next morning, Wednesday, June 23.

The second day of the convention opened up with a prayer for "harmony" and a "spirit of conciliation."[31] The Committee on Credentials then presented a majority report and a minority report concerning the vote of the New York delegation. It was no surprise to the Tammany men when P. M. B. Young, chairman of the Committee on Credentials, announced the majority report by declaring that the committee had "by a singular unanimity voted to allow the sitting members to retain their seats."[32] Young grudgingly went on to say that he would allow one moment for the views of the minority, adding that it was a very small minority.[33] The minority report, presented by Thomas M. Carroll of Kansas, recommended that the "Faulkner branch of the Democratic Delegation from the State of New York be allowed to cast fifty votes in this Convention, and that the Shakespeare Hall Democracy be allowed to cast twenty votes."[34] The convention then voted to debate the question of the contesting delegations from the state of New York. A delegate from Rhode Island moved that John Kelly take the platform. Kelly was not in the hall. The chair then recognized G. W. Miller, who spoke on behalf of the minority report. Miller, thoroughly loyal to

---

[30] *Ibid.*, p. 11.
[31] *Ibid.*, p. 20.
[32] *Ibid.*, p. 25.

[33] *Ibid.*
[34] *Ibid.*, p. 26.

Tammany's chief, declared that Kelly had "no superior in this, or any other assemblage, in integrity and devotion to the true interests of the great National Democracy of this country."[35] He vehemently assailed the tactics of the Tilden machine in New York, and went on to say that the discordant notes in the New York Democratic party could only be harmonized by "an accommodating spirit of compromise, by devising some means of conciliating the minority."[36] Miller reminded the delegates that in 1856, the last time the Democrats had been victorious in a presidential campaign, the convention had been faced with a similar difficulty. At that time the minority of the New York delegation was admitted to equal representation on the motion of the "glorious sire of that glorious man, Thomas F. Bayard."[37] The Kellyites were not being outdone by Hoadly or any other Tildenite in using the platform to advance the cause of their favorite candidate. In conclusion he made a plea for twenty out of the seventy votes in the delegation.[38]

Judge Amasa J. Parker supported Miller's appeal, and urged the members of the convention to listen to the minority reports with "reason, fairness and liberality."[39] It was apparent that a dangerous crisis had arisen in the proceedings of the convention, and Governor Richard B. Hubbard of Texas made an urgent plea to both the Tilden and the Kelly delegations to settle their differences in a friendly fashion so as to prevent any split that would work to the advantage of the Republican party in the November elections.[40]

But the smoldering animosities of the New York Democrats were too deeply ingrained to be reasoned away by the logic of Governor Hubbard. On the previous evening Kelly had told the Committee on Credentials that Tammany would not support the

---

35 *Ibid.*, p. 31.
36 *Ibid.*, p. 34.
37 *Ibid.*, p. 32.

38 *Ibid.*, p. 34.
39 *Ibid.*, p. 36.
40 *Ibid.*, pp. 39-40.

nomination of Tilden, and he had made a speech from the balcony of the Burnet House to the same effect. Kelly's defiance of the Cincinnati convention, coupled with his refusal to support Robinson in the late gubernatorial election in New York, had made him a marked man in the eyes of the Tildenites. After Colonel John R. Fellows had delivered a speech that was bitterly denunciatory of Kelly's action in threatening to bolt again, the minority report had little chance of acceptance. It was defeated by the ample margin of 457 to 205½, and it is significant that this minority report received strong Southern support, thereby showing a close link between Tammany and the Southern Democrats.

Tilden had refused to conciliate the opposition within the party just prior to the November elections in 1879. The result of that refusal had been a Republican triumph in New York. And now once again Tilden had refused to give his approval to any compromise, with the result that the Tammany delegates were excluded from participation in the convention. Would history repeat itself, or was there yet a chance that something might be done to bring about harmony between the warring factions in the party?

After the Committee on Credentials had discharged its most difficult task, the Committee on Organization reported that it had chosen John W. Stevenson of Kentucky as permanent chairman. The convention unanimously agreed to the choice of Stevenson. Since the Committee on Resolutions had not as yet presented a proposed platform, it was decided to get on with the nomination speeches. J. E. McElrath presented the name of Judge Stephen J. Field of California in a speech that hailed Field as a justice of the Supreme Court of the United States who had expounded "the law with the logic of Marshall and with an ability greater than that of Brougham."[41] Though born in New

---

41 *Ibid.*, p. 70.

England, he had developed as a "child of the great West," and to him the poor man of the Pacific slope "owes protection from forced sale of the cottage and the roof that shelters his family."[42] These intellectual qualifications, joined with a very real charity, made him the logical nominee; and if nominated he would "sweep California like the winds that blow through her golden gates."[43]

About a month before the convention Edwards Pierrepont was of the opinion that Tilden or Field would be the Democratic nominee. He said that Tilden had no idea of retiring, although he led some persons to believe that he would.[44] Pierrepont, however, was apparently unaware that Justice Field had incurred the hostility of the Democratic machine of his own state by boldly defying local sentiment on the Chinese question. His decisions in support of the constitutional rights of the Chinese hurt him more than he realized.[45]

The call of the states was continued. When Delaware was reached, George Gray nominated Bayard with a volley of praise. In his portrait of the senator from Delaware, Gray made no attempt to conceal his warm admiration. Bayard, he declaimed, was a statesman who needed no introduction to the American people. His name and record were known "wherever our flag floats, aye, wherever the English tongue is spoken." He presented Bayard's record of defending constitutional liberties and fighting radicalism in phrases of colorful oratory. Gray was mindful of those politicians of both parties who held that

---

[42] *Ibid.,* pp. 70-71.

[43] *Ibid.,* p. 70.

[44] Fish MSS, Edwards Pierrepont to Hamilton Fish, May 20, 1880. Field's legal opinions had reflected the Southern point of view, and consequently Pierrepont calculated Field's chances as follows: 138 votes would be secured from the solid South, "and as it takes but 47 more these are expected thus: No. Pacific Slope 15, Indiana 15, New Jersey 9, Conn., 6 . . . and the rest somewhere?"

[45] Edward S. Corwin, "Stephen Johnson Field"; in *Dictionary of American Biography,* Vol. 6, pp. 372-76.

Bayard was "distinctly unavailable."[46] He therefore pleaded
with the convention to let the country know that the sneer of the
Republican enemies was a lie and that a man with the qualifications possessed by Bayard was worthy to receive the highest
honors of the Democratic party.[47]

Gray waxed prophetic and asserted that, if the 738 delegates
nominated Bayard, success was assured, for "his very name
would be a platform."[48] Apparently the delegates were impressed by these words, for the Bayard movement solidified, and
his friends were able to count some 200 to 250 votes on the first
ballot. They felt that, if the South had had a little more political
courage and the Democratic party a greater degree of sincerity,
Bayard would have been the nominee.[49]

In response to the call of Illinois, Samuel S. Marshall presented the name of Colonel William R. Morrison. The heat of
the hall was oppressive and Marshall, almost prostrated by it,
began to speak "absolutely without preparation." He proceeded
to rub salt into the wounds of the 276 Southern delegates by
comparing Congressman Morrison to Abraham Lincoln. It
would have been difficult for anyone to have devised a better
plan for alienating the South's 276 votes. Having thus lost the
South, Marshall naïvely went on to detach the industrial East
from any enthusiasm it might have had for his candidate by insisting that Colonel Morrison's views on the tariff would be a
"tower of strength" to the Democrats in the coming canvass.[50]
Unfortunately for Morrison's candidacy, the high protectionists
read the *Congressional Record.* Four years previously the Illinois congressman had said that protection, other than that inci-

---

[46] *New York Times,* June 21, 1880. The *Times* added that if Bayard "should be
named it would be because the worse men could not combine their forces."
[47] *Proceedings, Democratic Convention, 1880,* p. 73.
[48] *Ibid.*
[49] *Cincinnati Commercial,* June 23, 1880.
[50] *Proceedings, Democratic Convention, 1880,* pp. 74-76.

dental to revenue, was spoliation.[51] Marshall concluded on the confident note that, if the convention would only nominate his candidate, the people would rally with enthusiasm and make him the next president of the United States.[52]

The Middle West was full of presidential candidates, and Daniel Voorhees spent some time in acclaiming the many genuine qualities of Indiana's favorite son, Governor Thomas A. Hendricks. With a view to enhancing his own availability Hendricks had adroitly managed to have Indiana's Supreme Court declare that the state would henceforth hold October elections. Indiana was a doubtful state, and with this tempting background Voorhees reminded the convention that under the leadership of Hendricks, "when the October sun goes down on the October election . . . you will have the enemy in full retreat."[53] Hendricks, said Voorhees, possessed a broad vision, and his services had not been limited to any one section of the country. "To the South who has been more faithful? To the North who has been truer? To the East who has been . . . more faithful? To the West I need not appeal, for he is our own son."[54] The country at the time needed a leader in the presidential chair who, oblivious of sectional differences, could travel a road leading to complete reunion.

It did not require a particularly keen mind to see that, unless the Republicans could capture at least one of the two doubtful states of New York and Indiana, they would have to yield the White House to the Democrats. E. B. Martindale, editor of the Republican *Indianapolis Journal*, with a good deal of political wisdom sounded a note of caution by writing that "with Seymour and Hendricks as the Democratic nominees all candid Republicans will admit that the result in those states would be

---

[51] *Congressional Record*, 44th Cong., 1st Sess., 3313.
[52] *Proceedings, Democratic Convention, 1880*, p. 76.
[53] *Ibid.*, p. 78.
[54] *Ibid.*, p. 77.

doubtful."[55] But Hendricks, like Bayard and Thurman, had incurred the disfavor of Tilden. His refusal to accept second place on the Tilden ticket created animosity between himself and the Tilden delegates.[56]

When New York was reached on the roll call of the states, there was considerable confusion mingled with calls and cheers for Tilden. It was a dramatic moment, but it quickly passed as the chairman of the New York delegation announced that he had no nomination to make. John McSweeney then pointed to another Midwesterner, Allen G. Thurman of Ohio, as the man who "stands forth as the born leader of the people, whom they will delight to follow." He did not have to bore the convention with any "tedious biography," for Senator Thurman's record was one of splendid achievement, and the American people were well acquainted with his "public integrity and chivalric honor." Against the Ohio senator "the furious tongue of slander and of most audacious calumny in an era of slander" did not have "the boldness to speed from its weakened bow, even one blunt arrow against the spotless shield of the chief I name today." If the delegates should so honor Allen G. Thurman by nominating him for the high office of president, then, McSweeney solemnly assured them, "In spite of returning boards, and in spite of electoral commissions, . . . the Republican party . . . shall not prevail against us."[57]

---

[55] *Indianapolis Journal*, June 16, 1880.

[56] *Cincinnati Commercial*, October 1, 1880.

[57] *Proceedings, Democratic Convention, 1880*, p. 84. Thurman was the choice of the Ohio delegation, and on June 9 Congressman Thomas Ewing wrote Thurman assuring him of his wholehearted support (Library of Congress, Thomas Ewing MSS, Ewing to Thurman, June 9, 1880). In 1883 Hoadly was a candidate for the governorship of Ohio and certain newspapers were carrying stories concerning Hoadly's disloyalty to Thurman during the convention of 1880. Hoadly wrote Thurman to assure him that these stories were not true (Ohio State Archaeological and Historical Society, Allen G. Thurman MSS, Hoadly to Thurman, May 22, 1883).

McSweeney's eloquence failed to reconcile the Eastern banking interests to Thurman's soft-money views, and the *Louisville Courier Journal* recorded that "Senator Thurman appears to be getting among the unavailable. So does Judge Field and they loomed largely but a short time ago. Senator Bayard loomed prominently up like Saul among his brethren."[58]

Oregon was next on the list and had no nomination to make. On the call of Pennsylvania, Malcolm Hay rose to say that the Pennsylvania delegation, as a delegation, had "no candidate to present, but . . . a Delegate from Pennsylvania now desires to make a nomination." At that moment an Irishman named Daniel Dougherty took the platform and made a short speech in favor of General Hancock. Dougherty was no great orator, but the tired crowds seemed swayed by his turgid words. In a three-minute speech he told the convention that he was presenting for their thoughtful consideration the name of one "who on the field of battle was styled the 'superb.' " Dougherty insisted that Hancock was not only a soldier but a statesman as well. He was not too clear as to just how Hancock had developed the stature of a statesman. Apparently this had come about when he was military governor of Louisiana and Texas. His nomination "would thrill the land from end to end, crush the last embers of sectional strife and be hailed as the dawning of the longed-for day of perpetual brotherhood." The destinies "of the Republic—the imperiled liberties of the people, hang breathless on your deliberations—pause! reflect! beware! make no misstep!" The last sentence, "If elected he will take his seat," was both a reference to the hesitant Tilden and a warning to the Republican schemers of 1876.[59]

There were ten thousand sweltering people jammed into Cincinnati's Convention Hall, and as Dougherty took his seat a

---

[58] *Louisville Courier Journal*, June 23, 1880.
[59] *Proceedings, Democratic Convention, 1880*, pp. 85-86.

great shout for Hancock burst from thousands of throats. The spectators were especially clamorous, and the various delegations were evidently impressed with this loud-voiced acclaim for the soldier candidate.

When the cheering had finally subsided, General Wade Hampton made a brief speech in which he pledged the South's 138 electoral votes to the Democratic party. Hampton was quite aware of the enthusiasm which greeted the name of Hancock, and he told the convention that "we of the South would feel that we would be safe in his hands, because we were safe when he had the power." Hampton stated that Thurman, like Hancock, was quite acceptable, and all knew that "Indiana's son is worthy of the honor." But in spite of great admiration for Hancock, Thurman, and Hendricks, Hampton declared that the South favored Bayard because it believed him to be the strongest man. Hampton held that Bayard would attract more conservative Republican votes than any other candidate and, if elected, would also take his place, for he was as brave as Hancock.[60]

Hampton was followed by Governor Richard B. Hubbard of Texas, who grew lyrical over the virtues and accomplishments of General Hancock.[61] John W. Daniel of Virginia, who had been an ardent Bayard supporter at St. Louis in 1876, had recently been converted to the cause of Hancock. He now informed the convention in long, rolling periods that, among all the candidates, Hancock was the only one who could completely meet the needs of the hour.[62]

After these winds of oratory had finally subsided, a motion was made to adjourn. The motion was rejected, and the convention proceeded to take the first ballot. Hancock led with 171 votes, and was trailed by Bayard with 158½. Payne received

---

[60] *Ibid.*, pp. 86-87.
[61] *Ibid.*, pp. 88-89.
[62] *Ibid.*, pp. 92-94.

81, Thurman 68½, Field 63, Morrison 62, Hendricks 49½, Tilden 38, Ewing 10, Seymour 8, Randall a mere 6, and William H. English only one vote. The total number of votes was 738, and under Democratic convention rules a two-thirds majority was required for nomination, in this case 492 votes.[63]

The forebodings of Bayard's friends proved to be well founded, for the South had failed to pay her debt to the senator from Delaware. Only two Southern states, Florida and South Carolina, gave him their undivided votes. Despite Lamar's efforts the Mississippi delegation gave him only one half of its vote, and in the other Southern states he shared equal honors with several other candidates. Both Bayard and Hancock received sixty-nine votes each from twelve Southern states, including Kentucky. When Bayard's friends heard the results of the first ballot, they could not help noting, as one of Bayard's correspondents expressed it, that the Southern delegates had subscribed to the principle that "all things among democrats must give place to expediency."[64] Their desertion of Bayard may well have stemmed from the fact that some of them went to Cincinnati by way of New York in order to consult with Tilden. It is certain that Tilden did not encourage them to keep their promises to Bayard.[65]

After the secretary had announced the vote of the first ballot on the evening of June 23, the chairman immediately stated that, since no one had received two thirds of the vote, no choice had been made.[66] A motion to adjourn was then adopted, and the way was open for the political manipulation that would control the proceedings of the following day. George Bates wired to Bayard that the "Hancock vote was larger than we expected because the convention got into a little furor over a speech made

---

[63] *Ibid.*, p. 99.
[64] Bayard MSS, J. Clement Carroll to Bayard, June 27, 1880.
[65] Flick, *Tilden*, p. 457.
[66] *Proceedings, Democratic Convention, 1880*, p. 100.

by Dan Dougherty."[67] The *New York Times*, whose political prognosticians were so sure that Grant was the only possible Republican nominee, ran true to form and asserted that "Hancock heads the first and only ballot taken by the Cincinnati Convention yesterday, and yet Hancock is about the last man that body is likely to nominate."[68]

At 10:30 the next morning, June 24, the convention reassembled. The Reverend Dr. Taylor asked God to aid the delegates in selecting candidates "unsullied in reputation."[69] Before the delegates could proceed to the second ballot Rufus W. Peckham informed the convention of the Tilden letter, interpreted by the New York delegation on June 21 to be a refusal. At the mention of Tilden's name there was a tremendous outburst of cheers and applause. The noise was so uproarious that the chairman threatened to clear the house of all spectators. This had a quieting effect on the multitude, and Peckham then announced that, since their "honored leader" had "renounced" the nomination, New York was for Samuel J. Randall.[70] The way was now clear for the crucial second ballot. Bayard's vote began to shrink as Connecticut, Iowa, Massachusetts, Missouri, New Hampshire, New Jersey, and North Carolina either reduced his vote or abandoned his cause altogether. South Carolina and Florida remained loyal to Bayard, and continued to give him their undivided vote. Bayard's vote had been reduced to 112. Randall showed surprising strength and received 103½ votes, with Pennsylvania not voting.

When the vote of Pennsylvania was announced, Randall received 25 additional votes, bringing his total to 128½. But the break came on the next vote, when Wisconsin suddenly voted as a unit for Hancock and New Jersey did the same. Pennsylvania

---

[67] Bayard MSS, George H. Bates to Bayard, June 23, 1880.
[68] *New York Times*, June 24, 1880.
[69] *Proceedings, Democratic Convention, 1880*, p. 101.
[70] *Ibid.*, pp. 102-07. See also Ganfield, *Wisconsin*, p. 6.

joined in the stampede for Hancock, and when Smith M. Weed cast the seventy votes of New York for Hancock, "every delegate was on his feet and the roar of ten thousand voices completely drowned the full military band in the gallery."[71] Ohio, Kentucky, Nebraska, Connecticut, Virginia, Nevada, and New Hampshire emulated New York and went for Hancock. A motion was now made and seconded that the call of the states be made anew. This motion was carried, and when the balloting was completed Hancock had 705 votes, Hendricks 30, Bayard 2, and Tilden a single vote.[72] Another "man on horseback" had captured an American political convention.

All of the presidential candidates who were present at Cincinnati joined their voices to the chorus of praise for General Hancock, and even John Kelly was allowed to mount the platform and pledge the support of Tammany. He assured the jubilant delegates that he was quite willing to forget past political dissensions which had hurt the party so much in New York. He was even ready to forgive the treatment he and his Tammany men had received earlier in this convention, and he promised to do everything in his power to elect the Democratic ticket.[73] Bayard on his part immediately wired Hancock his congratulations and assured the general that he would make every effort to secure his election.[74]

The convention quickly finished its arduous labors by unanimously nominating William H. English of Indiana as the vice-presidential candidate.[75] The choice of English was based on sound political logic. Hancock, as it was argued, by uniting Irving Hall and Tammany Hall would carry New York, and

---

[71] *Proceedings, Democratic Convention, 1880*, pp. 108-12. Thus Wisconsin received another first. A few weeks previous she had led the stampede for Garfield.
[72] *Ibid.*, p. 114.
[73] *Ibid.*, p. 123.
[74] Bayard MSS, Bayard to Hancock, June 24, 1880.
[75] *Proceedings, Democratic Convention, 1880*, p. 136.

Indiana would certainly follow English, her own native son. Thus Indiana's 15 electoral votes and New York's 35 in addition to the solid South's 138 would spell victory for the Democrats for the first time since 1856.

Bayard's ardent friends were inconsolable at the results of the convention. Just before the decisive second ballot was taken on June 24, August Belmont, a loyal Bayard supporter, wired Manton Marble in an effort to soften Tilden's heart toward Bayard. The telegram was sent from Cincinnati to Marble's New York residence. Belmont felt there was a good chance that Marble might be able to induce Tilden to transfer his forces to Bayard in order to insure victory.[76] Marble promptly replied that the telegram had arrived too late, since the whole thing had been settled the night before.[77] Marble implied that, if Belmont had wired sooner, there might have been a chance that Tilden would have been induced to accept Bayard. This appeared especially possible in view of Whitney's statement that Hancock was the "man of all men" whom Tilden did not want.[78] In any event, the Bayard adherents had given their very best for their candidate. As soon as the second ballot had been taken, Bates telegraphed to Bayard that the whole thing had "gone off in a hurrah for Hancock."[79] Henry L. Bryan wrote to Bayard and depicted the nominating scene at Cincinnati as "a wild hurrah, and the men flocked like sheep towards the bell-wether after the first stampede."[80]

When Wade Hampton reached Louisville, Kentucky, he sent Bayard a long and detailed account of the convention in which he expressed his sincere regret that the senator from Delaware had not been chosen as the presidential nominee. Yet Hampton

---

[76] Marble MSS, August Belmont to Manton Marble, June 24, 1880.
[77] Ibid., Manton Marble to August Belmont, June 24, 1880.
[78] William C. Whitney; in Hudson, Recollections, p. 109.
[79] Bayard MSS, G. H. Bates to Bayard, June 24, 1880.
[80] Ibid., H. L. Bryan to Bayard, June 26, 1880.

was consoled when he reflected that much had occurred at Cincinnati to make Bayard's friends proud of him.[81]

Bradley Johnson of Maryland was one of the two delegates who remained with Bayard to the end. Johnson, like Hampton, blamed the South for being "very weak-kneed" and "terribly afraid." He urged support of Hancock and rejoiced in the defeat of Tilden. He felt that, if the New York delegation and Randall had acted sensibly, they would have nominated Bayard.[82]

August Belmont retained a vivid impression of the influence of the galleries on the Cincinnati delegates. A noisy claque had worked wonders for Hancock, and Belmont was convinced that the nomination had been made under the pressure of an organized mob in the galleries and on the floor.[83] Samuel L. Barlow had witnessed all the proceedings of the Cincinnati convention,

---

[81] *Ibid.*, Wade Hampton to Bayard, June 26, 1880. He wrote: "That you were the first choice of a large majority of the delegates there can be no question, and could we have taken a ballot on the first day, this would have been shown. It was so clearly indicated that all the opposing elements were concentrated that night against you, and the influence of Tilden's friends was brought to bear solely to defeat you. It was said to the Southern men that you could not carry New York, and they were advised to scatter their votes until it could be ascertained what your Northern strength was. Some of your Southern friends thought that this was the best policy, but it was a great mistake. It led to the accidental position Hancock obtained and then the galleries nominated him. On all sides I heard the confident expression that you were the best man of the party for President, but I saw the effect of the insidious work of your opponents, in the fear expressed that your geographical position and your Southern sympathies rendered you unavailable at present. All said that four years hence you should be the man and you were really broken down by those who were your warm friends. I could not be led off by their fallacy, and South Carolina stood by you till Delaware voted for Hancock. Your strength defeated Tilden and his friends and for this at least I am delighted. It is important that Hancock should not fall into bad hands." In a postscript to this letter Hampton makes reference to a speech he made at the convention in favor of Bayard's nomination: "You should know in justice to myself that I was called on to second your nomination at the last moment, thus giving me no time for preparation."

[82] *Ibid.*, Bradley T. Johnson to Bayard, June 26, 1880.

[83] *Ibid.*, August Belmont to Bayard, June 27, 1880.

and he was quite sure that two thirds of all the delegates really preferred Bayard. Unfortunately, large numbers of these sympathizers had been induced to believe that Bayard was not certain of carrying New York.[84] J. S. Moore rejoiced that the selection of Hancock had dealt a deathblow to the political ambitions of Tilden. Moore felt that Tilden had been the chief cause of Bayard's defeat.[85]

Frank H. Alfriend of Richmond, Virginia, despised the foolish fears of Southern statesmen, who allowed themselves to be deceived by the Tildenites into believing that Bayard, if nominated, could not be elected. During the convention he soon realized that Bayard's nomination was impossible after the Southern delegates had been frightened by the assaults made upon his availability by his opponents.[86]

The role of Tilden in the Cincinnati convention of 1880 will ever be shrouded in mystery. No doubt he wanted it that way. Smith M. Weed, who perhaps more than any other person represented Tilden at the convention, asserted that it was very apparent that it would not have been possible to nominate him even if he would have taken it. It was Weed's opinion that the element that sold him out in Washington in 1877, together with those who were honestly fearful that he could not win, were enough to defeat him under any circumstances.[87]

Letters from old political adherents like Weed did not shake Tilden's confidence in himself, and in an interview on June 25

---

[84] Ibid., Samuel L. Barlow to Bayard, June 28, 1880.
[85] Ibid., J. S. Moore to Bayard, June 28, 1880.
[86] Ibid., Frank H. Alfriend to Bayard, July 3, 1880. The letter continues: "I trust you will never forget the especially importunate and vindictive opposition to you of Ben Hill. After the Hancock business was fairly started, I tried hard to get the New Yorkers to stop it in the only way then possible, viz., by casting the seventy votes of their state for you. That would have reclaimed to you all the wavering support of the South and probably have nominated you on the 3rd ballot."
[87] Tilden MSS, Smith M. Weed to Tilden, June 25, 1880.

he declared that he could have been nominated and elected. But he did not feel able to enter upon "five years of hard, exhausting labor."[88] On July 2, in a letter to S. C. Johnson, who had expressed regret that Tilden had not been chosen at Cincinnati, he remarked: "I do not doubt if I had felt disposed to make a canvass for the nomination, the Convention would have done as you think they ought to have done."[89]

A few hours after the convention adjourned, Whitney, a prominent Tilden lieutenant, gave his comments on the controversial letter. He said that the situation developed as he foresaw but not as he hoped. He said the letter was intended to be read in the convention and that Tilden believed that, if it had been read, it would have caused a stampede for him.[90]

On the second day of the convention, June 23, Daniel Manning telegraphed to Tilden, asking him whether he would accept if nominated.[91] It is not certain whether Manning sent this wire before or after the first ballot had been taken. In any event, Tilden did not answer until the next day, June 24. It is also a moot question whether Tilden sent his telegram before or after Hancock's nomination. The Tilden telegram acknowledged Manning's message, as well as many others like it, and stated that his action was "well considered" and "irrevocable," and that his friends must not be allowed to cast a doubt on his

---

[88] *New York Herald*, June 26, 1880.
[89] Tilden MSS, Tilden to S. C. Johnson, July 2, 1880.
[90] Hudson, *Recollections*, p. 110. Says Whitney: "If Mr. Tilden had been frankly out two weeks before the convention met, we could have nominated Payne. But Mr. Tilden wasn't out even when he wrote that letter. No, that letter was written to be read in the convention, and Mr. Tilden believed that if it had been the convention would have been swept into a stampede for him. It was a very cunning thing. If the convention was determined to nominate someone else, as appeared to be the case, then the result would go down in history as a consequence of Tilden's withdrawal. If in the reading of the letter in the convention it had had the effect intended, then history would say that the party refused to let him withdraw."
[91] Hirsch, *Whitney*, p. 157.

sincerity.[92] Toward the close of his life, when asked by a newspaper correspondent whether Tilden was really a candidate in
1880, Manning replied that, although Tilden's ambition led him
to desire the nomination, he acquiesced in the result since he
was physically unfit to undergo the turmoil of another campaign. Manning said furthermore that this was the opinion of
Tilden's best friends prior to the meeting of the convention.[93]

Nast, in *Harper's Weekly*, sarcastically penned a cartoon
putting the Tilden letter on a lightning rod, with the legend
reading, "Can't they see a joke? Catch me believing in lightning
rods again."[94] Years later the *Philadelphia Press* characterized
the letter as a Pickwickian epistle with a Pickwickian purpose.[95]
Yet Whitelaw Reid could write that it was "a sort of farewell
address to the Democratic party," an absolute refusal.[96]

Although Smith M. Weed was convinced that Tilden's nomination was not possible, he felt that, if Tilden's letter had been
there Saturday morning and if they had acted together, they
could have nominated Payne. Weed thought that Randall had
"acted bad and talked bad." Yet he acted "with the Brooklyn
and Fox gang and named him as our second choice" on what he
took to be Tilden's advice. Weed did not think that the Democrats could have nominated Randall.[97]

The Republicans had their agents at Cincinnati. One of
them, Joseph G. Carter, did not want to see Tilden nominated.
He therefore urged Gorman to keep Hendricks in the fight.
Carter states that the true history of Tilden's role was yet to be
written. When Tilden found that there was a combination
against him, he was careful to keep his friends under control by

---

[92] Tilden MSS, Tilden to Manning, June 24, 1880.
[93] Hudson, *Recollections*, p. 111.
[94] *Harper's Weekly* 24:433, July 10, 1880.
[95] *Philadelphia Press*, September 30, 1894.
[96] *New York Tribune*, June 21 and 22, 1880.
[97] Tilden MSS, Smith M. Weed to Tilden, June 25, 1880.

urging them to support Payne. If these friends, said Carter, had struck for him as long as Grant's men had at Chicago, they would have brought Tilden to the front as the compromise candidate he sought to be. But the wild frenzy that took possession of the convention in behalf of Hancock placed it beyond the control of the manager.[98]

About a week after the convention Judge Field, who had also been a possible nominee at Cincinnati, confessed to his friend Chauncey F. Black that he had never been "oversanguine" concerning his own prospects.[99] The *New York Times* was deeply critical of the Democratic choice at Cincinnati, and seriously questioned the logic of having English, a millionaire banker with a hard-money record, attempt to carry Indiana, which was known to be a hotbed of inflation and repudiation. This newspaper thought that the head of the ticket was an even greater mistake, for "does anybody know what Gen. Hancock thinks about the principles of finance, about the tariff, civil service reform, interstate commerce or free ships?"[100]

This lack of political experience on the part of General Hancock was soon to become a Republican theme, and the Democrats tried to answer it by pointing to the general's own words. For Hancock had stated that, if he were nominated by a party, he would be governed by the platform or would not accept the nomination.[101] But the Democratic platform was somewhat of

---

[98] Garfield MSS, Joseph G. Carter to Garfield, August 25, 1880.

[99] Jeremiah S. Black MSS, Stephen Field to Chauncey F. Black, July 5, 1880. After elaborating on this statement he pays a tribute to Hancock, who, he writes, "is a gallant soldier and a pure man, and if surrounded by wise and able counselors, will make an excellent President. It would seem from the signs of the times that his election is assured." As for himself, he concludes, "This episode from my quiet life as a judge will soon be forgotten, and I turn my back from politics for all time."

[100] *New York Times*, June 25, 1880.

[101] From an undated clipping from the *Louisville Argus* in Bayard MSS, Vol. 50, no. 10053. Blanton Duncan is the author of the article.

an afterthought, having been introduced after the presidential nominee had been selected. It contained fourteen planks and gave evidence of hasty construction. It was to harm rather than aid the Democratic cause. Wells gave Manton Marble some idea of how it was thrown together. When Wells arrived in Cincinnati he was "pushed" on the Committee on Resolutions with the explicit assurance that there was nothing that he would be obliged to do, since the platform had already been prepared by Marble. Wells goes on to say that this was not the case; and he found himself in a miserable situation, himself "sick" and Watterson "jubilant." Under circumstances that were physically uncomfortable in the extreme "the platform was cooked up." "If I had not been there," he continued, "the damdest lot of rot would have forced itself in."[102]

Henry Watterson, chairman of the Committee on Resolutions, read the Democratic platform. The Republican platform, now nineteen days old, had stated that the Constitution was the supreme law and "not a mere contract."[103] The Democrats might have caught a few of their necessary forty-seven Northern votes if they had only paraphrased the above Republican plank. Instead, Watterson led off with, "We pledge ourselves anew to the constitutional doctrines . . . of the Democratic party as illustrated by the teachings and example of a long line of Democratic statesmen."[104] Any sympathetic Northern or Western Republican who took the trouble to read the Democratic platform could hardly help but reflect that Calhoun and Jefferson Davis formed a part of this "long line of Democratic statesmen." As though aware that they might be accused of fostering a secession spirit, Watterson and his friends quickly added that these constitutional doctrines had been embodied in the platform of

---

[102] Marble MSS, David A. Wells to Manton Marble, October 30, 1880.
[103] *Proceedings, Republican Convention, 1880*, p. 161.
[104] *Proceedings, Democratic Convention, 1880*, p. 127.

the party's last national convention.[105] But who, even among the most well-disposed, would take the trouble to hunt down a copy of the 1876 platform?

The Republicans had strongly urged that the Constitution be amended so as to forbid any state from appropriating public funds to the support of sectarian schools.[106] Whether or not the Democrats were proud of Garfield's remark that "the combined power of rebellion, Catholicism, and whiskey" had won for Tilden in 1876, it is difficult to say.[107] At any rate, the party of Jefferson did not emulate the strictures that Lincoln's party would have fastened on the states. Watterson merely advocated the "separation of Church and State for the good of each," and "common schools fostered and protected."[108]

Both parties stood for a restriction of Chinese immigration, a continuance of "honest money" consisting of gold and silver, and paper convertible into coin on demand.[109] The Democrats made their greatest mistake when they boldly put down, without any attempt at explanation, that they stood for a "tariff for revenue only."[110] This was to boomerang later, and win many votes for Garfield. During the campaign the Democrats were to attempt in vain to explain that a "tariff for revenue only" was also of its very nature protective. A little forethought would have obviated the necessity for all this futile explaining. The explanation should have been set down in the platform itself.

The platform made a bow in the direction of the "wisdom, patriotism and integrity" of Tilden. In vigorous language it portrayed the great fraud of 1876-1877, whereby the candidate de-

---

[105] *Ibid.*, p. 128. In the 1876 platform the Democrats had reaffirmed their faith in the permanency of the Federal Union. See Stanwood, *Presidential Elections*, p. 322.

[106] *Proceedings, Republican Convention, 1880*, p. 162.

[107] Caldwell, *Garfield*, p. 251.

[108] *Proceedings, Democratic Convention, 1880*, p. 128.

[109] *Ibid.*

[110] *Ibid.*

feated at the polls was declared to be president. The concluding plank asserted that, since this was the first time in American history that the will of the people was set aside under a threat of military violence, the election of 1876 did indeed strike a deadly blow at our system of representative government.[111]

But in spite of certain glaring weaknesses in the Democratic platform, Warner M. Bateman confessed that the Hancock nomination had taken the Republicans "with considerable surprise and some alarm." Bateman feared Grant, "who, it seems, is acting with his accustomed ingratitude and selfishness."[112] This fear of Grant and his New York friends seemed to permeate Republican ranks. W. K. Rogers, personal secretary to President Hayes, wrote Garfield that the Cincinnati nomination was the wisest the opponents could have made, and would give the Republicans all they could do to carry New York.[113] Carl Schurz also wrote the Republican nominee and expressed grave doubts as to whether Conkling would support the Republican ticket in New York. The secretary of the interior regretted that Hancock's nomination eliminated the Southern question from the campaign, and suggested that Garfield's strongest appeal would be "to the conservative elements and business interests of the country."[114] The flow of letters to Garfield after the Democratic convention seemed endless. H. H. Harding expressed the opinion that the nomination of Hancock by the Democrats would tend to confuse the great issue in the campaign. According to Harding, the "great issue" was that of the "loyal people of the nation keeping possession of the government until the issue of the war

---

[111] *Ibid.* It continues: "The Democratic party, to preserve the country from the horrors of a civil war, submitted for the time in firm and patriotic faith that the people would punish this crime in 1880. This issue precedes and dwarfs every other. It imposes a more sacred duty upon the people of the Union than ever addressed the consciences of a nation of freemen."

[112] Chandler MSS, Warner M. Bateman to William E. Chandler, June 28, 1880.

[113] Garfield MSS, W. K. Rogers to Garfield, June 25, 1880.

[114] Schurz MSS, Carl Schurz to Garfield, June 24, 1880.

and the results were settled."[115] Ralph Plumb was certain that Hancock's nomination had united "politically corrupt" New York. He urged upon Garfield the necessity of cooperation with Conkling and Arthur in order to hold that city. Republicans clearly understood that Conkling must be conciliated as an essential condition of victory.[116]

Garfield wrote to Schurz and concurred in his views concerning Hancock's nomination. For he too felt that the Democrats had escaped some serious troubles by choosing a former Union general as their standard-bearer. He added, however, that they would run the risk of meeting others.[117] Prominent Republicans felt that these other troubles would spring from the fact that in politics Hancock was, as one wag expressed it, only "a good man weighing two hundred and fifty pounds."[118]

There were those, however, who, like Murat Halstead, did not think that Hancock's nomination signified a united Democratic party in the state of New York. Halstead, writing in the *Cincinnati Commercial,* gave a different reading to New York's political situation. He wrote that friends of Governor Tilden did not enthuse over the "rock-ribbed West Pointer," and that the embraces on the platform between Tilden and the Tammany chiefs were "spectacular and not spontaneous." Belmont and other devoted friends of Senator Bayard, the article continued, though slightly consoled by Tilden's defeat, were not compensated in Hancock's victory. In Halstead's opinion New York state was as doubtful as ever.[119]

George Jones, the pro-Grant editor of the *New York Times,* was sure that there was still a good deal of bitterness between Irving Hall and Tammany Hall. The *Times* felt that Kelly had

---

[115] Garfield MSS, H. H. Harding to Garfield, June 24, 1880.
[116] *Ibid.,* Ralph Plumb to Garfield, June 27, 1880.
[117] Schurz MSS, Garfield to Schurz, July 6, 1880.
[118] Roseboom, *Presidential Elections,* p. 258.
[119] *Cincinnati Commercial,* June 25, 1880.

had his revenge in Cincinnati, for Tilden was a candidate for renomination until the delegates heard the "awful threat of Kelly." The Democratic party of New York could not, in Jones's opinion, afford to run the risk of again alienating Kelly if it wanted to win in November.[120] Although Henry Watterson headlined his *Louisville Courier Journal* with, "The Love Feast . . . Tammany and Anti-Tammany Fall on Each Others Necks," he was quick to add that Kelly, "with a gleam of fire in his gray eye," declared that all past differences should be buried.[121] To many political observers this meant that, although Kelly was burying the hatchet, he was carefully marking the spot. If Tilden tried any more "raids," like the recent removal of Gumbleton as clerk of New York County, Kelly could easily unearth the hatchet. At best the political situation in New York was precarious.

On June 25 the *Springfield Republican* was ready to concede that at least Garfield and Hancock did not represent the worst element in their parties. Since Hancock had no political record, the *Republican* considered him to be the most available among the Democratic candidates. It felt that the moral effect of the nomination was excellent in many ways.[122]

William Tecumseh Sherman seemed happy over the selection of Hancock. He wrote the general that he agreed wholeheartedly that his nomination and election would prove that the Democratic party endorsed the idea that the great war of 1861-1865 had been fought for the integrity of the Union. This would be the final proof that the war was national and just.[123]

This rejoicing over the fact that Hancock's nomination signified the death knell of the "bloody-shirt" issue was quite gen-

---

[120] *New York Times,* July 2, 1880.
[121] *Louisville Courier Journal,* June 25, 1880.
[122] *Springfield Republican,* June 25, 1880.
[123] William T. Sherman MSS, Letter Book, W. T. Sherman to Hancock, June 25, 1880.

eral, and was reflected in the press of the time.[124] However, General Sherman's hope that the coming election would be clearly decisive, one way or the other, mirrored the disturbing apprehensions of many Americans.[125] The country had narrowly escaped being plunged into another civil war over the disputed election of 1876, and when responsible editors assured the public that the Democrats had a secret plan to seat their candidate whether elected or not, these forebodings of coming disaster only increased.[126] The *Atlanta Constitution* had only contemptuous language for the bogus Electoral Commission of 1876, and proclaimed Hancock as the man who would "bow the usurper out of the White House." Unlike the hesitant Tilden, Hancock would take his seat if elected.[127] Small wonder that Americans hoped for a decisive victory at the polls in 1880!

There were some political commentators who insisted that, if Tilden's letter had appeared a week earlier, he would have received the nomination. The *Constitution* pointed out that there was an almost overwhelming enthusiasm for Tilden at the Cincinnati convention. This zeal for Tilden was met by a small but persistent opposition which kept a rumor afloat to the effect that Tilden had written a private letter in which he definitely declined to be the nominee. With Tilden, the rallying cry would have been the issue of 1876; with Hancock, the issue was "new blood and union forever."[128] Tilden was at odds with this interpretation of the paramount issue in the coming campaign, and in a telegram to Samuel J. Randall at Cincinnati he congratulated the convention and the Democratic party upon the nomination of Hancock and English. He declared that the people would

---

[124] *New York Herald*, June 25, 1880.

[125] William T. Sherman MSS, Letter Book, W. T. Sherman to Hancock, June 25, 1880.

[126] *Cincinnati Commercial*, October 9, 1879.

[127] *Atlanta Constitution*, June 25, 1880.

[128] *Ibid.*

condemn the "fraudulent subversion of the election of 1876," and resume their "sovereign right to choose their rulers."[129]

Tilden did not telegraph his good wishes to Hancock. He left that task to Manton Marble. Marble asked General Hancock to accept his "cordial congratulations" on his nomination, which was so satisfactory to all who had been deprived of their first choice by Tilden's peremptory withdrawal.[130] There may well have been a double meaning intended by this message. At all events, there is no record of Hancock's reaction to it. It seemed apparent that Marble was taking on some of the "political mysticism" of his mentor, and was growing adept at giving a Delphic touch to his pronouncements.

The *New Orleans Times* had given loyal support to Bayard's candidacy. On the day after the Cincinnati convention it stated that, although Hancock was no Bayard, yet he was better than Garfield, for Hancock's record was pure. He was a good administrator; and since he was a Northern war general, the Republicans would not be able to malign the South by saying that the Democrats intended to pay the rebels out of the United States treasury for their losses during the Civil War. Hancock would unite the state of New York; and if he took New York and Indiana, the party could forget about the rest, for he would be "in." The editorial concluded by saying that English was "very strong with the masses in Indiana."[131]

But the *Indianapolis Journal* was not at all convinced of English's strength. E. B. Martindale, editor of that paper, admitted that the vice-presidential nominee had money, but quickly indicated English's great reluctance to part with any of it. Furthermore, he had incurred the wrath of Hendricks, who was still the powerful figure in Indiana politics.[132] The *San*

---

[129] Marble MSS, Tilden to Randall, June 24, 1880.
[130] *Ibid.*, Marble to Hancock, n. d., Vol. 53, no. 11518.
[131] *New Orleans Times*, June 25, 1880.
[132] *Indianapolis Journal*, June 25, 1880.

Francisco Bulletin was disgusted with the choice of English, and remarked that he was nothing but a proslavery Democrat. During the "bloody" Kansas imbroglio of 1854 he had been a willing tool of those who were even then conspiring to destroy the Union. If the Democrats were victorious in November and if Hancock died, English would then be president. The people would prefer Jefferson Davis![133] The *Boston Transcript* testified that at least English had a record in Congress, and was, therefore, open to criticism. Hancock, being a political nonentity, was a complete question mark as far as capabilities were concerned. English also possessed the prime Democratic requirement in that he had a "bar'l." But the *Transcript*, like the *Indianapolis Journal*, significantly added that liberality was not his outstanding virtue. The *Transcript* concluded its comments by lauding the Democratic plank which recommended separation of church and state.[134]

The *Cincinnati Commercial*, mindful of the fact that Tilden had anathematized Hendricks for his refusal to accept second place on the Tilden ticket, recalled how Tilden's newspapers had boomed English and sneered at Hendricks. Hendricks always suspected English of collaboration with Tilden's lieutenants in this newspaper attack. The *Commercial* summed up the situation by admitting that Hancock was handsome and English was rich, but nevertheless believed that "the attempt to carry Pennsylvania on a free trade platform and Indiana with cold crow for Hendricks, may not succeed."[135]

There were many important Democrats who were completely taken by surprise when they discovered that the soldier Hancock had been chosen over the statesman Bayard. James Wilson, writing Senator Bayard from the United States consulate in

---

[133] *San Francisco Bulletin*, June 28, 1880.
[134] *Boston Transcript*, June 25, 1880.
[135] *Cincinnati Commercial*, June 26, 1880.

Nuremberg, Germany, was so certain of Bayard's nomination after Tilden was out of the way that he had actually prepared a cablegram of congratulations.[136]

Despite the best of good will, everything seemed to have gone wrong with the attempt of the Bayard supporters to nominate him. In December 1879 Edward Spencer, an editorial writer for the *Baltimore Sun,* began a brief biography of Bayard. It was ardently hoped that the book, by presenting Bayard's excellent record in the United States Senate, would definitely enhance his chances for the presidential nomination. This effort, like so many others, went awry, for the book did not appear until the first week in June 1880. After some difficulty in finding a publisher, Spencer took the book to D. Appleton and Company, who published it.[137] At that date it was too late for any summary of Bayard's achievements to influence the viewpoint of Democrats, who between trying to read with perception the complex New York political scene and entraining for Cincinnati, had little time for any serious reading. Bayard was neither shocked nor disheartened by this unfortunate blow to his political prospects. He was convinced that hundreds of intellectuals, both Democrats and Republicans, looked to him for guidance. He was greatly consoled by their trust in his ability.

In spite of Tilden, and in spite of timorous Southern delegates, it is the belief of some competent observers that Bayard could have secured the nomination on June 24 if he had been willing to pay the political price. In a long memorandum in the McKinley papers Ernest Isitt of Philadelphia gives an interesting picture of what he believed went on behind the scenes of the Cincinnati convention, and ascribes Bayard's failure to obtain

---

[136] Bayard MSS, James Wilson to Bayard, July 15, 1880. He concludes, "But such is life (political)."

[137] *Ibid.,* Edward D. Spencer to Bayard, May 19, 1880. Dr. William Hand Browne wrote more than half of the Bayard biography but refused to allow his name to appear on the title page.

the nomination to his refusal to pledge himself to a prearranged Cabinet slate.[138]

Apparently not even that expert political prophet, Manton Marble, knew the inside story of what went on at Cincinnati, for Samuel Barlow urged him to "come to Glen Cove and learn the true inwardness of Cincinnati."[139] The defeated candidates, nevertheless, forgot their disappointments in an effort to insure a triumph in November. Hancock thanked Bayard for his assurances of support.[140] Upon reflection, Perry Belmont concluded that Hancock's nomination was a "most opportune one."[141] Bayard wrote a friendly foreword to a campaign biography of Hancock compiled by Alvan S. Southworth.[142] Despite his wretched health Tilden determined to remain in the political picture. Weed and Barnum, two Tilden lieutenants, had some intimate conversations with Hancock's supporters, and they were glad to enlist the support of Tilden.[143] Cooperation might well spell success in November. Democrats everywhere rejoiced when the Republican *New York Times* predicted that the Democratic candidate would be elected in the fall, with at least eighteen votes to spare.[144]

---

[138] Library of Congress, William McKinley MSS, Scrap-Book, Memorandum of Ernest Isitt, October 4, 1898. The memorandum reads in part: "A competent authority once said: 'Nothing but the pride of Mr. Bayard prevented his nomination for the Presidency in 1880. His refusal to pledge himself to a pre-arranged Cabinet slate was the cause of his failure.' It is well known to many politicians still living that confidential pledges of sufficient votes to nominate Mr. Bayard for President in the Democratic National Convention had been made. Several of the votes were conditional upon Mr. Bayard's pledge as to two Cabinet places if he was elected. These conditions were presented to Mr. Bayard, but he indignantly refused to ratify them."

[139] Marble MSS, Samuel Barlow to Manton Marble, n. d., Vol. 53, no. 11529. The date is probably early July 1880.

[140] Bayard MSS, Hancock to Bayard, June 24, 1880.

[141] *Ibid.*, Perry Belmont to Bayard, July 6, 1880.

[142] Southworth, *Hancock*, pp. 7-14.

[143] Tilden MSS, Smith M. Weed to Tilden, June 25, 1880.

[144] *New York Times*, July 20, 1880.

Third Party Movements during the Campaign of 1880

Democrats and Republicans were not the only ones holding conventions in that June of 1880. Three other parties, the Greenbackers, the Prohibitionists, and the Anti-Masons, assembled to select candidates for the presidency of the United States. On June 9 the Greenbackers convened at Chicago in Exposition Hall, where only the day before Garfield had been chosen as the standard-bearer of the Republican party.

They remained in session from Wednesday morning, June 9, until Friday morning, June 11. It seemed to be a year for generals, and General Butler, at the time a Republican, was most generally thought to be the logical choice of the Greenback party.[1] The Republicans had given Butler some financial support in his unsuccessful efforts to achieve the governorship of Massachusetts in November 1879.[2] But by May 1880 Butler was evidently planning to align himself with the Democratic

---

[1] Frederick E. Haynes, *James Baird Weaver*, pp. 159-60. Iowa City: State Historical Society of Iowa, 1919.

[2] Butler MSS, Simon Cameron to Benjamin F. Butler, October 28, 1879. On September 4, 1880 William E. Chandler rebuked Butler for joining the Democratic party. See *ibid.*, W. E. Chandler to Butler, September 4, 1880.

party. It was common knowledge that both the major parties were attempting to win Greenback support. Butler, who was soon to declare himself a Democrat, was apparently hard at work in an effort to control the Greenbackers in the interest of the Democratic party. J. J. McDavitt, who was party to the plan, wrote General Butler that "in addition I am to arrange for the Greenback nomination, and am under an expense of $50 a week by your authorization for that purpose."[3] Butler's dickerings with the Democrats reached the ears of certain prominent Greenbackers. On the first day of the convention the temporary chairman, Gilbert De La Matyr, wired the general that the convention was composed of "very level headed men" who were filled with enthusiasm. De La Matyr pointed out that the only argument that could prevent Butler's nomination was that his acceptance depended on the action of the Democratic convention. This, he said, must instantly be met by authorizing the Greenbackers to guarantee his unconditional acceptance.[4]

Prominent Republicans like Murat Halstead fully expected Butler to be the Greenback nominee, and wondered whether it would not be possible to induce Butler to recognize resumption as an established fact. Then, in the event of the nomination of Grant and Tilden, he could be the third candidate to "play the devil the most thoroughly."[5]

Butler's assurances to the Greenback party were either not forthcoming or, if they were, they failed to convince; as a result the sentiment of the convention turned toward yet another general, this time James Baird Weaver. At one o'clock Friday

_____

[3] *Ibid.,* J. J. McDavitt to Butler, May 20, 1880.
[4] *Ibid.,* G. De La Matyr to Butler, June 9, 1880. This telegram was also signed by Horace Binney, Thomas J. Durant, John McDevins, and H. H. Bryant. De La Matyr feared that the forthcoming Democratic platform might repudiate Greenback fiscal policy. In that event Butler would very probably renounce his Greenback nomination.
[5] Schurz MSS, Murat Halstead to Carl Schurz, May 27, 1880.

morning, June 11, when most Republicans and Democrats had already been asleep for several hours, the Greenbackers began their nominations and continued them for three hours. At 4:00 A.M. an informal ballot was taken and resulted as follows: General Weaver, 226; Hendrick B. Wright, 126; Stephen Dillaye, 119; General Butler, 95; Solon Chase, 89; Edward P. Allis, 41; and Alexander Campbell, 21. Before a formal ballot could be taken the names of Wright, Dillaye, Allis, and Campbell were withdrawn. When on the first ballot it appeared that General Weaver had over five hundred votes, states began rapidly changing their votes. When the results were announced at 6:00 A.M., General Weaver was declared to be the unanimous choice of the convention for president. B. J. Chambers of Texas was quickly nominated for vice-president, and at 6:45 A.M., after an all-night session, the convention adjourned.[6]

General Weaver had been in the thick of the fighting at Fort Donelson, at Shiloh, and at Corinth, and had many more battle scars than Garfield and almost as many as Hancock. Besides his military accomplishments, he was elected district attorney of the Second Iowa Judicial District in 1866, and in 1867 he received an appointment as federal assessor of internal revenue for the First District of Iowa. At this time Weaver was a Republican but was objecting strenuously to the stand his party was taking on the currency question. His popularity with the people was such that only the sharpest political trickery prevented him from obtaining the Republican nomination for Congress in 1874 and for governor in 1875. These defeats, which Weaver believed wholly unmerited, served to undermine his loyalty to the Republican party and drive him toward the Greenbackers, for whose principles he was developing a close affinity.

Weaver never advocated unlimited inflation, and as Professor John D. Hicks says, "His views on the money question would

---

[6] Haynes, *Weaver*, pp. 160-61.

not at a later date have been regarded as extreme."[7] He would not approve debt repudiation, but he opposed what he considered the systematic efforts of the creditor class to depreciate the purchasing power of the dollar. As a Greenbacker he won a seat in Congress in 1878, and on June 7, 1880 the House of Representatives granted him an indefinite leave of absence.[8] This leave was undoubtedly given to enable Weaver to attend the Greenback convention.

On July 3, 1880, from his home in Bloomfield, Iowa, General Weaver formally accepted the nomination "as a solemn duty." He gave his "cordial approval" to the platform, which he declared to be "comprehensive, reasonable and progressive— containing those elements of economic reform essential to the preservation of the liberty and the prosperity of the whole people." In a running commentary on the platform he began by insisting that the prosperity of the country depended upon an adequate circulating medium, which should be issued and controlled by the government. He urged the payment of the public debt as rapidly as practicable. He argued that the existing surplus revenues, together with that which would be realized under the silver law of 1878, would be more than adequate to pay off the debt within the next six years. He asserted that the only excuse the Republicans had for funding the debt was to perpetuate the national banking system, which was, together with other corporations, "fast swallowing up the profits of labor, and reducing the people to a condition of vassalage and dependence." He felt that these important monopolies were interlocked in purpose and always acting in closest sympathy.[9]

General Weaver believed that "the great problem of our civilization" was "to bring the producer and consumer to-

---

[7] John D. Hicks, "James Baird Weaver"; in *Dictionary of American Biography*, Vol. 19, pp. 568-70.

[8] *Congressional Record*, 46th Cong., 2d Sess., 4227.

[9] *Weekly Iowa State Register*, July 9, 1880. See also Haynes, *Weaver*, pp. 162-65.

gether." To accomplish this, adequate currency, as well as the rigid regulation of interstate commerce and transportation, were necessary. Because both of these, currency and commerce, were under the control of monopoly, the producer and the consumer were being ground into "poverty and ruin." He said he was thankful that the Greenback platform was "open, bold, and unmistakable on these great questions," while the Democratic and Republican platforms were either silent or "pronounced in favor of the monopolies and against the people."

When he reached the fifth plank, which referred to the "public domain," he pointed specifically to the fact that an area "larger than the territory occupied by the great German Empire had been wantonly donated to wealthy corporations." On the other hand, a bill to enable people of moderate means to reach and occupy the public lands had been "ridiculed and defeated" in Congress. The public domain should be reserved for actual settlers. Weaver felt that, where corporations had not complied strictly with the terms of the grants, the government should reclaim the lands.[10]

The Republican platform spoke of restraining and limiting Chinese immigration, but General Weaver went much further, and thought that "those seeking homes and desiring to become citizens of the United States, should be encouraged. But the importation of Chinese servile laborers" should be strictly prohibited. Weaver was at one with the Democratic platform on this subject of Chinese immigration into the United States.

In concluding his letter of acceptance Weaver asserted that one of the "grand missions" of the Greenback party was to "banish forever from American politics that deplorable spirit of sectional hatred, which for base purposes" had been perpetuated by Republican and Democratic leaders. In an appeal to the broad American masses General Weaver pleaded for a "free

---

[10] *Weekly Iowa State Register*, July 9, 1880.

ballot, a fair count, and equal rights for all classes."[11] This plea
for a free ballot and a fair count was a clever combination of
what he considered to be the just complaints of Republicans and
Democrats. Continuing in this vein, he urged united action of
all industrial classes, "irrespective of party," to re-establish in
the administration of public affairs the "old time Democracy of
Jefferson and Jackson, and the pure Republicanism of Abraham
Lincoln, and Thaddeus Stevens."[12]

This attempt to absorb what he considered the best elements
in the two major parties suffered from the defect that it would
have been difficult in 1880 to have found any Republicans who
would accept the states-rights theory of Jefferson. Any true
Southerner would choke if asked to accept the "pure Republicanism of Abraham Lincoln, and Thaddeus Stevens."

The Greenback convention had requested its candidates to
visit the various sections of the Union and talk to the people.
Weaver replied that it was his intention to comply with this request to the extent of his ability.[13]

Among the platforms adopted by the various conventions in
1880 that of the Greenbackers was by far the most progressive,
for the platforms of the two major parties refused to come to
grips with the pressing problems of the country. On some points
they were deliberately vague and general. Often they got bogged
down in a struggle with a straw man which they had set up for
themselves. The straw man of loyalty or disloyalty to the central
government was transformed into a major issue. Both parties
seemed to be unaware of the new problems that demanded an
answer. Unfortunately, both Republicans and Democrats insisted on perpetuating the atmosphere of the Civil War, which
had been over for fifteen years.

───────────

[11] *Ibid.*
[12] *Ibid.*
[13] *Ibid.*

The Greenbackers, on the other hand, were anything but vague and general. Their platform anticipated by almost fifty years the progressive legislation of the first quarter of the twentieth century. The Democratic party asserted that it was the "friend of labor," while the Republicans were going to continue to collect the high tariffs they had set up with the advent of the Civil War.[14] But thereafter the "duties levied for the purpose of revenue should so discriminate as to favor American labor."[15] This was all that either of the major parties had to say on the perplexing difficulties of both labor and management. This deliberate vagueness released both the Republican and Democratic parties from any written obligation to institute real reform. By way of contrast to these meaningless platitudes the supporters of General Weaver declared in their third plank that "labor should be so protected by national and State authority as to equalize its burdens and insure a just distribution of its results." It specifically advocated the enforcement of the eight-hour labor law. The rigid control of sanitary conditions in industrial establishments, the abolition of contract labor competition, and the establishment of a bureau of labor statistics were parts of their program. The inspection of factories, mines, and workshops, the prohibition of the employment of children under fourteen years of age, and the cash payment of wages were also included.[16] Frederick Emory Haynes is of the opinion that General Weaver's efforts in behalf of economic and industrial reform entitle him to a place in history next in importance to William Jennings Bryan and Theodore Roosevelt.[17]

The Greenback party seriously injured its cause by admitting the Socialists to the Chicago convention. Dennis Kearney,

---

[14] Stanwood, *Presidential Elections*, p. 369.

[15] *Ibid.*, p. 358.

[16] *Ibid.*, p. 363.

[17] Frederick E. Haynes, *Third Party Movements since the Civil War*, p. 143. Iowa City: State Historical Society of Iowa, 1916.

the "San Francisco Communist," as his enemies called him, was among these Socialists who attended the convention.[18] Their attempt to identify themselves with the Greenback cause gave an unfortunate revolutionary tinge to what was otherwise a sensible program of reform. Fear gripped the hearts of many hardworking Americans and disposed them to believe several unfair editorials circulated by Republican and Democratic organs. For example, the *New York Times,* on the day following the adjournment of the Greenbacker convention, told its readers that it was "fitting that this assemblage of lunatics should nominate for President that undefatigable agitator and inflationist. . . . He is in favor of unlimited currency, a free division of all property, and a return to the primitive system of money under which anything is money which men agree to call by that name."[19] A more biased evaluation of Weaver's political philosophy could scarcely have been offered to the American public. Faced with a barrage of such propaganda, Weaver had about as much chance of winning the presidency in 1880 as a Chinaman had of receiving a royal welcome in California in the same year.

The Prohibitionists held their convention at Cleveland, Ohio, on June 17. The twelve states of Arkansas, Connecticut, Iowa, Massachusetts, Michigan, Minnesota, New York, New Jersey, Ohio, Pennsylvania, West Virginia, and Wisconsin were represented by 142 delegates. A platform was quickly drawn up whose central theme was a round denunciation of alcoholic drink. The various planks, thirteen in all, graphically enumerated the disastrous effects of alcohol upon the individual and upon society.[20] The first plank said that the use of intoxicating beverages was encouraged by their "legalized importation, manufacture, and sale." Thus people were taught "the errone-

---

[18] *Ibid.,* p. 145.

[19] *New York Times,* June 12, 1880.

[20] *Cleveland Leader,* June 18, 1880. See also *New York Times,* June 18, 1880 and *Chicago Tribune,* June 18, 1880.

ous and destructive sentiment that such use is right."[21] The other twelve were in essence nothing but a repetition of this first plank.[22] With the platform out of the way, the 142 delegates nominated by acclamation yet another general, Neal Dow of Maine, with A. M. Thompson of Ohio as the vice-presidential candidate.[23] Neal Dow had both a military and a political record. As a general of the Union Army during the Civil War he was wounded twice in the battle of Port Hudson.[24] As the mayor of Portland, Maine, he was chiefly instrumental in effecting the passage on June 2, 1851 of the "Maine law," which forbade any person in that State "to manufacture or sell . . . intoxicating liquors."[25] General Weaver had been given a "Chinaman's chance" of winning the presidency in November. The pollsters of 1880 could not score General Dow as high as that.

June 1880 was a prolific month for producing soldier candidates. To the long litany of generals already mentioned there was added the name of General John W. Phelps of Vermont. He was nominated by the American Anti-Mason party. His running mate was Honorable Samuel C. Pomeroy of Kansas. The primary object of this party was to "Expose, withstand, and remove secret societies, Free masonry in particular, and other anti-Christian movements, in order to save the churches of Christ from being depraved," and also "to redeem the administration of justice from perversion, and our republican govern-

---

[21] *Cleveland Leader*, June 18, 1880.

[22] *Ibid.*

[23] *Appleton's Annual Cyclopaedia and Register of Important Events of the Year 1880*, Vol. 5, p. 697. New York: D. Appleton and Company, 1881.

[24] W. Randall Waterman, "Neal Dow"; in *Dictionary of American Biography*, Vol. 5, pp. 411-12.

[25] John Marsh, *The Napoleon of Temperance*, Appendix, p. 1 (New York: American Temperance Union, 1852). See also Neal Dow, *The Reminiscences of Neal Dow* (Portland: Evening Express Publishing Company, 1898). This work is interesting in that it presents Dow's extreme views on alcoholic beverages. Unfortunately the book concludes with the end of the Civil War and does not include Dow's reflections on the campaign of 1880.

ment from corruption."[26] If it was possible for a presidential candidate to have less chance of success than General Dow, then General Phelps was that candidate.[27]

The four months that intervened between the nominating convention and the November election would decide whether Garfield or Hancock would be the twentieth president of the United States. The next chapter will disclose the efforts of the Republican party from July through October to insure the election of James Abram Garfield.

---

[26] *Appleton's Annual Cyclopaedia* . . . *of the Year 1880*, Vol. 5, p. 697.

[27] Cecil H. C. Howard, *Life and Public Services of Gen. John Wolcott Phelps* (Brattleboro: Frank E. Housh and Company, 1887). This book states that Phelps believed "that the Masonic Lodge was the cause of many of the country's evils," and that he became "the nominee for President of the 'American Party,' in the election of 1880" (p. 36). See also Robert Morris, *William Morgan or Political Anti-Masonry: Its Rise, Growth and Decadence* (New York: Robert Macoy, Masonic Publisher, 1883). The Anti-Masonic party agreed with the Prohibitionists on the liquor question and with the Greenbackers on the currency and land monopoly. Their platform demanded justice for the Indian and a tariff that would give "equal protection to all classes of industry" (pp. 373-74). The newspapers of the period did not carry an account of the Anti-Masonic convention of 1880. See also William B. Hesseltine, *The Rise and Fall of Third Parties: From Anti-Masonry to Wallace*, pp. 10-11 (Washington: Public Affairs Press, 1948) for the origins and development of the Anti-Masonic party down to 1836.

CHAPTER VI

The Republican Campaign

Calm, together with a sense of material security, pervaded western civilization in the year 1880. Europe was enjoying what England loved to call a balance of power, and America had passed the convalescent stage since her destructive Civil War. The old order seemed to be passing. In Washington, Grant's political demise was an accomplished fact. In London, Disraeli was dying, and in Berlin the placid William I was soon to make way for the explosive William II. In Rome the social-minded Leo XIII had but recently replaced Pius IX. In America any feeling of tranquillity, at least in the educational field, seemed to be a bit ruffled, for the most that Henry Adams could say for the American educational system was that it was becoming "more perplexing at every phase," and that no theory of education "was worth the pen that wrote it."[1] Even though Thomas A. Edison blew out the gas jets of America and the world with his electric light, Adams was by no means consoled by his country's progress. He exclaimed with what seemed to be a sort of fatal resignation that, if "two thousand years after Alexander the Great and Julius Caesar, a man like Grant should be called—and should actually and truly be—the high-

---

[1] Henry Adams, "The Education of Henry Adams"; in J. L. Davis, J. T. Frederick, and F. C. Mott, editors, *American Literature*, Vol. 2, p. 358. New York: Charles Scribner's Sons, 1949.

est product of the most advanced evolution," then evolution was "ludicrous."[2]

Against this background of peace at home and abroad the Republican party had nominated James Abram Garfield as its candidate for the presidency of the United States; and on June 9 began what was to prove one of the bitterest campaigns in all American political history.

Despite the sop to Conkling in the form of Arthur's nomination for the vice-presidency, the Grant element in Republican ranks remained in a highly resentful mood. Thus the Republican party, as the contest began, was not in the best of condition for a successful campaign. On June 8, the very day of the adjournment of the convention, Senator Cameron had attempted a coup by calling an impromptu meeting of the Republican National Committee and instructing only the Grant men to come early. The Stalwart plan was to elect at this rump gathering the officers of the committee without regard to the wishes of Garfield. If this were accomplished, the Conkling forces fully intended to "exact concessions from Garfield before opening any vigorous campaign."[3] The ever-alert William E. Chandler and William P. Frye, however, got wind of Cameron's strategy and defeated it by hurrying to the meeting in ample time. In a letter to Garfield telling of this "effrontery" of Cameron, Chandler advised the Republican standard-bearer to "give a little personal thought to the organization of the national committee." Blaine leaders insisted that Cameron should not "under any circumstances" be re-elected. Chandler suggested Marshall P. Jewell for chairman, with Stephen B. Elkins as secretary, and insisted that further subserviency to the bosses would be unwise and would gain no votes.[4]

---

2 *Ibid.*
3 L. B. Richardson, *Chandler*, p. 259.
4 Chandler MSS, W. E. Chandler to Garfield, June 14, 1880.

Much pressure was exercised upon Chandler, whom the Republican *New York Times* had characterized as a "notorious political tramp," to take the office himself.[5] Eugene Hale urged him to do so to prevent the bosses from stepping into power again.[6] J. W. Forbes, national committeeman from Massachusetts, considered Chandler to be the best man to defeat Cameron.[7] Marshall P. Jewell thought that the man who had saved the Republican party in 1876 was the only fit man to be the chairman of the Republican National Committee in 1880.[8] On June 29 Garfield sent in four names, Hale, Chandler, McCormick, and Jewell, as acceptable to him, and added that he would be glad if the committee could secure the services of Thomas C. Platt as secretary. He felt that Platt's acquaintance with the political elements in the state of New York would make his services of great value.[9] On the very day that Garfield urged the procurement of Platt—who was Conkling's *alter ego*—as secretary, W. C. Cooper, the national committeeman from Ohio, wrote Chandler that Garfield had no idea of how to organize a political campaign. Cooper added that in his opinion William E. Chandler was the only one who possessed all the qualifications requisite for the chairmanship,[10] but Chandler was adamant in his determination not to accept the office.

The Republican National Committee waited for the announcement of Hancock's nomination, and then held their organizational meeting in New York on July 1. By that time Senator Cameron had withdrawn his claims, and the Grant faction was demanding the selection of Thomas C. Platt of New

---

[5] *New York Times*, May 12, 1880.
[6] Chandler MSS, E. Hale to W. E. Chandler, June 27, 1880.
[7] *Ibid.*, J. W. Forbes to William E. Chandler, June 23, 1880.
[8] Marshall Jewell to W. E. Chandler, June 15, 1880; in L. B. Richardson, *Chandler*, p. 258.
[9] T. C. Smith, *Garfield*, Vol. 2, p. 999.
[10] Chandler MSS, W. C. Cooper to William E. Chandler, June 29, 1880.

York as chairman. Platt of course was a man who would have been highly displeasing to the Blaine Half-Breeds. The "old guard," however, although beaten at Chicago, had by no means surrendered their ambitions to control the campaign. A sub-committee consisting of Chandler, Forbes, and Logan was appointed to report nominations to the main committee. Senator Logan pressed insistently for Platt, but the other two would not hear of such a choice and voted for Marshall P. Jewell, the only man on Garfield's list who would accept. Whereupon the Stalwart Logan declared that he and his friends were through, and that the Blaine faction could run the campaign in any way it wanted. This threat had its desired effect, and Forbes insisted that Logan should be given the authority to select the secretary. After some further storming Logan named Stephen W. Dorsey, formerly a senator from Arkansas. Dorsey was exactly what Arthur had been at Chicago, a sop to the Stalwarts.[11]

Republicans were by no means idle while waiting for the formation of their national committee. Garfield's nomination was hardly announced before California's politicians were inquiring, "How is he on the Chinese question?" Writing to Garfield from San Francisco, C. Curtiss felt satisfied that it would not be safe to "ignore or speak mildly upon this feature of political affairs" since the Chinese question was the great question on the coast.[12] Q. L. Matthews wrote from Colorado urging Garfield to satisfy the Pacific states soon by pronouncing himself "right" on the Chinese question.[13] Definite suspicions of Garfield's stand on Chinese immigration had been engendered in the minds of many prominent Californians ever since January 28, 1879, for on that day Congressman Garfield had opposed the passage of a bill which would limit to fifteen the

[11] L. B. Richardson, *Chandler*, pp. 258-59.
[12] Garfield MSS, C. Curtiss to Garfield, June 9, 1880.
[13] *Ibid.*, Q. L. Matthews to Garfield, June 10, 1880.

number of Chinese passengers that any ship could discharge at any one time at any American port. Garfield took his stand on the Burlingame Treaty of 1868, which had provided for unrestricted Chinese immigration into the United States, and offered an amendment providing that the bill should not take effect until due notice had been given to China, according to the usages of international law, of the termination of the treaty. He considered the bill to be a "palpable and flat violation" of the Burlingame Treaty.[14] The House passed the restrictive bill by a vote of 155 to 72, and it was duly noted in California political circles that Garfield was among the sixty-one not voting. Voters on the Pacific coast were well aware that the Department of State had made no effective effort to amend or supersede the Burlingame Treaty,[15] and hence they failed to appreciate Garfield's attempts to handle the Chinese problem through the medium of the State Department. In the states west of the Rockies there was a deep fear of excessive Chinese immigration. Garfield in his letter of acceptance of July 12, 1880 attempted to mitigate these California fears. He pointed out that the recent movement of the Chinese to the Pacific coast of the United States was "too much like an importation" to be welcomed without restriction.[16] He declared that, if the diplomatic negotiations in progress failed, it would be the duty of Congress to mitigate existing evils and prevent any increase. Some questioned the effectiveness of this appeal, and asserted that only election day would demonstrate just how much conviction Garfield's words carried in California.[17]

Hancock was nominated by the Democrats on June 24, and in a letter of the same date Welley Whitaker wrote Garfield that

---

[14] *Congressional Record*, 45th Cong., 3d Sess., 800.
[15] Tansill, *Bayard*, p. 229.
[16] *The Republican Campaign Text Book for 1880*, p. 187. Washington: David H. Gildersleeve, 1880.
[17] *Cincinnati Commercial*, July 13, 1880.

the Democrats feared for their leader because of his connection with the Surratt case. He proposed a cartoon with a "liberal and truthful" history of the murder of Mrs. Surratt, which could be done by his friends in the North. He considered this appeal to the Catholic element necessary, since Mrs. Surratt was a Catholic.[18] The Democrats, even without having the advantage of reading Manton Marble's letter assuring Joseph Pulitzer that "no newspaper exhibits the truth," were deeply suspicious of a long article carried by the *Chicago Tribune* on June 26.[19] This Republican anti-Grant paper gave a front-page display to what purported to be an interview between Mrs. William P. Torney, formerly Miss Anna Surratt, and a *Tribune* reporter. On being informed that the Democrats were saying that Hancock's part in the execution of Mrs. Surratt on July 7, 1865 was honorable, Mrs. Surratt's daughter was reported to have replied that, although he was not "exactly brutal," yet she felt that he wished for the execution and would have done nothing to prevent it.[20]

As one goes through the hundreds of campaign documents issued by the Republican National Committee, it is significant to note that no mention is made of the Surratt issue.[21] No doubt Jewell and Dorsey feared a boomerang, for, after all, the Republicans had hanged Mrs. Surratt.[22]

The *Boston Transcript*, disgusted at the tactics of certain Republicans, reflected that the hanging of Mrs. Surratt was a small

---

18 Garfield MSS, Welley Whitaker to Garfield, June 24, 1880. Whitaker himself was a Catholic. Mrs. Surratt was hanged for her alleged complicity in the assassination of Lincoln.

19 Marble MSS, Manton Marble to Joseph Pulitzer, February 1888, Vol. 68, no. 14446.

20 *Chicago Tribune*, June 26, 1880.

21 *Documents Issued by the Union Republican Congressional Committee for the Presidential Campaign of 1880.* Washington: n. p., 1880.

22 George F. Milton, *The Age of Hate: Andrew Johnson and the Radicals*, pp. 205-08 (New York: Coward-McCann Company, 1930). Professor Milton makes out an excellent case for the innocence of Mrs. Surratt and the criminal injustice of her trial.

issue. Hancock had had her executed in accordance with orders. If he had contravened these orders, it would have led to court-martial and disgrace. The *Transcript* felt that she deserved hanging, but that it was not Hancock who had been responsible for the decision.[23]

Apparently no holds were to be barred in this campaign, for simultaneously with these sporadic attempts to capture the Catholic vote by playing up the Surratt issue, attempts were made in other localities to win the Protestant vote by identifying Hancock with the Catholic Church. From St. Louis, Robert L. Lindsay, a prominent attorney, wrote Garfield that it was amusing to hear these old Southern Baptists and Methodists "kicking on Hancock's nomination" and swearing they would never vote for a Catholic president. Lindsay assured Garfield that his religion would help him in the campaign. Cass and Scott, he stated, had lost because of their Catholicism, and Hancock would lose the same way, "with other things to help."[24] Edwin Cowles, the bitterly anti-Catholic editor of the *Cleveland Leader*, gave his readers a detailed and terrifying picture of how the "Romanish" church would operate out of the White House should General Hancock, "by some mysterious dispensation of Providence," come to occupy it.[25]

---

[23] *Boston Transcript,* June 26, 1880.

[24] Garfield MSS, Robert L. Lindsay to Garfield, June 28, 1880.

[25] *Louisville Courier Journal,* July 9, 1880. The *Courier Journal* carries this excerpt from the *Cleveland Leader:* "A Romish Chapel," writes Cowles, "would be fitted up in it [the White House] with the superstitious paraphernalia of Romish worship. The White House would become the headquarters of priests, nuns, monks and so on. The Pope of Rome would be influential in that house through Mrs. Hancock who would be the Romish power behind the throne! The tradition of the American people inherited from their Protestant Revolutionary forefathers is opposed to an intolerant Church, which favors the suppression of religious freedom, from having control of the White House. Mrs. Hancock is a bigoted Romish, from all we can learn, and like Mrs. Sherman will make everything politically and financially, subject to the interests of the Romish Church."

Henry Watterson pointed out that Cowles was the type of editor who had ten nightmares every night, and in every one of them saw the pope advancing on America accompanied by a large army. For Cowles's benefit Watterson proved conclusively that Mrs. Hancock was an Episcopalian.[26] But apparently Cowles was not convinced by Watterson's arguments. While Garfield was engaged in drawing up his letter of acceptance, the irrepressible Cleveland editor urged him to take a position in favor of amending the Constitution to forbid the appropriation of public money, credit, or property for the benefit of any institution under sectarian control. This plank, he felt, in addition to the fact that Hancock was pro-Catholic, would have great weight with the Protestant Democrats, particularly with the members of the OAU.[27]

The religious side of any political campaign is always an interesting one, particularly if religion becomes a strongly controversial issue. At the present writing the Cowles papers are unavailable to scholars. They are in the possession of the Cowles family. If historians obtain access to them, they should indeed shed great light on this phase of the election.

Cowles had written to Garfield on July 5. On the next day the silver-tongued Robert G. Ingersoll echoed Cowles's sentiments, and wrote that, as long as the Democratic party was controlled by the Catholics and afraid to pass a resolution that the public moneys should not be given to sectarian schools, he would vote some other ticket.[28]

Apparently Garfield valued the Cowles-Ingersoll approach to the campaign, for the Republican nominee expressed wonder

---

[26] *Louisville Courier Journal,* July 9, 1880.

[27] Garfield MSS, Edwin Cowles to Garfield, July 5, 1880. As we have seen, much of the opposition to John Sherman's candidacy came from the OAU. See John Sherman MSS, William H. Van Nortwick to John Sherman, March 22, 1880. The OAU was the Order of the American Union.

[28] Garfield MSS, R. G. Ingersoll to Green, July 6, 1880.

at the fact that the *Cincinnati Commercial* did not give him a like support. F. D. Mussey wrote Garfield that he had remonstrated with Murat Halstead about his "halfhearted" support of Garfield. Halstead assured Mussey that the *Commercial* would do all within its power to elect Garfield, but that he did not intend to "follow Ed. Cowles in representing Hancock's family on religious subjects."[29]

While these opening skirmishes were going on, the Republican National Committee, under the leadership of Jewell and Dorsey, was planning the over-all strategy of the campaign. It was decided that one of the big guns in the Republican artillery would again be the "bloody-shirt" issue. This tactic was adopted in spite of the fact that all fair-minded Republican leaders admitted that Hancock's nomination had eliminated the Southern question.[30] Even Garfield had declared in 1878 that a man who would attempt to carry on a campaign on the old sectional issues would find himself without a party. Watterson warned the Republican party that if it went back to its "moldy drivel about 'rebels' and 'loyalty,'" it would only make its defeat the more overwhelming.[31] But if this "drivel" would get votes, certain Republican leaders were not adverse to using it. The *San Francisco Bulletin* set down English as nothing but a proslavery Democrat, while the *St. Louis Globe Democrat* warned its readers that Hancock's nomination "no more changes the character of Democracy than a figurehead of the Virgin on Kidd's pirate craft would change it into an honest ship."[32]

Both in song and in prose the Republicans insisted that sectionalism was a paramount issue in the campaign. Canard after canard on the subject rolled off Republican presses; and in the

---

29 *Ibid.*, F. D. Mussey to Garfield, July 16, 1880.
30 Schurz MSS, Carl Schurz to Garfield, June 24, 1880.
31 *Louisville Courier Journal*, June 28, 1880.
32 *San Francisco Bulletin*, June 28, 1880 and *St. Louis Globe Democrat*, June 25, 1880.

dissemination of catchy campaign songs the Democrats were entirely eclipsed. Jewell and Dorsey got out forty-two popular tunes and distributed them where it was hoped that they would do the most good.[33]

The Southern Democrats with a Union general for their standard-bearer hardly supposed that even the most insensate Republican would make himself ridiculous by attempting to identify General Hancock with the revival of the dead doctrine of secession.[34] But Republican campaign leaders were not reading Southern newspapers in the late summer and fall of 1880. In multitudinous handbills and campaign documents, spread far and wide, Jewell's committee reiterated again and again that Hancock was the nominee of a "solid South" who was chosen because of his record in resistance to Reconstruction. If Han-

---

[33] Poor Hancock was represented as yodeling a solo to his Southern brigadiers to the tune of "Yankee Doodle" (*Garfield and Arthur Campaign Song Book*, p. 21 [Philadelphia: J. M. Armstrong and Company, 1880]) :

> My Brigadiers, let us forget
> Which side it was we fought on,—
> The Union up or Union down,
> For I have quite forgotten.

> CHORUS. For I a weather (Han) cock am,
> Your favor now imploring
> I turn my tail toward the North,
> The solid South adoring.

> I see you vote the way you shot,
> For solid South and plunder;
> My men, if you will vote for me,
> I'll shoot for you by thunder.—Chorus.

> The Northern debt let us forget,
> You want repudiation;
> And eighty thousand soldier rebs
> We'll pension on the nation.—Chorus.

> My Brigadiers, come dry your tears
> I understand your feelings;
> O Brigadiers! for twenty years
> They kept you from the stealings.—Chorus.

[34] *New Orleans Times,* July 31, 1880.

cock were elected in November, Republican official propaganda declared, he would transfer the national authority and power to the Confederate enemies of the Republic. Republican party hacks everywhere throughout the North and West were solemnly announcing that the Confederates were ranging themselves on one side in this struggle because of their determination to regain through Hancock the "lost cause," and that for the sake of the nation it "behooved all loyal men" to range themselves on the other side.[35]

The Republicans, after rather naïvely appealing to the Democrats "not to make the Presidential canvass a campaign of calumny," proceeded to put into the throats of thousands of lusty Republicans the words of the "Conspirators Song."[36] Democratic assertions that they had long ago buried the doctrine on

---

[35] *The Republican Campaign Text Book for 1880*, p. 195.

[36] *New Orleans Times*, July 5, 1880. This song, which was also sometimes known as the "Ex-Confederates Boast," was set to the tune of the "Rogue's March," with a note that it should be sung "rather dolefully." The dirge carried a coverage of Democratic political history from 1860 to 1880. The first four stanzas were devoted to the failure of secession and the wicked attempt to win political ascendency in 1876 with the help of "Tilden's barrel." The remaining doggerel (*Garfield and Arthur Campaign Song Book*, p. 22) depicted the Democratic leaders as singing that

> Now in eighteen hundred and eighty,
> Our Hancock leads the van—nan!
> Behind the union uniform,
> Our cause looks up again—nien!
> We tried this on the battle-field,
> To take the Yankees in—sin!
> And now with Hancock at the front,
> Our glorious cause we'll win—thin!
>
> Arouse! Confederate Brigadiers!
> Turn out your men in gray—aye!
> The Ku-Klux Klan and Rifle Clubs,
> Are ready for the fray—aye!
> Unfurl the stars and bars again,
> With Hancock we must win—in!
> For if defeated at the polls,
> We shall be counted in—Too thin!

secession proclaimed by South Carolina in 1860 fell on deaf ears as far as official Republican propaganda was concerned.[37] A steady drone of accusations, presented in verse, song, and story form, continued to be produced and circulated, claiming that the Southern Democrats still espoused the doctrine of the "lost cause."

A pamphlet entitled "Rebel Echoes" was but one of hundreds that the Republicans turned out in the hope of convincing the North and West that the South still sympathized with the political views of Jefferson Davis, Robert E. Lee, and Stonewall Jackson. A Rebel flag was inserted on the front of this brochure, with the remark that it was a facsimile of the Rebel "star and bars" which floated over the names of Hancock and English in the *Hot Springs (Arkansas) Telegraph* and which had appeared at various Democratic processions. Among other things, "Rebel Echoes" carried a series of excerpts from a speech by Wade Hampton at Staunton, Virginia, on July 26, 1880. It was just another attempt to identify the Democratic party with secession. Actually, Hampton, after having pledged the South's vote for the Democratic nominee, was in Virginia to urge that state to make the solid South a reality. He told the Virginians that he was there to consult with them both as a Democrat and as a Southern soldier, and also as one who "looks back to the time when he shared with you privations and suffering and defeat in the Army of the Northern Virginia." He accused the Republicans of wiping out the last vestiges of states rights, and called the Democratic party the "party of peace and of Union that would blot out all sectional differences forever." In his peroration General Hampton pleaded with his audience to take the lead in forming the new solid South. He counseled them to consider what Lee and Jackson would have done were they alive and to remember that the success of the Democratic ticket de-

---

[37] *New Orleans Times*, August 23, 1880.

pended on their vote.[38] Although Hampton had said nothing to defend or threaten secession, some of his statements provided good campaign material for the Republican party.

Determined to ring all the charges on this "bloody-shirt" issue, yet another Republican circular portrayed in vivid language the "terrible revolt" of 1861-1865. During those years the South had inflicted upon the nation a loss of 500,000 lives, together with a loss in treasure of $5,000,000,000. The wicked Confederacy had multiplied "widows and orphans and woe and suffering throughout the land," and had created a public debt which would "embarrass and burden our children's children for generations to come." In the congressional elections of 1878 this Southern oligarchy, by "usurpation through terrorism, blood and fraud," had seized the majority of the two houses of Congress. Now in 1880 this same vile oligarchy had again combined with the Northern Copperhead Democrats in a "new conspiracy for the conquest of the Republic through a seizure of the Presidency." This dark conspiracy was seeking to accomplish by fraud what it had failed to effect by force of arms— the ruin of the nation. "Will the majority submit? God save the Republic!"[39]

In response to a Senate resolution of March 8, 1880 the secretary of the treasury, John Sherman, issued a statement showing government expenditures for the Civil War to have been $6,189,929,908.58. This enormous sum covered the period from July 1, 1861 to June 30, 1879. Even this highly technical report was turned into a Republican campaign song. Jewell, Dorsey, and Company entitled it "Six Thousand Millions Strong," and had it set to the tune of "Le Petit Tambour." The

---

[38] *Documents Issued by the Union Republican Congressional Committee for the Presidential Campaign of 1880*, no. 70.

[39] Republican Congressional Committee, *The Great Usurpation: The United States under the Confederate Senate and House of Representatives, An Oligarch*, p. 16. Washington: Rufus H. Darby, Steam Power Printer, 1879.

lyric characterized Hancock as a second Jefferson Davis leading a secessionist campaign.[40]

Southern failure to repudiate Jefferson Davis and heap insults on his head was but grist for the Republican propaganda mill. On March 2, 1879 a bill which would grant pensions to veterans of the Mexican War was introduced in the Senate, to which an amendment was quickly proposed providing "that no pension shall ever be paid under this act to Jefferson Davis." As *The Republican Campaign Text Book for 1880* comments: "Thereupon Democratic Senators rose to vindicate and eulogize the arch-rebel." Senator Lamar of Mississippi voiced the sentiments of the entire South when he declared that Jefferson Davis' name would continue to be honored for his participation in a cause cherished by all, in a great movement which inspired an entire people. The people of the South believed that they were fighting for liberty and constitutional government.[41]

Southern Democratic newspapers continued their loud protests that the Republicans and not the Democrats were the real sectional party, for Hancock's supporters were making a canvass of the entire country, while Garfield's adherents were avoid-

---

[40] The song (see *Garfield and Arthur Campaign Song Book*, p. 20) runs thus:

> A Union General leads, my boys
> Secession on the field,
> We'll meet it with brave deeds, my boys:
> Once more foredoomed to yield!
>
> He waves our flag in vain, my boys!
> His stars go down in night!
> Secession dies again, my boys,
> Though Hancock for it fight!
>
> CHORUS
>
> Secessions cost, secessions crime,
> Its outrage and its wrong,
> A debt on all our future time,—
> Six thousand millions strong!

[41] *The Republican Campaign Text Book for 1880*, pp. 5-6. Jefferson Davis performed valorous deeds for the United States during the Mexican War.

ing the South altogether. The *New Orleans Times* pointed out that "The rebel brigadiers are talking to the people of Maine and Vermont . . . but the voices of the Stalwart Statesmen are not heard in the South."[42]

The attempt to fasten the label of secession upon the brow of the Democratic party was one of the important factors in the Republican campaign. But the necessity of conciliating the diverse elements within the Republican party was of even greater importance. Garfield was well aware of the need of harmonizing the Grant Stalwarts, the Blaine Half-Breeds, and the Schurz Independents into a unified team if success was to be assured in November.

A few days after Garfield's nomination Whitelaw Reid wrote him a long note advising him not to make promises to anyone. He cautioned him not to be impressed by Schurz's assurances that he was indispensable in getting the German vote. He should remain silent about DeGolyer, Crédit Mobilier, and so forth, and should make neither journeys nor speeches. "There is no place," he concluded, "where you can do so much for your supporters and be so comfortable yourself from now until next November, as on your farm."[43]

Both during the campaign and after, Garfield would have frequent occasion to recall the penetrating observation of Judge Jeremiah S. Black. Black wrote that he was "to a certain extent . . . bound to fail, for in our country the leader of a party is like the head of a snake, it can go only as the tail impels it, and your tail will be a very perverse one."[44] In his effort to insure for himself the support of the powerful Conkling and Blaine political machines, Garfield injured his cause with the remnant of the Liberal Republicans under the leadership of Carl Schurz.

---

[42] *New Orleans Times*, August 23, 1880.
[43] Garfield MSS, Whitelaw Reid to Garfield, June 12, 1880.
[44] Jeremiah S. Black MSS, J. S. Black to Garfield, June 9, 1880.

For while quietly composing his letter of acceptance on his farm in Mentor, Ohio, Garfield resolved that the Grant and Blaine men were to have no grounds for complaint about the letter if he could help it.[45] When Garfield's letter of acceptance was published on July 12, Horace White, a prominent Liberal journalist and a Schurz Republican, was convinced that Garfield had thrown away the state of New York. The Independents would free themselves from all responsibility for the campaign and do nothing. He also felt that New York would go Democratic, by which fact Conkling "would not be ill-pleased."[46]

Carl Schurz, who on July 9 had urged Garfield to hurry the publication of his letter of acceptance, was greatly dismayed on reading its contents. The secretary of the interior wrote him another letter enclosing the note he had received from Horace White. Schurz felt that it was his duty to tell Garfield that his letter of acceptance was a great disappointment to "very many great men who hailed your nomination with joy and hope." Garfield's failure to endorse the policies of the Hayes administration with regard to the civil service, Schurz continued, greatly discouraged many who had expected to support him "with enthusiasm" and would have done so "with effect."[47]

But when Garfield composed his letter of acceptance, one of his primary concerns was to assure Senator Conkling on the question of patronage in New York. Conkling had never forgotten or forgiven Hayes, who with his "snivel service" had removed the Stalwart Arthur as collector of the port of New York. Garfield was well aware that New York would be vital in the

---

[45] Garfield MSS, Garfield to Whitelaw Reid, June 29, 1880. About this time Republican campaign planners were attempting to popularize Garfield by giving him various nicknames. "Plow Boy" was a Republican campaign song. See *Garfield and Arthur Campaign Song Book* for this and other songs with such titles as "Our Boatman," "Boatman Jim," "The Canal Bargee" (Garfield had worked on an Ohio canal barge in his youth), and so forth.

[46] Schurz MSS, Horace White to Carl Schurz, July 14, 1880.

[47] *Ibid.*, Carl Schurz to Garfield, July 20, 1880.

coming election.[48] If the Empire State was to be placed in the Republican column, it was imperative to enlist the services of the senior senator from New York.[49] Carl Schurz had already anxiously written Garfield that Conkling was in a "decidedly sulky mood."

When Garfield, therefore, came to that part of his letter of acceptance which dealt with civil-service reform, he phrased it in such a way as to win the cooperation of Conkling. Admitting that the question was "most difficult," he did not feel that the civil service should be put in a strait jacket of legal regulations. The president should "seek and receive the information and assistance of those whose knowledge of the communities in which the duties are to be performed best qualifies them to aid in making the wisest choice."[50] This last sentence signified to the Horace White-Carl Schurz Independents that Garfield was abandoning the recent gains in civil-service reform, and that Senator Conkling's advice would be followed with regard to New York appointments. But Conkling put no stock in vague campaign promises and insisted upon definite assurance with regard to federal appointments in New York before putting his shoulder to the Empire State's political wheel.

William E. Chandler was still on fairly good terms with Conkling, and at the time of the Republican National Committee's organizational meeting in July he dined with Conkling and some of his followers at Manhattan Beach with the purpose of conciliating that faction.[51] Chandler was sufficiently astute to realize that the one indispensable requirement for Republican success was the appeasement of Conkling. Returning to New Hampshire, he wrote to Garfield a long letter describing his conference with the New York Stalwarts. By implication he in-

---

48 *New York Herald*, June 9, 1880.
49 *Atlanta Constitution*, June 9, 1880.
50 *The Republican Campaign Text Book for 1880*, p. 187.
51 L. B. Richardson, *Chandler*, p. 259.

dicated that Conkling had not fallen for the bait which Garfield had so temptingly inserted into his letter of acceptance. Chandler thought that Conkling and his friends were entitled to feel assured that, if Garfield were elected, they would not be treated as they had been by President Hayes. No greater outrage was ever committed, declared Chandler, than that upon Arthur and Cornell by the present administration. One could easily gain the impression that the crafty Chandler was only intent upon having Conkling "feel" assured, for he quickly indicated his unwillingness to return to the rule of the bosses. It was on this principle that they had given up Blaine, Sherman, and Washburne at the recent Chicago convention. Chandler considered the state of New York "important, probably vital," and it might be worth while "to stoop a little to conquer much." Chandler apparently did not put any trust in scraps of paper. He thought that for Garfield to talk alone with Conkling for two hours, "eye to eye, face to face," would be the best course. The letter concluded by confiding to Garfield that, upon reflection, he thought that he would be elected. Chandler did not think that Garfield's chances for success were really affected by the Crédit Mobilier and DeGolyer charges.[52]

---

[52] Garfield MSS, W. E. Chandler to Garfield, July 24, 1880. In January 1873 the Poland Congressional Committee investigated the Crédit Mobilier Company of America. In the summer of 1867 seven stockholders of the Union Pacific Railroad, under the leadership of Oakes Ames, gained control of the Crédit Mobilier Company. They then proceeded to make a contract with themselves by which the Crédit Mobilier should build 667 miles of the Union Pacific at a cost ranging from $42,000 to $96,000 a mile. The total bill was $47,925,000. The profits were estimated at about twenty millions. Since the Union Pacific was a government-subsidized railroad, the Crédit Mobilier people, led by Congressman Ames, were in reality defrauding the American people of millions. Ames testified that Garfield held stock in this company. Garfield denied it. (See Caldwell, *Garfield*, pp. 220-28.) In 1874 a joint congressional investigating committee discovered that the DeGolyer Company had paid Garfield $5,000 for his services in arguing their case for a government paving contract before the Board of Public Works (*ibid.*, pp. 237-38). Garfield was a member of Congress during the Crédit Mobilier and DeGolyer episodes.

On the same day on which Chandler wrote this letter to Garfield, Stephen W. Dorsey, the Stalwart secretary of the Republican National Committee, telegraphed Garfield that he was going to New York. Dorsey stated that it was imperative for Garfield to come East. He should "take the judgment of those who know, as against those who do not."[53] But the influential Whitelaw Reid, who carried great weight with Garfield, was strongly opposed to Garfield's leaving his farm for a sojourn in the wicked metropolis of New York. Furthermore, he was convinced of the essential wickedness of Conkling, and his judgment was strongly against the proposed trip. Conkling, he wrote, was useful on the stump, where he had to support Garfield. Reid pointed out that he had been a constant hindrance to Hayes, and insisted strongly that he personally knew Conkling to be dishonest. Reid had no love for any of the Stalwarts, and declared that, even if they could throw away the state, they dare not. They wanted promises about offices to which neither they nor anybody else had a right.[54]

This letter was written by Reid at his farm in Cedarville, Ohio, on July 19. Garfield replied from Mentor, Ohio, on July 21. It is difficult to estimate the influence of the *Tribune* editor's letter in shaping General Garfield's decision. At any rate, he replied that he was anxious to avoid the visit to New York, for he really thought it would be better not to go. His letter of acceptance had paid to the Regulars all that they could reasonably ask, and had considerably tried the temper of the Independents. He believed that a visit would soon be misconstrued, giving the appearance of a bargain with one of the factions. He stated that he had made no terms or committals to anyone, beyond what was contained in his letter of acceptance. In that letter, he declared, he sought to say for what he was willing to

---

[53] Garfield MSS, S. W. Dorsey to Garfield, July 24, 1880.
[54] *Ibid.*, Whitelaw Reid to Garfield, July 19, 1880.

stand. He had discarded "brilliant points" for the sake of permanent ground on which to stand.[55] Garfield seemed very much upset over the suggested visit to New York, and confessed to Jeremiah S. Black that he was "out in the tempest." Garfield went on to profess that he "did not desire the nomination. . . . *Sed Deus aliter visum.*"[56]

Marshall P. Jewell, the chairman of the Republican National Committee, was "somewhat undecided" about the Garfield-Conkling meeting. In a letter to William E. Chandler he admitted that Garfield did not favor the conference; he added, however, that Senator Dorsey and Arthur were clearly of the opinion that he should come. Jewell wanted Chandler's advice on several questions, particularly on the matter of Garfield's trip to New York, for he considered it one of the "most delicate and difficult" things he had ever had to arrange.[57]

Garfield answered Chandler's appeal in a six-page letter. He thought it might be a good idea to meet the National Committee in New York, and he was "entirely willing, and indeed should be glad, to see Mr. Conkling." Garfield had no fear that Conkling would ask "unreasonable things," or wish him to do anything which it would be "in the slightest degree dishonorable" for him to perform. The danger in any New York journey lay in its probable effect upon the Liberals and the class of voters "who live between the lines of the two great parties." Garfield asked Chandler to consider the effect of his visit to New York upon these "classes of allies." Garfield asked Chandler if there was any good reason why the senator could not come to Ohio. General Grant had spoken of his intention to visit Garfield on his return from the West, and the two might meet there. This, thought Garfield, would save embarrassment and prevent any

---

[55] *Ibid.*, Garfield to Whitelaw Reid, July 21, 1880.
[56] Jeremiah S. Black MSS, Garfield to J. S. Black, July 20, 1880.
[57] Chandler MSS, Marshall Jewell to W. E. Chandler, July 21, 1880.

misconstructions by Half-Breeds and Independents. He stated that he had no patience with that feeling indulged in by so many that a candidate is in danger of being "owned and run by somebody." Garfield asserted that, if he could not maintain a reasonable independence and still take advantage of consultation with his fellow Republicans, he deserved to be "run and owned" by anyone who was better able to manage him than he was himself. He declared that he did not wish to be unduly stubborn, but that he felt he ought to know the grounds on which Chandler, Dorsey, and Arthur based their advice. He concluded by observing that, if it was thought best for him to meet Conkling, Blaine should also be there, and perhaps Grant and Sherman as well; then no one would have any reason to say that it was merely a factional meeting.[58]

Garfield, although open to persuasion, still felt somewhat reluctant to make the New York trip.[59] A few days later he received a very lucid explanation from Stephen W. Dorsey as to why the New York Stalwarts insisted on the New York conference. The secretary of the Republican National Committee repeated that in his judgment it was a duty which Garfield owed to himself and to the Republican party to be there on August 5, regardless of what Jewell or Curtis or anybody else said. He insisted that a conference with Governor Cornell and Senator Conkling was "an absolute essential" to the success of the campaign. Dorsey's reply to Garfield's "natural" inquiry as to what the people in New York wanted to see him about was that they wanted to know whether the Republicans of that state were to be recognized. In other words, were the "scratchers," Independents, and featherheads to "ride over the Republican party" of New York as they had for the previous four years? Only a personal conference would satisfy them, and Dorsey felt that a thirty-

---

[58] Garfield MSS, Garfield to William E. Chandler, July 26, 1880.
[59] Ibid.

minute discussion with the persons named would "settle for all time the doubt in their minds."[60]

When Dorsey warned Garfield that the Conkling adherents "not only want to know . . . but they intend to know" whether, if elected, he would follow Hayes's policy of removing the New York regulars to make room for "Scratchers and Independents and feather heads," he was in effect answering Whitelaw Reid, who had assured Garfield that Conkling "can't help supporting" him.[61] Months later, when Conkling had received the universal approbation of all Republicans for his very prominent part in effecting Garfield's success, Whitelaw Reid admitted that he was in error when he wrote Garfield on July 19, 1880 that Conkling couldn't help supporting him. For after Garfield had taken his seat as America's twentieth president, Reid was convinced that Conkling, from the outset, had desired his defeat, and only "by main strength" had he been pulled into the campaign at all.[62]

There was no doubt that the Dorsey letter of July 26 was, to say the least, direct. There was a ringing conviction in Dorsey's insistence that a conference in New York was essential to Garfield's political success there. The Empire State might possibly be carried with Conkling's help, but it certainly could not be carried without it. At least, that was the Stalwart contention.

On July 28, under the impact of the Dorsey letter, Garfield recorded in his diary his reactions to Dorsey's indication of inevitable and serious trouble with Conkling and his friends should he not go to New York. He was "very reluctant to go,"

---

[60] *Ibid.*, Stephen W. Dorsey to Garfield, July 26, 1880.

[61] *Ibid.*, Whitelaw Reid to Garfield, July 19, 1880.

[62] *Ibid.*, Whitelaw Reid to Garfield, April 11, 1881. There was a good deal of friendliness between Conkling and Tammany Hall. See *Harper's Weekly* 24:82, February 7, 1880; *Louisville Courier Journal*, March 8, 1880; and *Cincinnati Commercial*, May 24-25, 1880. Benjamin Butler turned Democratic in 1880; and if the New York conference had not been held, it is conceivable at least that Conkling might have joined with John Kelly's Tammany Hall.

and considered it an unreasonable demand that so much effort should be made to conciliate one man. But he also considered it "ungracious and perhaps unwise" to resist the opinion of the whole committee.[63]

Two days later the Republican standard-bearer wrote to Curtis in an attempt to calm troubled waters, for Curtis had sent Garfield a sharply worded protest against the proposed conference. Garfield attempted to reassure Curtis by saying that he was going to New York only at the unanimous advice of the National Committee.[64]

Dorsey had made the purpose of the meeting quite clear to Garfield; but notwithstanding this, the Republican presidential nominee could write to Hayes that, if any part of the purpose of this meeting was to secure any concession for the New York men who were sulking, they would receive no help from him beyond what he would give to any Republican.[65]

A few days before entraining for New York Garfield was apparently still very much "out in the tempest." On July 30 he sent a confidential letter to Blaine, saying: "My dear friend, you must stand by me. . . . Of one thing you may be assured, there shall be no surrender to any unreasonable demands." He went on to assure him that he would do nothing to compromise himself or the "noble men" who had stood by him. He wanted Blaine to find out, if possible before he arrived, what the exact situation was, how large a force Conkling had behind him, and just what the trouble was.[66]

On August 3, 1880 Garfield commenced his pilgrimage from Mentor, Ohio, to New York City. The meeting with the Republican National Committee was scheduled for August 5 at New York's Fifth Avenue Hotel. Garfield's diary carries a short

---

[63] Garfield MSS, Diary, July 28, 1880.
[64] Garfield MSS, Garfield to G. W. Curtis, July 30, 1880.
[65] *Ibid.*, Garfield to Hayes, July 31, 1880.
[66] *Ibid.*, Garfield to Blaine, July 30, 1880.

account of the crucial conference, in which he mentions that speeches were made by Blaine, Logan, and Sherman, and that the absence of Senator Conkling gave rise to unpleasant surmises as to his attitude. Blaine, with whom he had a "long and friendly talk," he calls the "prince of good fellows."[67]

There were more than a few raised eyebrows when it was discovered that the lordly Roscoe had remained arrogantly in seclusion and had not deigned to honor the festivities by his presence. Conkling saw to it, however, that his henchmen were present in abundance. One of them, Thomas C. Platt, asserted that he had obtained from Garfield the assurance that under his administration the machine in New York would be paramount and that the rebellious elements in that state would be recognized only so far as the machine approved.[68] This promise, according to Platt, was extracted from the candidate at a private meeting held in the Fifth Avenue Hotel suite of Levi P. Morton. This session was held on the afternoon of August 6. Garfield's diary for that day ends with the words: "Did not sleep well. Had in the pm a long interview with Morton, Crowley, Arthur and Platt."[69]

Platt also asserted that Garfield promised Morton that if he undertook the arduous task of being chairman of the Committee on Finance, he would reward him with the important post of secretary of the treasury.[70] If Garfield made any political bargains on August 6, he did not confide them to his diary. When he returned to his Ohio farm on August 9, he admitted that he was very weary, but felt that no serious mistake had been made and probably much good had been done. His diary for that day reads: "No trades, no shackles and as well fitted for defeat or victory."[71]

---

[67] Garfield MSS, Diary, August 5, 1880.
[68] Platt, *Autobiography*, p. 131.
[69] Garfield MSS, Diary, August 6, 1880.
[70] Platt, *Autobiography*, p. 132.
[71] Garfield MSS, Diary, August 9, 1880.

No one can be absolutely sure of what happened in Morton's room on August 6; but from that date on Conkling and his friends took off their coats and began to work as they had not done before for the success of the national Republican ticket. The *Nation* caustically commented that Conkling's zeal in the campaign indicated that he had made a deal with the Republican candidate.[72]

Thomas C. Platt states that Conkling had two reasons for not attending the Fifth Avenue conference. He did not wish to become a party to any bargain or treaty which he would surely be charged with if he took part in the meeting. His second and more fundamental reason was he did not trust Garfield. To satisfy his friends, however, Conkling assured them that he would abide by their action, but urged great caution and distrust of verbal promises.[73] On August 15 Whitelaw Reid reported to Garfield that Conkling's absence was due to the presence of Curtis. Apparently Conkling could have endured Blaine, but the idea of conferring with Curtis was too much for him.[74]

Garfield's message to the New York Stalwarts, whatever it was, was certainly effective. For the Conkling machine, dormant for over two months, suddenly came to life. Eight days after the Fifth Avenue conference Richard C. McCormick informed William E. Chandler that Conkling had had a long session with Dorsey and promised to take part, "after his own fashion," in the campaign.[75]

On August 20 Platt, who had done practically nothing for the Republican ticket since June 8, told Garfield that work had begun and that there was good reason to believe that they could carry New York. Conkling had assured Platt that, as soon as he could get his private business adjusted, he would speak wher-

---

[72] *Nation* 31:282, October 21, 1880.
[73] Platt, *Autobiography*, p. 127.
[74] Garfield MSS, Whitelaw Reid to Garfield, August 15, 1880.
[75] Chandler MSS, R. C. McCormick to W. E. Chandler, August 13, 1880.

ever the Republican National Committee sent him.[76] Conkling himself confided to his close friend Levi P. Morton on August 29 that he was clearing his desk so that he would have time to "read up and get ready for the campaign."[77]

Three days after the Republican standard-bearer's visit to the Empire State, the *Boston Herald* stated in a very frank editorial that the politicians continued to talk about the late political conference. No one knew better than Garfield himself that Conkling could throw the state against him with perfect ease. New York was absolutely necessary to Garfield's success, wrote the *Herald*, and Garfield must make terms with Conkling or lose that state. When Edwin Cowles, editor of the *Cleveland Leader* and intimate friend of Garfield's, read the *Herald* article, he sent it on to the Republican nominee, asking if there was any truth in it. Was Conkling sulky, he asked, or would he work for Garfield? Cowles wanted to know whether he had demanded a consideration in the shape of control of New York appointments. He assured Garfield that what he wrote would be confidential. He wanted to be able to state the facts on Garfield's "own authority as a member of the Conference." Cowles promised to burn the letter he would receive from Garfield immediately upon reading it.[78] If Garfield had desired to squelch the prevalent rumors of a "deal," he could easily have spoken through the friendly pages of Cowles's *Leader* or Whitelaw Reid's *New York Tribune*. He preferred to remain silent.[79]

As the Republican campaign reached the midway mark, the *San Francisco Bulletin*, while conceding that the campaign lie

---

[76] Garfield MSS, Platt to Garfield, August 20, 1880.

[77] Morton MSS, Conkling to L. P. Morton, August 29, 1880.

[78] Garfield MSS, Edwin Cowles to Garfield, August 10, 1880. Cowles enclosed the clipping from the *Boston Herald* for August 8.

[79] Theodore Clark Smith, former professor of American history at Williams College, Garfield's alma mater, in his *Life and Letters of James Abram Garfield*, Vol. 2, p. 1016, thinks it "inconceivable" in view of Garfield's personal and political standards that he gave any such "pledge" as described by Platt.

was often plausible, felt that the half-dozen which had been manufactured in the course of the Republican campaign were clumsy. The alleged facts that Hancock had hanged Mrs. Surratt and that Garfield had made about three hundred and fifty dollars by a Crédit Mobilier transaction had "fallen dead."[80] Marshall P. Jewell, however, was not at all convinced that they had "fallen dead." He accused the Democrats of employing as their main stock and trade "mud-slinging and vituperation." Jewell vowed that they would "get paid off in their own coin." He saw evidence of the success of Republican propaganda in the fact that quite a few Democratic businessmen were now afraid to trust the government in the hands of the South. They were hesitating about voting for Hancock on that account.

The Maine elections were coming up on September 13, and both Ohio and Indiana would hold state elections in mid-October. Supremely confident that Blaine would take care of Maine, Jewell informed Garfield that the great fight was in Indiana and that it was mainly a question of finances. Jewell had secret information which indicated that the Democrats had already sent "roughs" and "repeaters" from Baltimore, so that Senator Dorsey would have all he could do to prevent frauds on the southern border of Indiana.[81]

The Maine election was a fearful disappointment to the Republicans. They had hoped for a glorious triumph; but on the morning after the election the Democrats could claim that Harris M. Plaisted had been chosen governor by a two-thousand majority.[82] The *San Francisco Bulletin,* in announcing the Dem-

---

80 *San Francisco Bulletin,* August 18, 1880.
81 Garfield MSS, Marshall Jewell to Garfield, September 7, 1880.
82 Louis C. Hatch, *Maine: A History,* Vol. 2, pp. 625-26 (New York: American Historical Society, 1919). Plaisted ran on a fusion ticket. The Democrats and Greenbackers both nominated him. The Republicans lost a member to Congress, while the Democrats and Greenbackers each gained one. See *San Francisco Bulletin,* September 14, 1880.

ocratic victory in Maine, asserted that the Democrats, after enjoying the initial boom given to them by the impetus of Hancock's nomination, had been rather inactive, but that Plaisted's triumph over Governor Davis was a sure indication that Hancock's supporters had their shoulders to the wheel in earnest. The *Bulletin* went on to affirm that the Republican defeat in Maine should serve as a warning to the adherents of Garfield, for it was now abundantly clear that victory could be won only by hard fighting. No Northern Republican could now remain apathetic and afterwards "settle the matter with his conscience." The *Bulletin* expected to see every man "hastening to the front," for the struggle for the presidency in 1880 was not to be a "political promenade" for any party.[83]

On Tuesday, September 14, Garfield recorded in his diary that he had received a long dispatch from Blaine saying that $70,000 to $100,000 had been sent into Maine four days before the election and used by the Democrats "as money was never used before." He did not believe that it would turn the tide against his party. He was encouraged to hear that Chauncey Depew and other prominent leaders of the party were convinced that the Republicans would still win in November.[84]

Marshall P. Jewell, writing to Garfield from the headquarters of the Republican National Committee in New York, took a realistic approach to the Maine election and asserted that it was no use to disguise the fact that this "set-back in Maine was

---

[83] *San Francisco Bulletin*, September 14, 1880.

[84] Garfield MSS, Diary, September 14, 1880. Early in September, Garfield wrote to Amos Townsend of Cleveland: "The situation in Indiana is such that Mr. Rockefeller can do us immense service there if he will. . . . Do not think that this relates to the raising of means. Mr. Rockefeller can do what is even more important than that." Townsend replied that Rockefeller was "all right," but warned Garfield that it was "risky writing." This attempt of Garfield to put pressure on the workingmen of Indiana was a typical Republican tactic in 1880. See Garfield MSS, Garfield to Townsend, September 2, 1880. For Townsend's reply to Garfield, see Caldwell, *Garfield*, p. 304.

a set-back." Blaine had "worked like a Trojan," and he said that the Democrats were pouring out money to a greater degree than he had ever before witnessed in the state of Maine. But Jewell could clearly see the silver lining in all these dark clouds, and thought that the Maine debacle would open the "purses, the pockets, and the eyes" of Republican businessmen to the danger which immediately threatened. He believed that they would pull Garfield through, for the one reason alone that the "business of the country" could not afford to have him defeated. But, he concluded, it would be "no walk-over." The Democrats, of course, could not be trusted, for they had "bought votes bodily on the day of election." Yet Garfield should not be overanxious, for Jewell told him confidentially that they would have money enough "somehow." He concluded his letter to Garfield by reporting that he had been in Philadelphia recently and had seen Wharton Barker, who was very active and was going to do "heaps of work." They would raise money enough to carry the state of Pennsylvania.[85]

Garfield analyzed the Republican defeat in Maine, and attributed the event to the use of money "with which the Democrats ambushed our people," and the "element of rebellion against Blaine and his autocracy."[86] From the state capitol in Augusta, Governor Davis wrote the Republican nominee that Plaisted's victory would shock big business into action. Davis was sure that $100,000 or almost that amount must have been spent in Maine in the last week of the campaign by the fusion managers. The country was now satisfied that the Democrats would go to the last extreme to obtain power. He was equally sure that the business interests of the country would come to the rescue.[87]

---

[85] Garfield MSS, Marshall Jewell to Garfield, September 14, 1880.
[86] Garfield MSS, Diary, September 18, 1880.
[87] Garfield MSS, D. F. Davis to Garfield, September 27, 1880.

There was no doubt that big business was deeply interested in the fate of the Republican party. Almost simultaneously with the Maine defeat there appeared, as if by magic, both workers and money. E. D. Lockwood wrote Carl Schurz a few days after the Republican catastrophe in Maine, and informed him that there was a movement on foot to raise $150,000 from large corporations and banks. A large portion of this sum would be promptly secured, but very little was said about it "for obvious reasons."[88] Secretary of the Interior Schurz was stumping the country from New York to California in Garfield's interest. He had but recently made several speeches in San Francisco in which he appealed directly to the business interests. Schurz was becoming more than ever convinced that the appeal which was being made to the conservative sentiment would carry the election for the Republicans.[89]

The shock of defeat in the Maine elections proved to be just the proper tonic for the Republican party. By the end of September Jewell and Dorsey had relegated the "bloody-shirt" theme to a secondary role, and had introduced the tariff question as the main issue of the campaign. Placards contrasting American and European wages suddenly appeared in thousands of American shopwindows. Each told the simple but effective story of the "real antagonism of the Democratic leaders to the artisan, the mechanic, and the laborer."[90] The Republican tariff, by protecting the American manufacturing interests, was in reality insuring high wages to the American workingman. The Democratic "tariff for revenue only" meant free trade with its inevitable consequences of ruin to American factories and unemployment for the working masses. American laboring men were everywhere solemnly warned by signs, handbills, docu-

---

[88] Schurz MSS, E. D. Lockwood to Carl Schurz, September 17, 1880.
[89] *Ibid.*, Schurz to Garfield, August 11, 1880.
[90] *Documents Issued by the Union Republican Congressional Committee for the Presidential Campaign of 1880*, p. 153.

ments, and newspapers that, unless they wished to be reduced to the pittance that Europeans called wages, they had better vote the Republican ticket.

After almost three weeks of this sort of thing, even the *Springfield Republican* protested that the Republicans were "overdoing the business scare." The propaganda which portrayed the Democratic party as intent on bringing in ruin and poverty for the American worker was obnoxious to the editors of the *Republican*. They frankly said that they regarded such an appeal as "claptrap." Neither party was clear on the issue, and every intelligent Republican saw the need of a revision of the tariff toward a reduction of duties.[91] As early as March 19, 1880 the Republican *New York Times* pointed out that for over a year the Democrats had had a large majority in both houses and that they had done nothing to lower the tariff. The *Times* felt that all that could be said was that the general tendency of the Republican party had been toward protection and that of the Democratic party toward a low tariff. Neither principle had been so plainly taken up by either party as to preclude great freedom of action on the part of its representatives.[92]

Marshall P. Jewell conveyed the cheerful news to Garfield that the stock market had suffered a severe slump after the Maine elections. It was now the opinion of all the leading brokers that Hancock's election would "put stocks down and raise a great breeze in the market," while Garfield's election would strengthen it. A prominent broker by the name of Heath had confided to the Republican National Committee that, if the public knew what the effect of Hancock's election would be, they would not "dream" of tolerating it for a moment. A month before the election Jewell remarked that Republican talk of tariff, Democratic vilification of Garfield, and money seemed to be the

[91] *Springfield Republican*, October 19, 1880.
[92] *New York Times*, March 19, 1880.

three main points of the campaign. The Democrats, he wrote, were basing their campaign almost exclusively on attacking Garfield's personal character, and saying nothing about principles. They were merely flooding the country with the "literature of the gutter."[93]

Somehow or other, during the New York meeting of August 5, Garfield had managed to conciliate both the Independents and the Stalwart Republicans. This was no easy task but it had been accomplished, and both factions were working hard for the success of the national ticket. On September 28 Horace White was not at all optimistic about the chances for the Republican success in November. Writing from New York to Carl Schurz, he informed him that the impression seemed to be gaining ground there that Hancock would be elected. He hoped that the "October states" would tell a different story.[94]

Indiana and Ohio were the October states; and with the elections there less than two weeks off, the chairman of the Republican National Committee, made cautious by the Maine results, was prepared for the worst. In a revealing letter to Garfield he related that, if disaster should come in October, the Republicans had the "lines of retreat" and the "bridges" they would need. They could "march over the bridges" in any of those states if they had money enough, and could get the electoral vote of "every mother's son of them." Jewell felt that the Republicans might be frightened badly enough after the October elections to need these "bridges."[95]

In the Buckeye State the Republicans were counting heavily on the fact that Garfield was a native son, and in Indiana their hopes were founded principally on the unpopularity of English and the recent large immigration of Negroes from the South.[96]

---

93 Garfield MSS, Jewell to Garfield, September 29, 1880.
94 Schurz MSS, Horace White to Schurz, September 28, 1880.
95 Garfield MSS, Jewell to Garfield, October 1, 1880.
96 *San Francisco Bulletin*, September 28, 1880.

As early as November 24, 1879 the *Louisville Courier Journal* had called attention to the fact that many Negroes were pouring into Indiana to serve as repeaters in the election. Watterson expressed the conviction that it was the only way the Republicans could hope to carry Indiana in November 1880.[97] Two weeks later the *New Orleans Times* sarcastically remarked that since the "counting in process" was no longer possible, it became necessary to defeat the Democrats in either New York or Indiana. Continuing, the *Times* stated that the Republicans apparently intended to overcome the 1876 Tilden majority of five thousand in the Hoosier State by colonizing some six thousand Southern Negroes there. This, said the *Times,* was the meaning of the sudden diversion of this current of emigration from Kansas to Indiana. The next question would be how to get their votes polled. That would have to be fought out by the people and the politicians in that state.[98]

But E. B. Martindale, editor of the Republican *Indianapolis Journal,* was quite sure that the emigration movement was entirely independent of political considerations. The colored people, he maintained, had simply determined to try to better their condition by moving to Indiana.[99]

With the Grand Old Party having already lost Maine in September, and faced with the possible loss of the October states, the Stalwart machine swung quickly into action. Grant and Conkling entrained for Ohio, while Levi P. Morton made for Indiana. On September 28, at Warren, Ohio, Conkling and Grant addressed forty thousand people. Senator Conkling spoke for more than two hours, and General Grant spoke for seven minutes. Neither of them so much as mentioned the name of James Abram Garfield, yet the speeches were admittedly of in-

---

[97] *Louisville Courier Journal,* November 24, 1879.
[98] *New Orleans Times,* December 10, 1879.
[99] *Indianapolis Journal,* January 26, 1880.

calculable assistance to him.[100] Garfield, however, was deeply hurt, and wrote to his friend Harmon Austin that it was a narrow and unmanly thing on Conkling's part to make such a manifest effort as he had in Ohio to avoid mentioning the head of the ticket in any generous way.[101]

After the Warren meeting Grant and Conkling moved on toward Cleveland. Mark Hanna, who was in charge of transportation, arranged to have the train stop at Mentor. Thus it came about that Grant and Conkling spent an hour or so with Garfield on his farm. We do not know with certainty what happened at Mentor, but the public, which did not know either, instantly began talking about a "treaty." The *New York Sun* was sure that a "Treaty of Mentor" had been signed, and that its significance was that Garfield was to be a placeholder for Grant. Dana was certain that Garfield had met Conkling's terms, for he wrote in the *Sun:* "What means Mr. Conkling's tall plume in the thick of the fight, which only the other day was so conspicuously absent, if it means not this? What means the sudden charge of the Old Guard all along the line?"[102]

In both the "Treaty of Fifth Avenue" and the "Treaty of Mentor" we have Garfield's word against Platt's. Platt swears that, when Conkling returned from Mentor, he told him that he had extracted a pledge from Garfield that he would make no New York appointments unless they were first approved by the United States senators from New York, by the vice-president, by the governor, and by the state committee. Platt then asked Conkling: "Have you any faith in Garfield?" Conkling made a wry face, sneered, and replied: "Not much but we will try him out."[103] Garfield recorded in his journal for September 28,

---

[100] Chidsey, *Conkling*, p. 309.
[101] Garfield to Harmon Austin, October 1880; in T. C. Smith, *Garfield*, Vol. 2, p. 1032.
[102] *New York Sun*, October 20, 1880.
[103] Platt, *Autobiography*, p. 135.

1880 that the party consisted of General Grant, Senators Conkling and Logan, Congressman Morton, and about fifteen gentlemen from Cleveland. Some two hundred citizens came to the house and were introduced to Grant. "Conkling gave them a lunch and coffee in the dining room. . . . I had no private conversation with the party but the call was a pleasant and cordial one all around."[104]

Just before the October elections Garfield apparently gave some credence to the story that Pius VII had sent over fifty million dollars to aid in the election of Hancock. At any rate, Garfield gave the bearer of this fantastic tale a letter of introduction to Cowles. The editor of the *Cleveland Leader* wrote the Republican nominee that a German called on him with a tremendous story of a great plot, of the pope's being engaged in aiding in Hancock's election, and of his having sent fifty million dollars to the United States for this purpose. The German gentleman got through to Cowles on the strength of Garfield's letter. This fellow was, said Cowles, "cracked." He had called on Cowles two years earlier with a story of a plot by the priesthood to assassinate him. Cowles concluded his letter with a request that it be destroyed, and cautioned Garfield to be more prudent in writing letters for people.[105]

During the first week in October, Republican prospects for success were so dismal that the *New York Truth* carried an article to the effect that Garfield was contemplating withdrawing from the contest in favor of Grant. On October 4 Halstead's *Cincinnati Commercial* branded this story as a mere rumor.[106]

Since the Democratic campaign had become almost "one of exclusively personal assault," Jewell felt the need of having someone in high repute make a direct attack on Hancock. Gen-

---

[104] Garfield MSS, Diary, September 28, 1880.
[105] Garfield MSS, Edwin Cowles to Garfield, October 1, 1880.
[106] *Cincinnati Commercial*, October 4, 1880. The *Commercial* printed the article from the *New York Truth* with regard to Garfield's contemplated withdrawal.

eral Grant answered this call, and in the interests of the Republican party made several short speeches in which he attempted to weaken the Democratic candidate before the people. The hero of Appomattox said he had known the Democratic nominee for forty years as a "weak, vain man," the most selfish man he knew. Grant admitted that Hancock was a "very fair corps commander," but declared that he was never thought of for any outstanding position. In the Democratic convention of 1864, Grant proclaimed, Hancock had received one vote, and ever after he had the "Presidential bee in his bonnet." From that time on, Grant concluded, Hancock had scrupled at nothing to gain Democratic and Southern favor.[107]

The chairman of the Republican National Committee put a very high estimate on General Grant's campaign work, and wrote to Garfield with obvious satisfaction that he thought Grant's utterances on Hancock were the most valuable contribution which had been made to the campaign. Republican journals had been saying, "Oh, Hancock was a good soldier and is a nice, clean gentleman." Nobody but Grant, concluded Jewell, had been big enough to "do Hancock justice."[108]

With the lesson of the Maine elections acting as a constant reminder of what the Democrats could accomplish, Garfield grew anxious about the outcome of the October elections. Confiding his fears to Arthur, he wrote that considerable sums of money had suddenly appeared among the Democrats in Ohio. Garfield had no doubt but that they were undertaking the Maine tactics in Ohio and Indiana. It was an experience, he wrote, with which Ohioans were not familiar.[109] Arthur's reaction to this last statement is not recorded.

---

[107] *New Orleans Times,* October 6, 1880 and *Cincinnati Commercial,* October 6, 1880.

[108] Garfield MSS, Marshall Jewell to Garfield, October 7, 1880.

[109] Library of Congress, Chester A. Arthur MSS, Garfield to Arthur, September 25, 1880.

Republican fears were proved to be groundless, for the Grand Old Party took Ohio by a majority of twenty thousand and Indiana by ten thousand. After giving the above tabulations, the *San Francisco Bulletin* added rather significantly that the Democrats could still win by taking New York, New Jersey, and California. Unfortunately for them, however, they were to capture only the latter two states and were to fail to win the all-decisive Empire State.

The Democratic press recognized the fact that the tariff issue had been a major factor in Republican success in the October states. The *New Orleans Times*, after admitting that the material interests of the country were never in a more flourishing condition, accused the Republicans of willfully misinterpreting the Democratic "tariff for revenue only" to mean misery and poverty for the country. The *Times* insisted that Hancock was a better protectionist than Garfield, and pointed with pride to the fact that the present Democratic Congress within the last two years had done nothing to change the protective nature of the tariff.[110] The *New York Sun*, while conceding the deceptiveness of the phrase "tariff for revenue only," vehemently asserted that such a tariff also gave protection. Dana turned to logic for votes, and explained carefully that the government would always be in need of revenue and that as a consequence there would always be a tariff. And every tariff, wrote Dana, was in essence protective.[111] Henry Watterson, who was largely responsible for the Democratic platform, was not worrying about the tariff question. He was sure that in this presidential campaign there was but one great issue: whether the unorganized masses of the people could hold their own against the organized politicians. In-

---

[110] *New Orleans Times*, October 20-21, 1880. On September 13 Garfield had written that "Indiana must have immediate and abundant help" (Library of Congress, Anson G. McCook MSS, Garfield to Anson G. McCook, September 13, 1880). At this time McCook was a Republican congressman from New York City.

[111] *New York Sun*, October 16, 1880.

diana had been "bought right out of hand." It was charged, said Watterson, that the Department of the Treasury actually printed money enough to do this, and he was certain that Indiana was at that moment flooded with freshly printed five-, two-, and one-dollar bills.[112]

Arthur seemed to give partial credence to Watterson's charges when he delivered a brief after-dinner address at Delmonico's Restaurant in New York on February 11, 1881. The vice-president-elect informed his table companions that he supposed Indiana was really a Democratic state.

> It had been put on the books always as a State that might be carried by close and perfect organization and a great deal of— (laughter and cries of "soap"). I see the reporters are present, and therefore I will simply say that everybody showed a great deal of interest in the occasion and distributed tracts and political documents all through the State.[113]

Levi P. Morton, perhaps more than any other man, was responsible for carrying Indiana. Roscoe Conkling wrote him on October 14 to congratulate him on his effective work in securing the Hoosier State for the Republican party.[114] Hugh J. Hastings, editor of the *New York Commercial Advertiser*, asserted that Garfield knew he was indebted to Morton more than to any other man for the success of Indiana.[115]

The Republican press struck a jubilant note when the *St. Louis Globe Democrat* declared that the fears caused by the Maine defeat had vanished with both the Hoosier State and the Buckeye State in the Republican column.[116] The *San Francisco*

---

[112] *Louisville Courier Journal*, October 22, 1880.

[113] *Nation* 32:122, February 24, 1881.

[114] Morton MSS, Roscoe Conkling to L. P. Morton, October 14, 1880.

[115] *Ibid.*, Hugh J. Hastings to ?, November 25, 1880. (Probably written to Morton.)

[116] *St. Louis Globe Democrat*, October 13, 1880. The editor conceded that ten days before the election everyone was sure that Indiana would be carried by the Democrats.

Bulletin was certain that one of the causes which had contributed to the defeat of the Democrats in the October elections was
their equivocal attitude on the subject of the tariff. There were
hundreds of articles made in San Francisco, wrote the *Bulletin,*
which but for the tariff would be imported.[117] The *Chicago
Tribune* thought the October elections so significant that it advised the Democrats to replace Hancock with Tilden and thus
revive the issue of the great fraud of 1876.[118]

The Democrats had been overconfident, but the results of the
October elections had shown them how great was the danger of
defeat. They now realized that it was imperative for them to put
forth every effort in their preparations for the final struggle.[119]

William H. Barnum, chairman of the Democratic National
Committee, was convinced that the Democrats had been defrauded in the October elections. He carefully read Republican
newspapers which were asserting that, in spite of the great victory in Ohio and Indiana, the Democrats could still win with
New York, New Jersey, and California.[120] Barnum left New
York in the hands of Tammany and Irving halls. He personally
set himself to the task of bringing New Jersey and California
into the Hancock column. The next chapter will narrate how he
accomplished this task. It will also present the general strategy
of the Democratic campaign.

---

[117] *San Francisco Bulletin,* October 14, 1880.
[118] *Chicago Tribune,* October 14, 1880.
[119] *New Orleans Times,* October 16, 1880.
[120] *San Francisco Bulletin,* October 5, 1880.

CHAPTER VII

The Democratic Campaign

Just as Garfield had attempted to conciliate the Stalwarts, Half-Breeds, and Independents in order to insure the success of the national ticket, so Hancock endeavored to find a formula that would weld together the antagonistic forces of Tammany, the supporters of Tilden, and the disappointed adherents of Bayard. He was faced with no easy task in his efforts to mold these diverse elements of the Democratic party into an effective national political unit.

John Hunter, a loyal Bayard supporter, was visibly disturbed when he discovered that William H. Barnum had been re-elected chairman of the Democratic National Committee on July 13. Hunter regarded this action as a handing over of Hancock's administration to Tilden. He felt that a dishonorable deal had been made. Why would politicians never learn that honesty was the only policy that would lead to success, he asked, and why did they think finesse and corruption the only road to advancement of their pretended principles? Hunter was sick at heart, for he could see neither the success of the ticket nor the advancement of politics to a higher plane.[1]

August Belmont, a wealthy and important Democrat, was convinced that Tilden and his associates would have a large

---

[1] Bayard MSS, John Hunter to Bayard, July 13, 1880.

share in controlling the campaign of Hancock. He did not think
this augured success for the Democratic nominee. The New
York state committee of the Democratic party was determined
to count out Tammany. In fact, the committee took the attitude
that anyone who had opposed Tilden's nomination at Cincinnati
was not a real Democrat. Belmont regarded this as a suicidal
policy, one that would ruin the party's chances for success at
the polls in November. Along with Hunter, Belmont thought that
Barnum's appointment was the height of folly.[2]

By the middle of July, Hunter was certain that Hancock had
sold out to Tilden. Some strange maneuverings had occurred,
said Hunter, on the night before the National Committee met.
Hancock, after assuring at least some of his friends that he
would support William A. Wallace for the chairmanship,
switched suddenly to a negative position, professed no choice,
and thus allowed a pro-Tilden chairman to slip in.

Hunter did not think that Hancock could carry the all-
important state of New York. It was his opinion that Hancock's
only strong point was his "complete affiliation" with the Tilden
wing of the party, for his accomplishments as a military officer
were of no interest to New York.[3] It was very apparent that
Tilden was still a potent political figure in national as well as
in New York state politics. His henchmen, Weed and Barnum,
had reached an understanding with Hancock, and on July 27
Hancock wrote to Tilden asking him for suggestions with reference to the letter of acceptance which he would soon issue.[4]
Tilden promptly sent him a paragraph to be inserted in the
letter, and the Democratic standard-bearer was glad to accept
it.[5] Hancock also paid a visit to Greystone in order to receive
personal advice and promises of support. The Bayard Demo-

---

[2] *Ibid.*, August Belmont to Bayard, July 14, 1880.
[3] *Ibid.*, John Hunter to Bayard, July 17, 1880.
[4] Tilden MSS, Smith M. Weed to Tilden, June 25, 1880.
[5] *Ibid.*, W. S. Hancock to Tilden, July 27, 1880.

crats were sure that Hancock would have to pay for these pledges of support with political favors to Tilden and his Irving Hall Democrats. Hancock would have little time for Tammany or for Bayard and his friends.

Any dissension in Democratic ranks that would assist the Grand Old Party in garnering New York's thirty-five electoral votes was joyfully welcomed by Republican strategists. Marshall P. Jewell was watching the complicated political situation in the Empire State most carefully, and he informed Garfield that Kelly seemed to be angry over Hancock's direct approach to Tilden and that Kelly would refuse to support the ticket if Tilden controlled Hancock's policies. In the existing state of uncertainty, however, the Tilden Democrats dared not promise Kelly the comptrollership, nor did they dare decline to promise it to him.[6]

Murat Halstead felt that Hancock would be committing political suicide if he continued to avoid Kelly out of deference to Tilden's wishes.[7] The *Cincinnati Commercial* in a penetrating article brought out the fact that Hancock had no definite policy on any great practical question. The opinion was advanced that, if he were elected president, he would be entirely in the hands of Tilden, who would in the opinion of many also be his secretary of state.[8]

At least four months before the Democratic convention, George William Curtis, in an attempt to describe the difficult pattern of New York politics, declared that the Democrats in New York feared some kind of secret understanding between the Republican machine and John Kelly. They reasoned that this would be but a continuation of the amity of the previous

---

[6] Garfield MSS, Marshall Jewell to Garfield, August 26, 1880.

[7] *Cincinnati Commercial*, August 6, 1880.

[8] Garfield MSS, Murat Halstead to Garfield, September 8, 1880. The summary is from an open letter signed by Cyrus W. Field which appeared in the *Cincinnati Commercial* during September 1880. Halstead forwarded it to Garfield.

election by which Kelly's municipal power would remain undisturbed while at the same time the Democratic vote in the city would be conveniently reduced. Curtis felt that, if Tilden continued to demand the complete submission of Kelly to Irving Hall, the suspected alliance between Conkling and Kelly might become a reality.[9]

Apparently Hancock realized to some extent the urgent need of uniting the factions in the Democratic ranks. On July 25 he wrote to Bayard and suggested that he visit Governor's Island for a conference. Hancock hoped to have his letter of acceptance in shape by August 1, and he wished to discuss with the senator from Delaware the topics that should be included.[10] Bayard did not spare himself in rendering every possible service to Hancock, who appreciated his support. Occasionally the general would write to Bayard and give his reflections as to the progress of the campaign. It seemed to him, for example, that the situation was progressing satisfactorily enough in New York, considering the allowances which must be made for the fact that large cities are the scenes of ambition and "control." Hancock reminded Bayard that time was required to reach that "moment when matters of settlement by common consent as it were, fall into the hands of a few people." Hancock had suddenly become the recipient of hundreds of detailed letters "from all quarters." These letters were optimistic about his chances, and he reported this to Bayard. The people were being organized everywhere and were intent upon a change of administration. This fact caused Hancock fairly to exude confidence. He was confident that all who desired a change—Republicans, soldiers, and the men of the new generation, all of whom wished to see the war ended "in discussion as well as in reality"—would settle the question in the coming election. It was the task of the New York

---

[9] *Harper's Weekly* 24:82, February 7, 1880.
[10] Bayard MSS, W. S. Hancock to Bayard, July 25, 1880.

Democrats to unite and thus capture New York's thirty-five electoral votes.[11]

Hancock did not succeed in clarifying his position on the tariff question. It was difficult to comprehend just what his position was. The New York *Nation* considered his speech on the tariff so "dark and mystical" as to defy any clear understanding of his precise viewpoint.[12] General Grant's two administrations had sickened the entire country. Hayes's four years had started the movement toward reform. To avoid the possibility of any relapse the White House needed a capable administrator who possessed an expert knowledge of current questions, and not a soldier whose military maxims could have but little application in a land that had long since turned to peaceful pursuits. Hancock's political bewilderment was the subject of a cartoon by Thomas Nast, who depicted Hancock on a speaker's platform whispering in a companion's ear, "Who is Tariff and why is he for revenue only?"[13]

A week before the Democrats won their sensational victory in the Maine elections, Hancock in a letter to Bayard revealed the fact that he had no particular program he was zealous to push forward. Despite his military background, he was no fighter in the political arena, and he pursued a cautious and noncommittal policy. If the movement for a change of national administration continued to grow in strength, it would then be necessary "to make assertions of a general character," and to meet demands "for accurate utterances on great questions." But until that time arrived Hancock considered it would be wise to "let well enough alone." It would be expedient, so argued the Democratic nominee, to let the Republicans pursue an active role and make mistakes which alert Democrats could seize upon

---

11 *Ibid.*, W. S. Hancock to Bayard, August 31, 1880.
12 *Nation* 31:283, October 21, 1880.
13 Paine, *Nast*, p. 438.

to use as political explosives. Hancock's attitude was one of watchful waiting.[14]

Bayard was far less cautious than Hancock. He believed that the best defense was a good offense, and as early as July 2 he began his attack upon Garfield in a speech in Wilmington. He stated that Garfield had long been a leader among the advocates of force bills, the suspension of *habeas corpus*, military usurpation, and every other means to which his party had resorted to prolong its power. He declared that Garfield had been on the side of every measure tending to exalt the military above the civil power, and that he had taken an active part in every question tending to create animosity between the sections. Bayard informed his audience that the Democrats proposed to put an end to all this by placing in power a man who "although a distinguished soldier, never forgot that his citizenship was a higher distinction."[15]

Republican leaders grew fearful of this offensive, and determined to "drive out from the Senate the Jesuit Bayard."[16] The Wilmington speech was particularly irritating, and I. A. Kitzmuller wrote the senator from Delaware that he had been in the habit of saying that, if there were an honest Democrat in Congress, it was Bayard. He felt now, however, that he was mistaken; for by attempting to make the American people believe the things that he did about Garfield, Bayard was not only lowering himself in the eyes of the American people, but was saying what was not the truth.[17]

In the middle of July, Edward Spencer, editorial writer for the *Baltimore Sun* and Bayard's biographer, wrote that Garfield's convictions were held by so loose a tether and that he had spoken so often, that one could prove almost anything in

---

[14] Bayard MSS, W. S. Hancock to Bayard, September 5, 1880.
[15] *Nation* 31:22, July 8, 1880.
[16] Garfield MSS, W. E. Chandler to Garfield, October 15, 1880.
[17] Bayard MSS, I. A. Kitzmuller to Bayard, July 3, 1880.

regard to him "except that he is honest."[18] Garfield gave his summary of the 557 pages of *The Democratic Campaign Text Book for 1880* when he wrote in his journal, "The campaign on the democratic side has become also one of exclusively personal assault."[19] Marshall P. Jewell told the Republican standard-bearer that he felt indignant when he looked at the Democratic campaign book. In Jewell's eyes the Democrats' main stock in trade appeared to be mudslinging and vituperation.[20]

That eminent Republican, Judge Jeremiah S. Black, as soon as he heard of Garfield's nomination, wrote to him that as a statesman he was so "heterodox" that a very inferior Democrat would be better than he.[21] He now joined in the general Democratic attack on Garfield's character. Black had been invited, together with Benjamin F. Butler, another former Republican, to a meeting of Tammany Hall on September 23. In the invitations issued by Tammany's secretary, Denis Quinn, the urgency of the meeting was stressed because New York was the "pivotal" state. The result of the campaign would hinge on its vote.[22]

The *New York Commercial Advertiser* explained that Judge Black was unable to appear at the Tammany meeting. Instead, he wrote a letter which he directed should be read at the gathering. The letter increased the tempo, if that were possible, of the withering fire by which the Democrats sought to eliminate Garfield's chances for success in November. Black opened his letter by remarking that he was moved by the impulses of personal friendship and by the duties of fair political opposition in expressing himself. He proceeded to extol Garfield's intellectual position among politicians and his stainless, morally sound private life. He hastened to add, however, that convictions and

---

[18] *Ibid.*, Edward Spencer to Bayard, July 16, 1880.
[19] Garfield MSS, Diary, October 6, 1880.
[20] Garfield MSS, Marshall Jewell to Garfield, September 7, 1880.
[21] Jeremiah S. Black MSS, Jeremiah S. Black to Garfield, June 9, 1880.
[22] Butler MSS, Denis Quinn to Benjamin F. Butler, September 6, 1880.

conscience did not guide his public life. "For his party," wrote Black, "he is willing to do any wrong which will promote their interests, or play any card howsoever false which will win them power."[23]

William E. Chandler, whom Garfield had assisted in seating Hayes during the dangerous impasse resulting from the disputed election of 1876, wrote with great disgust to Garfield about the meanness and subtlety of Black's letter. He lamented over Delaware, and rejoiced over success in Ohio and Indiana and consequent salvation from "rebel" rule.[24]

General W. S. Rosecrans kept the Democratic cannonade against Garfield going by addressing himself to the *Alta Californian* and the *San Francisco Call*. Since Garfield had been Rosecrans' friend and chief of staff during the Civil War, the *Alta Californian* apparently felt that Rosecrans should support the Republican nominee during the campaign of 1880. General Rosecrans, who was running on the Democratic ticket for the Congress of the United States, took issue with the editors of the *Alta Californian* in an open letter to that newspaper. He was surprised, he explained, that a slur should be cast upon his good name in its pages because as chairman of a public meeting he refused to interfere with the free discussion of public and political characters. It was true that Rosecrans had spoken highly of General Garfield seventeen years previously when he had deserved it as chief of staff, but he did not feel that this should influence his subsequent judgments.[25]

Garfield was shocked by this California attack, and gave vent to his feelings in a short speech at Mentor. Apparently this was just what General Rosecrans was waiting for, and in an interview with a *San Francisco Call* reporter he stated that he

[23] *New York Commercial Advertiser*, September 25, 1880. Clipping in Garfield MSS, Vol. 94, no. 122.

[24] Garfield MSS, W. E. Chandler to Garfield, October 15, 1880.

[25] *Alta Californian*, August 18, 1880. Clipping in Garfield MSS, Vol. 90, no. 136.

had never before attacked Garfield, but that he did so now and pronounced him an "unmitigated fraud."[26] After the election Rosecrans cooled down and wrote Garfield a letter on December 9 asking him to let bygones be bygones. He wanted to know whether the old cordial regard still existed as it had before the elections. This friendship had begun when Garfield was admitted to Rosecrans' headquarters in the winter of 1862-1863.[27] But there was no forgiveness in Garfield's heart for his old superior officer, and on December 28 he wrote to Rosecrans stating that he had read the latter's communication to the *Alta Californian*. This, declared Garfield, with its wicked and unjust implication, was widely circulated as Rosecrans' opinion of him. It was an insuperable barrier to the restoration of their old relations.[28] About a week later Rosecrans replied that he failed to see the slightest impropriety in his language and refused to consider it even a mistake. He concluded by intimating that he would not stoop for favors even though Garfield was the president-elect.[29] This was the last letter that ever passed between the two generals. Their personal relations and correspondence came to a complete stop.

On July 20 Mrs. William Tecumseh Sherman contributed her part to the Democratic offensive by writing a letter to the editor of the *Catholic Herald*. She congratulated that paper for its stand against the Republican candidate and warned that, if Garfield were elected, he "would do all he could to injure our holy Catholic Church." Two weeks later the *New York Truth*, New York's penny newspaper, commented on Mrs. Sherman's letter. It stated that no more fatal blow could be given to General Hancock than to have it supposed that he would aid the

---

[26] *San Francisco Call*, October 29, 1880. Clipping in Garfield MSS, Vol. 105, no. 277.

[27] Garfield MSS, Rosecrans to Garfield, December 9, 1880.

[28] *Ibid.*, Garfield to Rosecrans, December 28, 1880.

[29] *Ibid.*, Rosecrans to Garfield, January 9, 1881.

Catholic Church as against all others. The *New York Truth* felt that no better campaign document could have been circulated for Garfield than a statement that he was the champion of Protestantism and the inveterate enemy of Catholics. A secret fear existed among Protestants and Freethinkers of the gradual encroachment of the Catholic Church in America.[30]

General Sherman's wife was convinced that Garfield was bitterly opposed to the Catholic Church, and she could never forget the former Campbellite preacher's effort to prevent the passage of a bill giving the sum of $25,000 to a Catholic institution in Washington conducted by the Little Sisters of the Poor. The incident occurred on the floor of the House on June 22, 1874. Just before the vote on the bill was about to be taken Garfield rose to object to its passage. He stated that the "divorce between church and state ought to be absolute." When Benjamin F. Butler of Massachusetts reminded him that Congress had made appropriations in favor of the Women's Christian Association, Garfield rejoined that that was quite a different matter, for the association did not as such belong to any church, the members being from various churches. The Little Sisters of the Poor, Garfield argued, were composed exclusively of people of one religious denomination. Isaac C. Parker of Missouri, who professed to be neither Catholic nor "much of a Protestant," was not at all convinced by the cogency of Garfield's logic. Parker reminded the House that when "the white bonneted nuns were seen carrying consolation to the gallant soldiers of the Republic upon every battlefield" no questions had been asked about their religion. Parker wanted the congressman from Ohio to realize that the Little Sisters of the Poor were not permitted under the obligations of their order to partake of a single mouthful of

---

[30] *Catholic Herald*, July 20, 1880 and *New York Truth*, August 6, 1880. Both of these clippings are in John Sherman MSS, Vol. 228, no. 150460. Mrs. Sherman had not said that Hancock would aid the Catholic Church as against all others. The *New York Truth* is unfair to Mrs. Sherman in this instance.

food until the inmates of their asylum were first fed. Was the House aware of the fact that these holy women went to hotels and restaurants to "gather what is left of the crumbs" to feed the poor, aged, and outcast men and women who were not able to take care of themselves? Butler now took the floor again in an attempt further to soften Garfield's heart. General Butler could never forget that when his men were dying in New Orleans from fever and malaria the good Sisters of Charity took them into their hospitals, and the question was never asked, "What is their faith?" The only question asked was, "Are these men sick and dying?" When that question was answered the soldier was taken in and was treated as well and as carefully as if he had been of their own faith. Butler recalled that his friend from Ohio had said that nobody but a Catholic could belong to this association. The congressman from Massachusetts conceded that this was true in the sense that nobody would undertake "the self-denying vows, that entire devotion to charity but those who have been driven by stern religious faith." Butler concluded by vowing that he would cut off his right hand before he would "strike down this appropriation in behalf of any religious prejudices against their religion."[31]

These vivid descriptions of heroic Christian charity were of no avail in changing Garfield's mind. He arose to assert that he desired to say a single sentence in reply. Unfortunately for the record, his rebuttal was drowned out by calls for an immediate vote. The appropriation for the Little Sisters of the Poor went through by a vote of 102 to 43.[32] Barnum's National Committee made good use of this incident by including it in *The Democratic Campaign Text Book for 1880* under the caption, "General Garfield's Religious Intolerance."[33]

---

[31] *Congressional Record*, 43d Cong., 1st Sess., 5384-85.
[32] *Ibid.*
[33] *The Democratic Campaign Text Book for 1880*, p. 265. New York: John Polhemus Press, 1880.

General Hancock's letter of acceptance, dated July 29, made its expected appearance during the first week in August. The message attempted to counteract Republican campaign charges that he was nothing more than a Rebel masquerading in a Union uniform. Since June 25 the Republicans had been stressing the "bloody-shirt" issue. They were not to abandon this tactic until after the Democratic triumph in Maine in the elections in mid-September. It was only after this Maine disaster that Jewell and Dorsey made the tariff question the paramount issue of the campaign. Hancock's letter, unfortunately for the success of the Democratic party, failed to explain its ambiguous plank calling for a tariff for revenue only. The Democratic standard-bearer, after consultation with Tilden and Bayard, had determined to give a quiet but effective burial to the "bloody-shirt" issue. This was the main concern of his letter of acceptance. Hancock therefore said that the thirteenth, fourteenth, and fifteenth amendments to the Constitution of the United States, embodying the results of the war for the Union, were inviolable. He went on to say that, if he were called to the presidency, he would deem it his duty to resist with all his power any attempt to impair or evade the full force and effect of the Constitution. The Constitution, continued the Democratic nominee, in every article, section, and amendment, is the supreme law of the land. When Hancock declared that "scrupulous care of the public credit" would benefit labor and insure to all persons the fruits of their own industry he was quoting almost *verbatim* from the innocuous and vague paragraph that Tilden had written out for him. Finally Hancock concluded by asserting that, if elected, he would, "with the divine favor," labor with what ability he possessed to discharge his duties with fidelity and according to his convictions.[34]

---

[34] *Ibid.*, pp. 4-6. For Tilden's contribution to Hancock's letter of acceptance, see Bigelow, *Tilden*, Vol. 2, p. 604.

J. S. Moore, part owner of the Colorado Silver Cliff Mining
Company, reflected in a letter to Bayard the views of thoughtful
Democrats concerning Hancock's letter of acceptance. While he
did not doubt that Hancock, when elected, would make a good
president, he was nevertheless disappointed to see in the letter
no allusion to the tariff, the more so since he considered the
time had come when men of responsibility could no longer ignore the question.[35]

The disappointment expressed by Moore was to increase to
fearful proportions as the campaign progressed. More than six
months before, a sharp warning had been issued by John P.
Cochman, who was very much afraid that the tariff question
would be the "straw that will break the Democratic Party's
back." Cochman knew only too well that Bayard was the Democrats' foremost expert on the complicated tariff question, and he
was therefore doubtful of success with any other man.[36] Hancock knew next to nothing about duties and revenue, and when
the Republicans dropped their "bloody-shirt" propaganda and
started hammering on the tariff issue, he called to Bayard for
help. Shocked into action by their defeat in Maine, the Republicans were determined to employ the tariff as the effective
weapon that would defeat the Democrats in the October elections as well as in the national struggle in November. Tammany
had arranged for a tremendous Democratic rally in New York
on September 23. Hancock asked Bayard to explain the complicated tariff issue at this rally.[37] This was the first of many requests that Bayard was to receive. Just prior to the state elections
in Indiana and Ohio, W. M. Singerly of Philadelphia informed
Bayard that an assurance from him would help "amazingly,"

---

[35] Bayard MSS, J. S. Moore to Bayard, August 5, 1880.
[36] *Ibid.*, John P. Cochman to Bayard, January 17, 1880. Bayard was for moderate
protection. See *ibid.*, Philip Zell to Bayard, May 15, 1880 and L. T. Wallis
to Bayard, May 17, 1880.
[37] *Ibid.*, Hancock to Bayard, September 13, 1880.

for all the leading manufacturers were attempting to frighten their employees with the prediction that Democratic success would mean no work and the destruction of the industries of the country.[38]

Democratic merchants, manufacturers, and businessmen pleaded with the senator from Delaware to reassure them on the puzzling phrase, "a tariff for revenue only."[39] From New Jersey the chairman of the Hancock and English Club wrote to complain that the people were highly confused, not only on the tariff question, but also on the outlook for business should Hancock be elected. He felt that Bayard could satisfy them on both matters.[40] Lewis C. Cassidy, a Philadelphia attorney, told Bayard that Pennsylvanians were deeply interested in the tariff. If they could not be convinced that their mercantile interests would be as "safe and protected" by Democratic as by Republican tariff legislation, their votes and the state would be hopelessly lost.[41] J. S. Moore was "perfectly sanguine" that the Democrats would carry Indiana; but he sincerely regretted that the tariff question, now the issue in the campaign, was not more directly and fairly met by the Democrats.[42]

The Democratic debacle in the October elections had repercussions all over the country. From Louisville, Kentucky, Albert A. Stole begged Bayard to take the trouble to write him something that would encourage the people there. He was afraid that the tariff plank was injurious.[43] Thoroughly depressed at the sound thrashing the Democrats had received in Indiana and Ohio, W. Wurts Dundas, a Philadelphia businessman, sent

---

[38] *Ibid.*, W. M. Singerly to Bayard, October 7, 1880.
[39] *Ibid.*, Merchants, Manufacturers, and Business Men of Philadelphia to Bayard, October 5, 1880.
[40] *Ibid.*, James R. Hoazsain to Bayard, October 11, 1880.
[41] *Ibid.*, Lewis C. Cassidy to Bayard, October 6, 1880.
[42] *Ibid.*, J. S. Moore to Bayard, October 12, 1880.
[43] *Ibid.*, Albert A. Stole to Bayard, October 16, 1880.

Bayard a long letter on the subject of the tariff. He was gratified that the Republican party had now made it the issue of the presidential campaign and had more or less abandoned its other false lines. Dundas was quite convinced that, in spite of everything heretofore said, the belief continued strong in Philadelphia that a tariff for revenue only meant no protection, or at best inadequate protection, for American industry. He had just returned from the scene of battle and could report that the grossest misrepresentations of Democratic doctrine on this subject had been made in the states of Indiana and Ohio. Ohio, he wrote, was absolutely flooded with Republican tracts and posters calling on workingmen to rally against "Democratic free trade as dictated by the South." Even though the *Springfield Republican* regarded this Republican propaganda as so much claptrap, the idea seemed to be fixed in the minds of the ordinary workingman that General Hancock's election meant the closing of mills and foundries and the banking of furnaces.[44] Dundas believed that the elections in those states were lost to the Democrats in consequence of neglect of the tariff issue. He insisted that this question would have to be fairly and squarely met by positive assertion in New Jersey and Connecticut.[45]

In an effort to answer this veritable deluge of Republican campaign literature on the tariff question, Hancock gave an interview, later frequently quoted, to a reporter of the *Paterson Daily Guardian*. He had finally determined to end his policy of watchful waiting. He was convinced that the time had arrived for accurate utterances on great questions.[46] According to Hancock, there was really no mystery about the famous third plank of the Democratic platform. In his analysis of a tariff for revenue only, the Democratic nominee declared that "there had to

---

[44] *Springfield Republican*, October 18, 1880.
[45] Bayard MSS, W. Wurts Dundas to Bayard, October 17, 1880.
[46] *Ibid.*, Hancock to Bayard, September 5, 1880.

be a certain amount—millions of dollars—raised by a tariff that can be got in no other way. This tariff," Hancock continued, "must necessarily give protection to the manufacturing interests of the country." Actually, the two major parties took the same position on the tariff issue. The whole argument was merely a question of words, and big business would continue to prosper under his protecting eye. There was no need, declared Hancock, for the Paterson people to have any anxiety whatever that he would ever favor anything that interfered with the manufacturing or industrial interests of the country. They would have as much protection under a Democratic administration as under a Republican one, he promised. And he concluded, "The tariff question is a local question."[47]

This last sentence is the much-quoted one, and it immediately served as added grist for the Jewell-Dorsey propaganda mill. Edwin Cowles promptly wired Garfield that the recent speech in which Hancock refers to the tariff as "a mere local question" was "one interview too many."[48]

The *Springfield Republican* in an effort to be impartial declared that Hancock's letter on the tariff was "eminently wise and to the point, but a little behindhand." The editors of the *Republican* asserted that this lucid explanation should have been inserted in the platform or at least in Hancock's letter of acceptance. With the election only a little more than a week off, it was rather late for a candidate to be coming out with clarifications of vital issues.[49]

The Republican press in general took the attitude that the speech was but another revelation of Hancock's political ineptitude. Professor John D. Hicks, however, recently wrote that Hancock "spoke far more truly than he knew," for "tariff rates

---

47 *Cincinnati Commercial*, October 17, 1880.
48 Garfield MSS, Edwin Cowles to Garfield, October 1880.
49 *Springfield Republican*, October 18, 1880.

must be levied by Congress, but they have generally been fixed, item by item, because of some local demand."[50]

John Kelly boasted that the Democrats would carry New York in spite of the fact that William H. Barnum was badly mishandling the tariff issue.[51] Bayard was doing all he could to reassure big business on the tariff question, but the Republican threat to "drive out from the Senate the Jesuit Bayard" forced the senator from Delaware to forgo a number of important speaking engagements in order to mend his own political fences.[52] John O. James deeply regretted that Bayard could not go to Doylestown, but admitted that his reason was unanswerable. "Do take care of Delaware."[53]

John Hunter agreed with Kelly's criticism of Barnum, and felt that the leaders of the campaign were daily proving themselves more incompetent than he had ever imagined they could. And "as for that 'apple dumpling' at the head of our ticket he is unworthy of criticism."[54]

The index of *The Democratic Campaign Text Book for 1880* under the titles "Garfield" and "Hancock" reveals a sharp study in contrasts.[55] The misdeeds under Garfield's name would seem to make him a more fit candidate for the penitentiary than for the presidency. The noble achievements after Hancock's name might cause the unsuspecting to believe that he had achieved the highest degree of sanctity that is attainable by mortal man.

Among the many charges leveled at Garfield by the Democrats, the DeGolyer case and the Crédit Mobilier scandal were the most outstanding—at any rate, Republican leaders did most

---

[50] John D. Hicks, *The American Nation: A History of the United States from 1865 to the Present*, Vol. 2, p. 163. Boston: Houghton Mifflin Company, 1943.

[51] *New York Herald*, October 17, 1880.

[52] Garfield MSS, W. E. Chandler to Garfield, October 15, 1880.

[53] Bayard MSS, John O. James to Bayard, October 20, 1880. See Vol. 57 of Bayard MSS for number of speeches that Bayard was forced to forgo.

[54] *Ibid.*, John Hunter to Bayard, October 23, 1880.

[55] *The Democratic Campaign Text Book for 1880*, pp. ix-x.

of their worrying over these two incidents. John W. Alling, a New Haven attorney, had written the governor of Ohio that he was much pleased with the nomination of Garfield but that the stories about the DeGolyer and Crédit Mobilier matters "take a great many people by surprise."[56] As soon as Barnum put his back to the muckraking business, Whitelaw Reid wrote in haste to Garfield advising that for the present nothing be said about DeGolyer and Crédit Mobilier. He suggested that Garfield let him know if he saw any occasion which would make it desirable for the *Tribune* to adopt a different course.[57] Actually, the policy of silence advocated by Reid was the one adopted for the most part by Jewell's Republican National Committee. Neither in *The Republican Campaign Text Book for 1880* nor in the hundreds of documents issued by Republican propaganda agencies can there be found any serious attempt to meet the DeGolyer and Crédit Mobilier accusations.[58] This strategy of silence seemed wisest to the Republicans, especially when the Democratic *New Orleans Times* stated that, although Garfield "was somewhat spattered by the Crédit Mobilier scandal . . . it did not stick sufficiently to impede his advancement."[59]

Nevertheless William H. Barnum and his committee were determined "to impede his advancement." They carefully planned what the Republicans called their campaign of "exclusively personal assault . . . mudslinging and vituperation."[60] Garfield was called the friend of the District of Columbia ring,

---

[56] Garfield MSS, John W. Alling to Charles Foster, June 12, 1880.

[57] *Ibid.*, Whitelaw Reid to Garfield, June 12, 1880.

[58] *The Republican Campaign Text Book for 1880, passim* and *Documents Issued by the Union Republican Congressional Committee for the Presidential Campaign of 1880.* See document no. 7. This is a reprint of Garfield's 1874 defense of his conduct in connection with Crédit Mobilier and DeGolyer. Document no. 7 is the sole exception to the official Republican policy of silence.

[59] *New Orleans Times,* June 9, 1880.

[60] Garfield MSS, Diary, October 6, 1880 and Garfield MSS, Marshall Jewell to Garfield, September 7, 1880.

and it was loudly proclaimed that he "was owned by that combination of public plunderers."[61] They went on to explain that in February 1871 the city of Washington had been placed under a new government, with a governor and a council appointed by the president and a House of Delegates elected by the people. All public improvements were directed by a Board of Public Works appointed by the governor. President Grant appointed his personal friend, Alexander R. Shepherd, a plumber of the city, to the powerful office of governor. Under Shepherd's regime the Board of Public Works initiated a scheme of general improvements which was to change Washington from an ill-paved, unattractive city to one that was a model of neatness and cleanliness, but these changes were effected at an expense that left the city saddled with a large public debt. Rumors of corruption and extravagance soon led, in 1874, to an investigation by a joint committee of the two houses. Enough evidence of fraud was discovered to warrant a change of government. Shepherd retired to engage in mining in Mexico. The affairs of the district were assigned to three commissioners who continued to administer its affairs. The former plumber left behind him enemies who called him a thief and friends who hailed him as the founder of modern Washington.[62]

One of the principal matters connected with the Shepherd administration was the awarding of contracts involving new pavements costing the city $4,500,000 and the individual property owners $1,500,000 more. Senator Allison of Iowa was the chairman of the joint investigating committee which in 1874 took voluminous testimony with regard to these highly suspected contracts. Among the companies competing for these contracts was the DeGolyer-McClelland Company of Chicago. This company was interested in a patented wood pavement and sought a

61 *The Democratic Campaign Text Book for 1880*, p. 80.
62 Caldwell, *Garfield*, pp. 236-37.

contract for 200,000 yards at a price of $3.50 a yard, a total contract of $700,000. The investigation brought out that through their agent, G. R. Chittenden, the company entrusted the presentation of its argument before the Board of Public Works to a Cleveland attorney, later a congressman, Richard C. Parsons. Parsons was given a direct fee of $6,000 and was promised $10,000 more contingent on the success of his efforts. At this time Garfield stepped into the picture. He was at this time the leader of the House as well as chairman of the Appropriations Committee. Parsons, eager for the lucrative rewards that success would bring, hired him as a lawyer to plead the DeGolyer case before the Board of Public Works. Garfield was paid at least $5,000 for his effective aid in obtaining the contract for the DeGolyer-McClelland Company.[63]

Garfield was re-elected to the House of Representatives in October 1874, but only after a bitter struggle. The DeGolyer pavement matter was the central issue of the campaign almost to the exclusion of all others. Garfield was able to satisfy the majority of his constituents by pointing out that the money for pavement did not depend on national appropriations, but was subject to the control of a local legislature.[64] *The Democratic Campaign Text Book for 1880* termed this 1874 explanation of Garfield's "too thin," and considered it to be a mere subterfuge. William H. Barnum and his National Committee could hardly be called liars in this case, for even though the local Board of Public Works paid for the pavements by taxing the people of the city of Washington, they also relied on Garfield's Appropriations Committee for large grants. More than a suspicion of impropriety was created when Congressman Garfield, the chairman of the committee, successfully pleaded the DeGolyer case before

---

[63] *Senate Reports*, 43d Cong., 1st Sess., no. 453, Vol. 2, 1075.

[64] "Remarks of Hon. James A. Garfield to His Constituents, Warren, Ohio, September 19, 1874"; in *Documents Issued by the Union Republican Congressional Committee for the Presidential Campaign of 1880*, no. 7, p. 11.

Shepherd's hand-picked Board of Public Works in the spring of 1872. For only a few months later Garfield's committee generously voted to reimburse the Board of Public Works to the amount of one and a quarter millions.[65] Garfield always insisted that he was a lawyer as well as a congressman and that there "was nothing either of law or morals to prohibit a member of Congress from practicing his profession."[66] But the DeGolyer-McClelland Company was looking for more than a mere lawyer. On May 30, 1872 its representative, G. R. Chittenden, recorded with joy that Garfield's services had been secured. He noted that Garfield held the "purse strings of the United States," and that the securing of his services was a "rare success and very gratifying," as all appropriations for the District of Columbia had to come through him.[67]

William H. Barnum devoted forty-three pages of *The Democratic Campaign Text Book for 1880* to an effort to prove that Garfield had been owned by Shepherd's "public plunderers."[68] But the DeGolyer pavement scandal was only one of many that the Democrats attributed to the Republican standard-bearer. In fact, Hancock's adherents boldly asserted that Garfield had been the "supporter of every job, the defender of every steal, which by hook or by crook got through Congress from 1863 to 1875."[69] Small wonder that Marshall P. Jewell felt indignant when he looked at the Democratic campaign book.[70] In their treatment of the fraudulent Crédit Mobilier Company, Barnum and his National Committee declared: "In our exposition of General Garfield's connection with the Crédit Mobilier, the monster fraud of the nineteenth century, we desire to do him no

---

[65] Garfield MSS, Diary, December 9, 1872.
[66] Garfield MSS, Garfield to Burke A. Hinsdale, April 20, 1874.
[67] Caldwell, *Garfield*, p. 241.
[68] *The Democratic Campaign Text Book for 1880*, p. 80.
[69] *Ibid.*, p. 53.
[70] Garfield MSS, Marshall Jewell to Garfield, September 7, 1880.

injustice.''[71] This was a disarming introduction to a twenty-four-page indictment that made Garfield a party to one of the biggest swindles in all American history.

In the period immediately following the Civil War the building of railroads had been encouraged by great public gifts of land and money from the national government. One of the chief beneficiaries of this policy had been the Union Pacific Railroad, whose completion in 1869 had been the cause of great national rejoicing. The gifts to this important road had included twenty sections of land to the mile and loans of public funds varying from $16,000 a mile in the plains to $48,000 in the mountainous regions.

The actual building of the road had languished during the period of the war, but by 1867 it was apparent that the Union Pacific had sufficient wealth to complete the building of the railroad as well as leave a very large surplus in its treasury. But by 1867 the seven leading directors of the company worked out an ingenious scheme for robbing the public and the road of all this surplus wealth. Under the leadership of Oakes Ames, a capitalist and a congressman from Massachusetts, these seven stockholders of the Union Pacific obtained control of a corporation known as the Crédit Mobilier Company of America. Then the directors in their double capacity made a contract, virtually with themselves, by which the Crédit Mobilier should build the remaining 667 miles of the Union Pacific at a cost ranging from $42,000 to $96,000 a mile. The total bill was $47,925,000 and the profits were estimated at about twenty millions. Most of this was paid by the American public and to a large extent actually from the public treasury. So far as the railroad itself was concerned, the result was that the Union Pacific was changed from a wealthy public corporation into a debtor staggering under an almost impossible load.

---

[71] *The Democratic Campaign Text Book for 1880*, p. 55.

These fake contracts were signed in the late summer and fall of 1867. By Christmas of the same year the swindlers, fearing unfriendly legislation, determined to sell blocks of Crédit Mobilier stock to influential persons at a ridiculously low cost. Congressman Oakes Ames was entrusted with the distribution of these favors among members of the House with whom he had some acquaintance.[72] This was accomplished, and for two years things seemed to go very well for Ames and his companions in crime. But during the presidential campaign of 1872 Charles A. Dana, editor of the *New York Sun*, managed to get hold of some of Ames's correspondence dealing with the Crédit Mobilier affair. Dana published these incriminating documents in the *Sun* on September 4, 1872, and the country was shocked when it read that Vice-President Schuyler Colfax, Blaine, Boutwell, Kelley, Garfield, and others were named as important stockholders of the Crédit Mobilier Company of America.[73]

Garfield immediately issued an indignant denial, and asserted that "he never subscribed for a single share of the stock, and that he never received or saw a share of it." He admitted that on three occasions he had been urged to subscribe, but each time he had declined.[74] Colfax, Blaine, Boutwell, and Kelley issued similar denials, and they were apparently accepted at their face value, for the Republicans won a resounding victory in the election of 1872.

Things might well have remained in this state of vigorous accusations followed by indignant denials had not James G. Blaine demanded a congressional investigation. Blaine, a member of the House at the time, was anxious to clear his name. The House accepted his motion, and a committee was appointed with Luke P. Poland of Vermont as chairman. This committee

---

[72] Caldwell, *Garfield*, pp. 220-21.
[73] *New York Sun*, September 7, 1872.
[74] *Cincinnati Commercial*, September 16, 1872.

to investigate the Crédit Mobilier charges started hearings in December 1872. The chief witness was naturally Oakes Ames, whose testimony as to Garfield was first given on December 17, 1872. Among others Ames mentioned Garfield: "I agreed to get ten shares of stock for him and hold it until he could pay for it. He never did pay for it or receive it." When pressed as to actual financial transactions, Ames answered somewhat vaguely: "He had some money for me once, some three or four hundred dollars, and called it a loan."[75]

Garfield, after waiting "with some impatience" for the opportunity to appear before the committee, finally testified on January 14, 1873.[76] His account of the affair was in substantial agreement with the testimony of Ames, but he expanded and modified in important respects his Cincinnati interview of the previous September. In that interview of less than three months earlier, Garfield, while admitting that he had received an offer, had asserted that he had repeatedly declined it. He now changed his story, and conceded that he had received an offer of stock, which he had held in abeyance for at least a year and had then declined. Garfield later confided to his friend Harmon Austin that he had asked Ames to lend him money. Ames had offered him a subscription to the Crédit Mobilier stock and was willing to hold it until Garfield could pay the subscription or until dividends should accrue.[77] On one occasion, Garfield could not remember the date, he had received a loan of $300 from Ames, which he afterwards repaid. Interrogated by Chairman Poland as to whether there was any connection between that loan and the offer of stock, Garfield replied that there was none except as

---

[75] Caldwell, *Garfield*, p. 225. See also *The Democratic Campaign Text Book for 1880*, p. 57. For a full report see "The Crédit Mobilier Report"; in *House Reports*, 42d Cong., 3d Sess., no. 77, 5, 6, 20, 21, 28, 40, 91, 92, 128-31, 136, 180, 181, 223, 228, 303, 353-61, 450, 451, 471.

[76] Garfield MSS, Garfield to J. P. Robinson, January 9, 1873.

[77] *Ibid.*, Garfield to Harmon Austin, February 17, 1873.

to the time of payment. Ames had stated to him that if he subscribed to the Crédit Mobilier stock, he could allow the loan to remain until the payment on it was adjusted.[78]

Before Garfield retired that evening he consoled himself with the thought that he had made a clean breast of the whole miserable business. He wrote confidentially in his journal that he believed his statement was regarded as "clear and conclusive."[79] This view, however, proved to be somewhat too optimistic, for on January 22 Ames again came before the committee armed with a memorandum book. A careful reading of this new evidence revealed that by June 19, 1868 the dividends on ten shares of stock were sufficient to pay for the full par value of the stock, $1,000, and leave $329 due to Garfield, provided he was the owner of the stock at the time. Ames testified under oath that he had given Garfield $329 about that time. A week later the committee discovered a check of Ames dated June 22, 1868 for the sum of $329. Ames had initialed other checks to show their disposition, but this one had no initials. Ames concluded his testimony by saying that in his judgment it was the one by which the dividend that Garfield called a loan had been paid.[80]

As one weighs the evidence gathered by the Poland committee, it is apparent that, as between Garfield and Ames, there were only two substantial differences. Had Garfield in January 1868 subscribed to Crédit Mobilier stock of which he had become a legal owner, or had he merely accepted an option which he was later free to exercise or not exercise as circumstances might warrant? On or about June 22, 1868 had he received from Ames a loan of $300, or was the money he admitted having received a dividend of $329?

---

[78] Caldwell, *Garfield*, p. 226.
[79] Garfield MSS, Diary, January 14, 1873.
[80] "The Crédit Mobilier Report"; in *House Reports*, 42d Cong., 3d Sess., no. 77, 295-96.

On February 18, 1873 the report of the Poland committee, which left so many honorable reputations threadbare, was read before a tense House of Representatives. The finding of the committee was unanimous, but it recommended punishment only in the cases of Oakes Ames of Massachusetts and James Brooke of New York. A resolution for the expulsion of these two members accompanied the report. Blaine was completely exonerated, while the committee found Garfield guilty in that he had received a check for $329 as a payment of dividends.[81] During the campaign Democrats capitalized on the scandal by chalking the telltale figures, $329, on fences, walls, and buildings.

Garfield's personal reactions to the findings of the Poland committee were rather moderate. His description of the scene that took place in the House is recorded in his diary. The report, he wrote, "produced a profound sensation and was listened to with silence and painful interest." With regard to his own case Garfield was not satisfied with some of the statements of the committee, but felt, nevertheless, that with Ames's memorandum and testimony before it the committee probably thought it was "doing right."[82]

William H. Barnum, chairman of the Democratic National Committee, had some excellent campaign literature in these congressional reports of the DeGolyer and Crédit Mobilier cases. No one realized that more than Barnum, and he used them with telling effect. Had not the Republicans been extremely clever in

[81] *Ibid.*, vii. The text reads as follows: "He [Garfield] agreed to take ten shares of Crédit Mobilier stock, but did not pay for the same. Mr. Ames received the 80 per cent dividend in bonds and sold them for 97 per cent, and also received the 60 per cent cash dividend, which together paid the price of the stock and interest and left a balance of $329. This sum was paid over to Mr. Garfield by a check on the Sergeant-at-Arms and Mr. Garfield then understood this sum was the balance of dividends after paying for the stock."

[82] Garfield MSS, Diary, February 18, 1873. See *The Democratic Campaign Text Book for 1880*, pp. 55-79 for a full if somewhat partisan interpretation of the Crédit Mobilier scandal.

their development of the tariff issue, Barnum's hard-hitting attacks on Garfield's reputation might have elected Hancock.[83]

Barnum and his committee agreed with the *New Orleans Times* when it declared that the results of the October elections had awakened the managers of the Democratic party to the fact that a Democratic victory was by no means certain. It had shown them how great was the danger of defeat and how imperatively necessary it was for them to put forth every effort in their preparations for the final struggle.[84]

There was no doubt that Hancock's popularity had reached a climax with the Maine victory in mid-September. After that the Republicans put a definite *quietus* on their sectional arguments and made the tariff question the main issue of the campaign. The results justified the change, for a month later the tariff, plus huge quantities of money, carried Ohio and Indiana for the Grand Old Party. But Barnum was evidently a fast finisher, and he was determined to put forth every effort. His *Campaign Book* had asserted that on the subject of Chinese immigration, which was of such vital importance to the people of the Pacific coast, Garfield was as usual "Janus-faced." His record as a member of Congress was in direct conflict with his letter of acceptance.[85] In view of Garfield's opposition to the Chinese Exclusion Bill of February 1879, the *Cincinnati Commercial* in commenting on Garfield's letter of acceptance stated that the

---

[83] The so-called "salary grab" of 1873 was also featured by Barnum. In February 1873 an amendment to the General Appropriation Bill was introduced by Benjamin F. Butler. The amendment would increase the salaries of congressmen by 50 per cent and would make the increase retroactive to the beginning of the existing Congress whose term was almost completed. Garfield as chairman of the Appropriations Committee opposed the "retroactive" feature of the amendment but finally yielded and voted for the amendment as Butler had introduced it. The Ohio newspapers were so incensed that Garfield returned his share of the retroactive increase to the treasury. See Caldwell, *Garfield*, pp. 233-35. See also *The Democratic Campaign Text Book for 1880*, pp. 131-38.

[84] *New Orleans Times*, October 26, 1880.

[85] *The Democratic Campaign Text Book for 1880*, p. 258.

Chinese question was "deftly handled."[86] The *New Orleans Times* thought that in his letter of acceptance Garfield opposed the further importation of the Chinese with a rigor that was "astonishing" when one considered his record.[87]

With the Republican nominee's former views on Chinese immigration providing a rather plausible setting, the stage was set for Barnum to present his most effective scene in what was already a very dramatic campaign. On the morning of October 18, less than a week after the Democratic debacle in Indiana and Ohio, Joseph Hart, the publisher of the *New York Truth*, found a letter on his desk dated January 23, 1880. The letter was purported to have been written on that date by James A. Garfield to one H. L. Morey of Lynn, Massachusetts.[88] It was written on House of Representatives stationery, carried Garfield's signature, and read as follows:

> Yours in relation to the Chinese problem came duly to hand. I take it that the question of employes is only a question of private and corporate economy, and individuals or companys [sic] have the right to buy labor where they can get it cheapest. We have a treaty with the Chinese Government which should be religiously kept until its provisions are abrogated by the action of the General Government and I am not prepared to say that it should be abrogated until our great manufacturing interests are consulted in the matter of labor.[89]

Hart showed the letter to a number of persons, including Abram S. Hewitt, who pronounced the signature to be genuine. Hart then announced that on the next day the *New York Truth* would publish a sensational letter from the Republican candidate for the presidency. The letter appeared on October 20 and

---

[86] *Cincinnati Commercial*, July 13, 1880.
[87] *New Orleans Times*, July 13, 1880.
[88] Caldwell, *Garfield*, p. 307.
[89] Garfield MSS, J. Medill to Garfield, October 21, 1880. Medill enclosed a reprint of the Morey letter from the *Chicago Tribune* of October 20, 1880.

was followed by a facsimile of the letter and the envelope two days later. Barnum immediately sent copies of the letter, accompanied by an appropriate commentary signed by himself, to every newspaper in the country. His published commentary, accompanied by a facsimile of the Morey letter, appeared on the front page of all Democratic newspapers. It stated:

> The following was published in Truth this morning. The letter is authentic. It is General Garfield's handwriting. Denial is worse than useless. It should have the widest circulation among all classes, as it unmasks the Republican hollowness and hypocrisy on the labor question through their chief.[90]

Republicans rushed to contact Henry L. Morey, but to their dismay discovered that the gentleman had conveniently died. California was startled, and J. W. Simonton, the owner of a San Francisco Republican newspaper, wired Garfield that the evident purpose of Barnum was mischief in the Pacific states. He requested telegraphic notification as to whether the letter was a forgery or a misrepresentation.[91]

October 20 was a Wednesday, and it was not until the following Monday, October 25, that Garfield's specific denial of authorship of the Morey letter appeared in the press. This silence on the part of the Republican standard-bearer enhanced the forgery with a considerable amount of credibility. The *Cincinnati Enquirer* considered that, if the letter was a "stupid forgery," Garfield should have so stamped it without the solicitation of the party managers. He had maintained a "dogged silence" until forced by the party leaders to make a disavowal, and he did not make this disavowal of his own free will.[92]

The *New York Truth* stuck to its guns, and remarked that, if a man would swear to a falsehood for $329, would he not

---

[90] *Concord People and Patriot,* October 28, 1880.
[91] Garfield MSS, J. W. Simonton to Garfield, October 20, 1880.
[92] *Cincinnati Enquirer* as quoted in T. C. Smith, *Garfield,* Vol. 2, p. 1041.

tell a lie for the presidency?[93] The Democrat publisher, Charles A. Dana, rushed to Garfield's defense, and proclaimed the letter a forgery.[94] The *Springfield Republican,* while admitting that Hewitt was a good witness, declared that it was late in the campaign and the Democratic cause was "evidently in desperate straits."[95] While Whitelaw Reid urged Garfield to make his repudiation "short, clear and indignant," yet he warned him to be sure that his memory was exact and that they had no trap for him, for the Democrats boasted loudly of proofs.[96]

Garfield's diary, on October 20, gives the basis for his hesitancy about issuing an immediate and peremptory denial. Upon receiving the telegram from Simonton, he requested a copy of the Morey letter, which he received later in the day by wire. He wired back that it was a forgery, and that he had written no such letter. Garfield confided to his diary that it was evidently the purpose of the Democrats "in their desperation" to seek by this means to take the Pacific coast from the Republicans in the election.[97]

Two days later Garfield apparently changed his mind about saying anything to newspapermen. He recorded in his journal for Friday, October 22, that he had been awakened at about one o'clock that morning by a messenger with a telegram from James Gordon Bennett. Abram S. Hewitt had said the previous night that he had seen the original of the Morey letter and believed it to be genuine. Bennett reported great excitement in New York and desired Garfield to answer. Garfield made no answer, "not wishing to be a newspaper correspondent in his own behalf."[98]

---

[93] *New York Truth* as quoted in T. C. Smith, *Garfield,* Vol. 2, p. 1041.
[94] *New York Sun,* October 27, 1880.
[95] *Springfield Republican,* October 21, 1880.
[96] Garfield MSS, Whitelaw Reid to Garfield, October 24, 1880.
[97] Garfield MSS, Diary, October 20, 1880.
[98] *Ibid.,* October 22, 1880.

The following morning Garfield's mind was finally set at rest. The morning mail brought him a lithographic facsimile of the forged Morey letter, relieving his mind of the one fear that oppressed it: that there might have been a letter from Morey, and that Nichol might have answered it without his seeing it. The facsimile, however, was not in the handwriting of any person Garfield knew, and he considered it a manifestly bungling attempt to copy his hand and signature. When Garfield received a telegram from Jewell requesting him to deny the forgery, he immediately did so. Garfield regretted to do this, for he wrote that he "hoped to answer all of my accusers by silence."[99] During the period of Garfield's studied silence the Democrats grew bolder. In an address before the Young Men's Democratic Club in New York, Abram S. Hewitt declared that he had seen the Morey letter and that he was familiar with Garfield's signature. He had compared it with letters of Garfield's in his possession and he had no doubt of its genuineness.[100] Hewitt had a good reputation and commanded a good deal of respect. His word carried great weight with members of both parties. Republicans were deeply worried. When Joseph Medill, editor of the influential *Chicago Tribune*, read the Hewitt speech in the *Chicago Daily News*, he wired the Republican nominee that no denial or explanation had yet appeared there. The Democrats were capitalizing on Garfield's silence. Medill had said nothing, preferring to wait until he had heard from Garfield.[101]

Finally, on Monday, October 25, five days after the original publication of the Morey forgery, the Republican National Committee presented to the press a facsimile of a letter written

---

99 *Ibid.*, October 23, 1880. T. M. Nichol, one-time secretary of the Honest Money League was one of Garfield's political agents.

100 *Chicago Daily News*, October 21, 1880, an extract from a clipping sent to Garfield by Joseph Medill. See Garfield MSS, Joseph Medill to Garfield, October 21, 1880.

101 Garfield MSS, Joseph Medill to Garfield, October 21, 1880.

by Garfield pronouncing the Morey letter a forgery.[102] Republican newspapers gave a front-page display to this facsimile of Garfield's authentic handwriting, and alongside of it placed a facsimile of the forged Morey letter. How convincing this belated denial was, would be known on November 2, and that was only a week off.

A month prior to the publication of the Morey letter George W. Curtis in a penetrating article declared the political situation in New York to be of great importance, for without New York the Democrats could not hope for success. Nowhere was their party more seriously divided. The Democratic feud was between Tilden and the Regulars on the one side and John Kelly and Tammany on the other. The conflict turned on patronage in New York City. Would Tilden or Kelly control it?[103]

In the great metropolis of the Empire State the embattled Democrats realized only too well the grave responsibility that was theirs. Their task was twofold in that they had to nominate a candidate for mayor and help select a state ticket. In the latter case they experienced little difficulty, and the quest for unity so dominated the mayoralty struggle as to prompt the Irving Hall and the Tammany Hall factions to hold their county conventions on the same day, October 13. On the evening of October 12 Tilden's Irving Hall committee drew up a list of twelve possible candidates and forwarded them to John Kelly's Tammany committee. Tammany in turn sent the names of twelve acceptable candidates to Irving Hall. William C. Whitney was on the Irving list, although a little over a fortnight before he had positively

---

[102] Open letter to the public from Marshall Jewell and S. W. Dorsey, October 25, 1880. See Chandler MSS, Vol. 50, no. 110164. The perpetrator of the forged Morey letter was never discovered. On December 9, 1880 Joseph Hart, editor of the *New York Truth*, wrote President Garfield that "the result of my investigation has conclusively satisfied me that the letter is a forgery" (Garfield MSS, Joseph Hart to Garfield, December 9, 1880).

[103] *Harper's Weekly* 24:594, September 18, 1880.

declined to be a candidate. Kelly would cheerfully have accepted him, but Whitney's unwillingness to run apparently caused Tammany to accept William R. Grace from the Irving Hall list.[104]

The principal opposition to the selection of Grace arose from the fact that he was a Catholic and a close friend of Cardinal McCloskey, dean of the New York Catholic clergy. If elected, Grace would be the first alien-born mayor since colonial times. There was a definite fear among Protestant circles that a coalition of Catholics on the Board of Estimates might divert part of the educational funds to parochial schools. Whitney sought to destroy this sectarian scare, and in an interview he cited references to prove that public moneys could not be appropriated for other than public schools. He pointed out that Grace had promised to support the existing educational system. He concluded by saying: "Religious prejudices are easy to excite and hard to allay. In my judgment it is part of good citizenship to keep them out of politics altogether."[105]

James Gordon Bennett beat the drums of religious hatred in the *Herald*, and declared that Kelly might wish to defeat the Democratic party, but was it fit or proper that he should "use his Church as a club with which to beat out his party's brains?"[106] The *Springfield Republican* accused Bennett of injecting a "sectarian fire-brand into politics," and felt that his arguments were absurd.[107] The *New York Times*, the *New York Sun*, and the *New Orleans Times* followed the lead of the *New York Herald* and stated that Kelly was jeopardizing the national ticket by his selection of Grace.[108]

---

[104] Hirsch, *Whitney*, p. 159.
[105] *New York World*, October 31, 1880.
[106] *New York Herald*, October 19, 1880.
[107] *Springfield Republican*, October 20, 1880.
[108] *New York Times*, October 20, 1880; *New York Sun*, October 18, 1880; *New Orleans Times*, October 27, 1880.

The Democrats were wasting valuable campaign time discussing the pro's and con's of Grace's candidacy. Two days before election day the *New Orleans Times* expressed the hope that the Morey letter would offset any advantage the Republicans might have gained by their skillful handling of the tariff issue.[109] On election eve Murat Halstead begged his fellow Americans to make the victory conclusive. There must be no excuse for "counting out by the Confederate caucus that runs Congress." A disputed presidency would waste the prosperity they were just beginning to enjoy.[110]

As ten million Americans prepared to vote on November 2, John Kelly telegraphed confidently to Bayard that New York would give Hancock a thirty-thousand majority, New York City about a sixty-thousand.[111] If Kelly's prediction had come true, Hancock and not Garfield would have been America's twentieth president.

[109] *New Orleans Times*, October 31, 1880.
[110] *Cincinnati Commercial*, November 1, 1880.
[111] Bayard MSS, John Kelly to Bayard, November 2, 1880.

CHAPTER VIII

Garfield Wins
and Loses

At three o'clock on the morning of November 3, 1880 James Abram Garfield knew he had been elected president of the United States. As he heard the news of victory, perhaps he recalled that several years before he had written in his diary: "The Presidency is the one office in the nation that for peace of mind no one should set his heart on."[1] At any rate, he little realized that he had written more truly than he could know. From the day on which he recorded in his journal, "The news of 3 A. M. is fully justified by the morning papers. . . . We have at least 212 electoral votes, a small majority in the House and the Senate nearly or quite a tie," until the moment when he was felled by an assassin's bullets, the reader cannot but observe in his personal notes a distinct tone of sadness.[2] On New Year's Eve, just two months before leaving his farm for the White House, America's twentieth president wrote in his diary: "I close the year with a sad conviction that I am bidding good-bye to private life and to a long series of happy years which I fear terminate in 1880."[3]

[1] Stoddard, *Presidential Sweepstakes*, p. 84.
[2] Garfield MSS, Diary, November 3, 1880.
[3] *Ibid.*, December 31, 1880.

Among the thousands of congratulatory letters that reached
the Mentor farm, there was found one that was at once both
ominous and prophetic. Little Willie Madden of Number One,
Hanson Place, Brooklyn, New York, sent to the president-elect
a letter written in pencil which contained an accurate prophecy:
"I am a little boy five years old. . . . I am sorry Arthur has to
be President when you die. I would like to know whether you
are a bad man or a good one. . . . If not, I think Arthur must
take your place."[4]

Garfield's future murderer, the Stalwart Charles Guiteau,
later sent to the White House his analysis of the Republican triumph. He hoped Mrs. Garfield was feeling better, and was convinced that, if Hancock had remained silent on the tariff, he
would have been elected, probably notwithstanding Grant and
Conkling and the treachery of Kelly. He reasoned that businessmen were afraid to trust a man in the White House who did not
know the first thing about the tariff.[5] Guiteau was not far wrong
when he assigned a place of primacy to the tariff issue in explaining Hancock's defeat. James Duffy, a prominent Pennsylvania politician, reasoned similarly in a letter to Bayard in
which he told of a luncheon conversation with George W. Childs.
Childs felt that the businessmen were afraid of Hancock, not
because they did not consider him a good man, but because they
were afraid of him as a statesman. He believed that Bayard
would have been elected beyond a doubt. Childs had given
$29,000 to Garfield, but would not have given one cent if Bay-
ard had been the Democratic nominee. He felt that the banks
and large shipping merchants would not have given any money

---

[4] Garfield MSS, Willie Madden to Garfield, November 2, 1880. A check of the 1880
census for the old Eleventh Ward of Brooklyn reveals a William C. Madden,
age four, living at Number One, Hanson Place. The father of the boy is listed
as William Madden, age thirty-four. It is very possible that the father wrote
the letter for the boy.
[5] *Ibid.*, Charles Guiteau to Garfield, May 13, 1881.

to defeat Bayard either. Bayard was convinced that Childs meant what he said.[6]

On election day, Tuesday, November 2, 1880, General Hancock retired at 7:00 P.M. He was exhausted from his five-months' labors, and left strict orders not to be disturbed until the next day. Ten hours later he was awakened by his wife, who greeted him with the words, "It has been a complete Waterloo for you." "That is all right," replied Hancock, "I can stand it," and in another moment he was asleep again.[7]

Actually it had been an extremely close election, with Garfield holding only a 7,018 margin in the popular vote. Of all potential votes, 78.4 per cent were cast. This record has yet to be equaled in any American presidential election. In the Electoral College Garfield had 214 votes to 155 for Hancock.[8] New York's thirty-five votes, as had been predicted time and time again, made the difference between victory and defeat for Hancock. If he had taken New York, as Tilden had in 1876, he would have been president with 190 electoral votes to Garfield's 179. The South kept its promise, and placed her entire 138 electoral votes in Hancock's column. It was the first solid South since Reconstruction. Ten million votes were cast, the largest number up to that time in the history of presidential contests. Thirty-eight states took part in the election, with the Democrats carrying twenty of them. California and Nevada, undoubtedly influenced by the Morey forgery, went for Hancock. New Jersey was the only Northern state carried by the Democrats. All Hancock needed for victory, after receiving the 138 votes of the

---

6 Bayard MSS, James Duffy to Bayard, November 8, 1880.

7 Almira Russell Hancock, *Reminiscences of Winfield Scott Hancock*, p. 172. New York: Charles L. Webster and Company, 1887.

8 Don C. Seitz, *The Also Rans: Great Men Who Missed Making the Presidential Goal*, p. 280 (New York: Thomas Y. Crowell Company, 1928). In the 1956 presidential election an estimated 77.4 per cent of the total who were eligible voted. See *Time* 68:14, December 24, 1956. See *Time* 60:25, November 17, 1952 for percentages of potential votes cast in American presidential elections.

South's 17 states, was 47 electoral votes from the remaining 21 states. He could only garner seventeen of these forty-seven. Nevada gave him her three, and New Jersey her nine, while California gave five to Hancock and one to Garfield.[9]

The influence of third parties on the national election was practically nil. Their influence would be in that their more desirable reforms were eventually to be adopted by the two major parties. The Greenback candidate, General James Baird Weaver, received 308,578 votes, while 10,305 people voted for the Prohibitionist, General Neal Dow. The American Anti-Mason candidate, General John W. Phelps, could claim only 707 votes.[10] Not a single state was captured by Weaver, much less by Dow or Phelps. California would have been saved for the Republican party if the Greenback vote in that state had been added to the Republican. Indiana would have gone to the Democrats if the Greenbackers in the Hoosier State had voted for Hancock. Finally, New Jersey would have been counted for Garfield if all the Greenback votes there had been won for the Republican nominee. But the Greenback vote would not have produced any change, no matter on which side it was cast, in any other state in the Union.[11]

General Hancock, like Tilden, went to his grave with the firm conviction that he had been really elected and then defrauded.[12] Barnum and Kelly were thinking seriously of contesting the election. The chairman of the Democratic National Committee, together with the leader of Tammany Hall, claimed that there were at least twenty thousand illegal Republican votes

---

[9] In California the electoral ticket had been chosen before the presidential candidates were known. The split vote signified a "repudiation of a single elector who was particularly obnoxious to a class of Northern Democrats." See *San Francisco Bulletin*, November 18, 1880.

[10] Stanwood, *Presidential Elections*, p. 373. See also *The World Almanac and Encyclopedia*, p. 121 (New York: Press Publishing Company, 1907).

[11] *San Francisco Bulletin*, December 22, 1880.

[12] Hancock, *Reminiscences*, p. 175.

cast in New York.[13] On the night of the election Henry Watterson received a telegram which was intended to lay the basis for a dispute of the vote in New York. The editor of the *Louisville Courier Journal* refused to publish the telegram on the grounds that it would be suicidal for the Democrats to plunge the country into the turmoil of another disputed presidential succession. Watterson asserted that the Democratic party, since it controlled both houses of Congress, could very probably count Hancock in if it so desired. Shortly after the election General Benjamin F. Butler left New York for Boston. He traveled by boat, perhaps in the hope that the quiet sail would calm his rising anger. As he reclined on the deck of the ship in the evening, he fell to talking politics with W. W. Thomas of *Harper's Weekly*. Thomas' exultation over the Republican victory only increased Butler's irritation. Butler's ire mounted as the conversation progressed. He suddenly turned to Thomas and asked meaningfully: "What if the present Congress should throw out the vote of New York for fraud! What would you do? Where's your remedy!"[14]

In mid-July Garfield's good friend, George W. Atkins, had advised him to do just what William H. Barnum and John Kelly claimed he did do. Atkins had written Garfield reminding him that New York was generally conceded to be the pivotal state whose electoral votes would decide the contest. "I hope you will leave no stone unturned, no spring untouched, no ballot uncast, to carry it for the right."

Atkins had a perfect blueprint for victory. He suggested that Garfield colonize some three thousand voters from each of the

---

[13] *Boston Transcript*, November 8, 1880. See also *Brooklyn Daily Eagle*, November 6, 1880 and *Norwalk Gazette*, November 9, 1880 for the Barnum and Kelly claims of fraud in New York.

[14] Garfield MSS, W. W. Thomas to Garfield, November 7, 1880. This letter contains the account of the Butler-Thomas conversation en route to Boston. The Watterson story is also related in this letter.

states of Vermont, Massachusetts, and Pennsylvania, where they were superfluous. They would be decisive in New York, asserted Atkins. At least six thousand Canadians might be quietly distributed in the cities of Buffalo, Rochester, Syracuse, Oswego, Utica, and Troy. A proper distribution of his forces, observed Atkins, marked the good general.

It was obvious that Atkins considered the Democrats to be a depraved crowd, and he warned Garfield that it was said that the Democrats in Congress intended to count in their candidate and to count the Republican one out, no matter who was elected. Could not this game be foiled, he suggested, by summoning the supreme courts of the several Republican states to witness and attest the count?[15]

If Garfield answered this letter, his reply is not preserved in his letter book. *Harper's Weekly* hinted strongly that Atkins' methods were used. That magazine quoted Dorsey, secretary of the Republican National Committee, to the effect that Democratic majorities in New York were cut down by more than seventy-five thousand, and the state carried by twenty thousand. Asked how this was done, Dorsey "smiled and was silent."[16]

The Republican leaders, however, wired Garfield that the Democrats were honestly outvoted and that the cry of fraud was "utter humbug." Bennett and Dana had made Kelly the scapegoat. They claimed that Kelly and Tammany Hall cried fraud simply to shift the pressure from themselves to the Republicans. They designated Barnum an "old fool easily caught and dishonest enough to want to be deceived."[17]

On June 23, 1880 Daniel Dougherty had assured a wildly applauding Cincinnati convention that Hancock was the type of

---

[15] *Ibid.*, George W. Atkins to Garfield, July 15, 1880. Atkins was in the diplomatic service of the United States, and at the time he wrote the above letter was stationed at Port Elizabeth, Cape Colony, South Africa.

[16] *Harper's Weekly* 28:748, November 15, 1884.

[17] Garfield MSS, M. D. Landon and Eli Perkins to Garfield, November 7, 1880.

man who, if elected, would take his seat.[18] Hancock believed he had been elected; but his essential conservatism caused him to acquiesce in the results, and he declared on November 8 that he would not reopen the election, even if fifty thousand fraudulent votes had been cast. Over and above Republican dishonesty, Hancock believed he had been defeated by reason of the "blunders, jealousy, and selfishness" of the New York and Brooklyn leaders. But he would not express an opinion as to how far any one man was responsible.[19] Professor Hamilton J. Eckenrode, who considers Garfield to have been "one of the suavest, trickiest politicians of his age," feels that the honest and efficient government of President Hayes made a second Hayes-Tilden contest impossible.[20]

Dana, who at this time still owed Tilden $45,000 and who was one of the few Democrats who had consistently branded the Morey letter a forgery, now insisted that the Republicans had not colonized voters in New York.[21] He shared Tilden's bitter hatred for Tammany's leader, and declared that the only investigation should be of John Kelly.[22] E. B. Martindale was confident that the cry of fraud in New York coming from Barnum and Kelly would have no effect throughout the country. It was the "cry of baffled cheats, the protest of defeated rascals."[23]

George Jones, editor of the *New York Times*, reminded his readers that Kelly had been warned that the nomination of Grace would injure Hancock in New York City. Jones concluded that, had New York City done as well as all Democrats and many Republicans expected it would do, the state would have gone Democratic by a small majority and Hancock would

---

[18] *Proceedings, Democratic Convention, 1880*, p. 86.

[19] *Boston Transcript*, November 9, 1880.

[20] Eckenrode, *Hayes*, pp. 308-10.

[21] Tilden MSS, Dana to Tilden, August 4, 1880.

[22] *New York Sun*, November 9, 1880.

[23] *Indianapolis Journal*, November 8, 1880.

have been the next president of the United States.[24] James Gordon Bennett had no doubts about the matter, and boldly asserted that Kelly had barely elected his man mayor of the city at the price of sacrificing the electoral vote of the state to the Republican presidential candidate.[25]

Whitelaw Reid was convinced that one of the prime causes of Grace's poor showing was the alarm about the public schools which the religious complications of the campaign aroused.[26] George William Curtis reflected that "a multitude of Democrats" preferred the defeat of Grace, for even their party loyalty would not induce them to recognize Kelly as an irresponsible dictator.[27] Murat Halstead followed this Tilden-Dana version, and declared that Kelly lost the election for Hancock by insisting on Grace. Perhaps realizing that criticism is the only art that requires no apprenticeship, Halstead quickly gave Tammany a hearing by stating that Kelly accused Tilden's Irving Hall of not voting for Grace or for the electoral ticket.[28] In the interests of truth the editor of the *Cincinnati Commercial* should have added that Grace's name was on the list of the twelve acceptable candidates submitted to the Tammany Tiger by the Irving Hall Democrats. If Tilden thought that the nomination of a Catholic for the office of mayor of New York City would endanger Hancock's chances for the presidency, then he should not have invited Kelly to nominate Grace. On December 19 Kelly denounced Tilden for using his influence to defeat Hancock in New York.[29]

The *Atlanta Constitution* felt that "Your Uncle John Kelly lost his grip on the boys," and that the "one element the Demo-

---

[24] *New York Times*, November 7, 1880.
[25] *New York Herald*, November 3, 1880.
[26] *New York Tribune*, November 3, 1880.
[27] *Harper's Weekly* 24:754, November 27, 1880.
[28] *Cincinnati Commercial*, November 8, 1880.
[29] *New York Times*, December 20, 1880.

crats needed in the campaign was the fine Italian hand of your Uncle Samuel J."[30] Samuel Ward thought Kelly was nothing more than "a beast and traitor," and J. S. Moore was sure that the defeat of Hancock was simply due to Kelly.[31] Moore went on to say that Grace cost Hancock fifteen thousand or twenty thousand votes, and that, if New York had gone Democratic, Hancock would have been elected.[32] W. A. Kirkham assured President Garfield that his election was due to the treachery of which one man, John Kelly, had been guilty in New York state in November, when by bolting he gave the state into the hands of the Republican party.[33]

Kelly admitted that the Republican victory in the gubernatorial contest in New York in November 1879 was a major cause of Hancock's defeat. But this defeat in 1879, according to Kelly, was due to the stubbornness of Tilden's Irving Hall Democrats. Tammany's boss pointed a finger of accusation in the direction of Hugh McLoughlin, Tilden's Brooklyn henchman. He felt that, had he not the year before prevented the nomination of John C. Jacobs or General Slocum for governor, neither King's County nor the state at large would have been lost in the presidential election.[34] Barlow insisted that Kelly was an honest man, but admitted to Bayard that the Democratic defeat was assisted and perhaps absolutely caused by the "pigheadedness" of Kelly who, though honest, was "narrow, bigoted

[30] *Atlanta Constitution*, November 4, 1880.
[31] Bayard MSS, Samuel Ward to Bayard, November 17, 1880. Professor Minor does not believe that Hancock lost New York because of Tammany's nonsupport. See Henry Minor, *The Story of the Democratic Party*, p. 334 (New York: The Macmillan Company, 1928).
[32] Bayard MSS, J. S. Moore to Bayard, November 4, 1880. Moore blamed New York's Catholic clergy for influencing Kelly to sponsor the nomination of Grace. Moore agreed with Kirkham in ascribing the fundamental cause of Hancock's defeat to Kelly's bolt in 1879.
[33] Garfield MSS, W. A. Kirkham to Garfield, November 5, 1880.
[34] *New York Herald*, November 5, 1880.

and secretive in his ways of action and never willing to be advised by anybody."[35]

The Republican press continued to "wave the bloody shirt" even after the campaign was over. The *Cincinnati Commercial* headlined Garfield's victory with the words: "All Safe . . . Old Man Secesh Will Smile No More."[36] The *St. Louis Globe Democrat* pictured the Republican triumph as a Northern rebuke to the solid South, and erroneously added: "Dixie Alone Declares for Hancock and English."[37] The *Chicago Tribune* breathed a sigh of relief and declared: "The Second Rebellion Against Freedom and Nationality Put Down by Five Million Union Ballots Fired Yesterday. No Change Wanted; Good Times Have Come to Stay. Twenty More Years Of Good Republican Rule Insured."[38] The Democratic *Atlanta Constitution* and Watterson's *Louisville Courier Journal* agreed with the last two sentences of this broadside by the *Chicago Tribune,* for the *Constitution* believed that "good times and a good administration" had been sufficient to turn the scales in the closely balanced and decisive Northern states.[39] The *Courier Journal* struck a somber note and declared that the election of Garfield over Hancock made it certain that as party division then stood the Republicans could elect any ticket they put in the field.[40] In an attempt to console the Democrats, Henry Watterson wrote that, notwithstanding the follies of the Democratic leaders, a majority of the white people of the United States were Democrats. He felt that the Negro vote was "not morally worthy to be considered as forming any intelligent or just element of public opinion." The editor of the *Louisville Courier Journal* recalled

---

[35] Bayard MSS, Samuel Barlow to Bayard, November 5, 1880.
[36] *Cincinnati Commercial,* November 3, 1880.
[37] *St. Louis Globe Democrat,* November 3, 1880.
[38] *Chicago Tribune,* November 3, 1880.
[39] *Atlanta Constitution,* November 7, 1880.
[40] *Louisville Courier Journal,* November 3, 1880.

that of the white vote Tilden had a majority of more than a million and Hancock a majority of very nearly a million.[41]

William E. Chandler felt that Southern Democrats were far too adept in hindering colored citizens from exercising their franchise. He urged president-elect Garfield "to lead the Nation to the great work of securing Free suffrage in all its domain without which we are no Republic." During the campaign he "had begun to fear that God intended to work out his purposes in some mysterious way through democratic success," but now he rejoiced: "Thank God we are saved, and the nation is not to see, is never to see rebel-democratic rule."[42]

T. W. Osborne saw the Republican problem even more clearly than William E. Chandler, and writing from Tallahassee, Florida, warned him that four years later the Southern electoral vote would be where it was then, and that if they could then capture New York they would have the nation. Osborne reported that in Tallahassee alone the Democrats had kept more than two thousand Republican voters from registering and had then refused to let them swear in their votes. Osborne was quite convinced that in Tallahassee no more voting would be done by a majority of the people for many years. In fact, Louisiana, Mississippi, Alabama, South Carolina, and Florida had "no relationship to republican governments." In order to make sure that the Democrats would not win in 1884 it would be necessary to secure the right of suffrage for all citizens, and the remedy would have to be radical and complete. Osborne opined that, if he understood the feeling of the North correctly, the time was ripe for the effort to be made to rectify this whole matter.[43]

The *New Orleans Times* was disgusted with the Northern section of the Democratic party, and asserted that Southern

---

[41] *Ibid.*, March 19, 1881.
[42] Garfield MSS, W. E. Chandler to Garfield, November 17, 1880.
[43] Chandler MSS, T. W. Osborne to W. E. Chandler, November 12, 1880.

Democrats had always let the Northern wing of the party make the nominations and write the platforms, promising all the support that lay in its power. At the beginning of the campaign which had just ended the South had offered 138 electoral votes, expecting the North to furnish the other 47. The South had faithfully kept its part of the bargain, but the North had failed miserably, providing only seventeen electoral votes. The *Times* felt that the time had now come for the South to develop its own leaders.[44]

Garfield's love of the Catholic Church was not increased when he heard from F. F. Low of the Anglo-Californian Bank Limited in San Francisco that California went Democratic because of "the zeal infused into the canvass by Rosecrans, backed as he was by the entire body of the Catholic clergy, who canvassed the city house to house, for their favorite."[45] Garfield was informed that General Rosecrans, who was elected to Congress by the Catholics of San Francisco, went out on the streets of the city with letters of Garfield in one hand and the facsimile of the forgery in the other, and stated in the most positive manner that the forged letter was genuine.[46] After reading this letter the president-elect wrote his former commanding officer that there was an "insuperable barrier to the restoration of our old relations."[47] Low thought that the din in regard to the Morey letter undoubtedly did the Republicans great harm among the laboring classes. The faked letter was particularly insidious because the forgery was so timed that it was impossible to disabuse the nonthinking public before the election.[48]

[44] *New Orleans Times*, November 3 and 5, 1880.
[45] See T. C. Smith, *Garfield*, Vol. 2, p. 758 and Garfield MSS, F. F. Low to Garfield, November 4, 1880.
[46] This is an extract of a letter sent by L. P. Lenney of San Francisco to Miss Lubal Pelton under date of December 26, 1880. It was forwarded to Garfield. See Garfield MSS, Vol. 122, no. 282.
[47] Garfield MSS, Garfield to Rosecrans, December 28, 1880.
[48] *Ibid.*, F. F. Low to Garfield, November 4, 1880.

John Livingston assured Garfield that he would have carried New Jersey by five thousand votes had it not been for the Morey letter.[49] The *New York Times*, however, insisted that the Pennsylvania and Lehigh Valley railroads were far more effective in securing New Jersey for Hancock than any other single factor, for the owners of the railroads in question feared the Republican nominee Potts, with the result that they threw their support behind the more subservient Democratic candidate, George C. Ludlow, who had recently served them in the capacity of a corporation lawyer. George Jones, editor of the *New York Times*, pointed out that a vote for Ludlow was a vote for Hancock. Jones traced Hancock's success in New Jersey directly to Ludlow's election in the gubernatorial contest.[50]

There may be some who maintain that Garfield never set his heart on the presidency, but no one denies that he lost his peace of mind on becoming president-elect.[51] It was soon apparent that James G. Blaine was to receive the important post of secretary of state in Garfield's Cabinet, and he wrote the president-elect a long letter packed with advice. Blaine had a natural gift for clarity, and undoubtedly would have made a good teacher. He minced no words in warning Garfield that, if he gave any of the three departments with heavy patronage—the Department of the Treasury, the Post Office Department, or the Department of the Interior—to Grant men, it would be used against him. Blaine had obviously not made up his mind with regard to accepting Garfield's offer; and remarked that, if he did so, Garfield must fill the three departments mentioned with his friends, men who voted for him at Chicago or who desired his nomination against Grant. Blaine believed that Grant would be a candidate for the Republican presidential nomination in 1884, for

---

49 *Ibid.*, John Livingston to Garfield, December 1, 1880.
50 *New York Times*, December 1, 1880.
51 Garfield MSS, Diary, December 31, 1880.

he was convinced that the Republicans were absolutely determined to run Grant in the next election and that this would
brand the Garfield presidency as a failure, to take "its place in
history as no better than Hayes." Could he say more, he
queried emphatically?

Blaine wanted the Stalwarts removed quietly but effectively
from the political scene. He suggested that it would not be wise
to "make war on the Grant crowd. Indeed that would be folly.
They must not be knocked down with bludgeons. They must
have their throats cut with a feather."[52]

Garfield had an agonizing time of it in selecting a Cabinet.
When after many changes and revisions the task was finally
completed, he admitted that he had to resist "a very strong tendency to be dejected and unhappy."[53] The New York Stalwarts
regarded Garfield's refusal to appoint Levi P. Morton secretary
of the treasury as a violation of a pledge given at the Fifth
Avenue conference. Garfield denied that he had made such a
promise, and was very much annoyed at a misunderstanding between Morton and himself in regard to the conversation which
took place in New York in August.[54] He had even dared to think
of offering Conkling the State Department, but after a blast
from Blaine confessed that he had never given the consent of
his mind to the idea of offering him a place.[55]

The full list of Cabinet appointments was submitted to the
Senate on March 5 and was promptly confirmed. It read as fol-
lows: James G. Blaine of Maine, secretary of state; William
Windom of Minnesota, secretary of the treasury; Wayne Mac-
Veagh of Pennsylvania, attorney general; Thomas L. James of
New York, postmaster general; Samuel J. Kirkwood of Iowa,

---

52 Garfield MSS, Blaine to Garfield, December 16, 1880.
53 Garfield MSS, Diary, March 14, 1881.
54 Ibid., December 13, 1880 and November 27, 1880.
55 Garfield MSS, Garfield to Blaine, undated but probably January or February
1881 and Garfield to Blaine, February 7, 1881.

secretary of the interior; Robert T. Lincoln of Illinois, secretary of war; and William H. Hunt of Louisiana, secretary of the Navy.[56] As soon as the news became public, General Grant wrote Conkling that he was much disappointed but would say little for the present. He planned to be in Washington within a few days and wanted to meet Conkling, Logan, and Cameron.[57]

David A. Wells told Bayard that he agreed with him that Garfield's Cabinet "passes comprehension," and that he had written Garfield the day before asking him not to put any "lunatics" on the Supreme Court bench.[58] The *San Francisco Bulletin* expressed the opinion that the appointments were rewards for services faithfully rendered. This California paper claimed that at the eleventh hour both Blaine and Windom had helped secure the nomination for Garfield, while MacVeagh, so the *Bulletin* asserted, was an important member of the Barker-Lea coalition, which with Garfield's cooperation had so skillfully engineered his selection at the Chicago convention.[59]

Hayes had wisely turned from both Blaine and Conkling, but Garfield rejected this policy. By his appointment of Blaine as his chief counselor he considerably sharpened the antagonisms within the Republican party. He endeavored to justify this act to himself by asking Blaine whether he would be a candidate for the presidency in 1884. Garfield asked this because he did not want Blaine to use his Cabinet post as a steppingstone to the presidential nomination. Needless to say, Blaine disclaimed any such intention.[60]

Conkling's disappointment over the Cabinet nominations was deep. But if he was allowed to control New York, he would

---

[56] *Appleton's Annual Cyclopaedia and Register of Important Events of the Year 1881*, Vol. 6, p. 846. New York: D. Appleton and Company, 1882.

[57] Conkling MSS, U. S. Grant to Conkling, March 5, 1881.

[58] Bayard MSS, David A. Wells to Bayard, March 12, 1881.

[59] *San Francisco Bulletin*, March 25, 1881.

[60] Garfield MSS, Diary, November 27, 1880.

still be a powerful political figure.[61] The Half-Breeds Blaine and Whitelaw Reid, however, were anxious to have Garfield declare war on the New York Stalwarts. Blaine had already made his position clear. He wanted the job done neatly, and had suggested cutting their throats with a feather.[62] Eleven days before Garfield's inauguration the editor of the *New York Tribune* was urging a lucrative reward for the "man who made the defeat of Grant at Chicago possible." This man, according to the *Tribune*, was the New York state senator Judge William H. Robertson. Reid, like Blaine, would probably have made an excellent teacher, for he too possessed the knack of lucid and forceful exposition. He instructed Garfield that, had it not been for Robertson's action, "the New York bolt would have never occurred; that but for the New York bolt the Pennsylvania bolt would never have occurred; and that but for these Grant would have gone through roughshod."[63]

Conkling was soon to learn to his dismay that Garfield, under the tutelage of Blaine and Reid, was a very responsive pupil. Now, if there was one appointment that Senator Conkling worried about, it was the collectorship of the port of New York, for the man who succeeded E. A. Merritt in that position would enjoy more patronage than any other man in the Republican party.[64] It was a $20,000 a year job, and its possessor would control 1,300 appointments.[65]

.When, therefore, on Sunday, March 20, President Garfield invited Senators Conkling and Platt to confer with him on New York appointments, the two senators from the Empire State

---

[61] Caldwell, *Garfield*, p. 343.
[62] Garfield MSS, Blaine to Garfield, December 16, 1880.
[63] *Ibid.*, Whitelaw Reid to Garfield, January 24, 1881. Robertson had led the New York revolt against Conkling.
[64] *San Francisco Bulletin*, April 4, 1881.
[65] Garfield MSS, John Hay to Garfield, May 6, 1881 and the *Chicago Inter Ocean*, June 1, 1881.

were more than a bit anxious. Platt had to go to New York, with the result that Conkling and Garfield conferred alone for two and a half hours. Conkling seemed pleased, and told his friend Arthur P. Gorham that, if the conference had been with General Grant, it could not have been more agreeable.[66] According to Platt, Conkling proposed the name of Levi P. Morton to succeed Merritt. The president then replied that, although he was not ready to consider New York appointments, he would hold to his promise of the previous August and would make no changes in the Empire State without the approval of Senators Conkling and Platt.[67] Garfield's diary for March 20 states that he adopted many of Conkling's suggestions, but that he had told Conkling that he felt obliged to recognize some of the men who had supported him at Chicago. Garfield was not willing to accept the suggestion that he should "exile" them with foreign appointments. He was prepared to go as far as he could to keep the peace, but he declared that he would not "abandon the New York protestants."[68]

Since Platt had been unable to attend the March 20 meeting with the president, he had asked both Garfield and Conkling that no action be taken until his return to Washington. Senator Conkling, however, was so optimistic over his talk with Garfield that he presumed to speak for his fellow senator. Therefore, on Monday, March 21, he sent the president a note telling him to forget about waiting for Tom Platt to get back. Garfield took him at his word, and on that very day sent a list of five appointments to the Senate. They were: Steward L. Woodford, attorney for the Southern New York District; Louis F. Payn, marshal for that district; Asa W. Tenney, attorney for the Eastern District; Clinton D. MacDougall, marshal for the Northern Dis-

---

[66] Chidsey, *Conkling*, p. 330.
[67] Platt, *Autobiography*, p. 149. Platt claims to be telling what Conkling told him of his conference with Garfield.
[68] Garfield MSS, Diary, March 20, 1881.

trict; and John Tyler, collector of customs at Buffalo. All were incumbents and all were Stalwarts, tried units of Conkling's New York machine.[69]

The journalistic howl of rage which greeted these appointments was very loud indeed, and of course Whitelaw Reid and Blaine were indignant and alarmed.[70] The secretary of state was obviously fighting mad, and Garfield's diary reveals that Blaine visited him and expressed great distress because of the New York appointments. Garfield thought he had made a mistake in one of them and would try if possible to correct it. Blaine renewed his visit later that evening and stayed with Garfield until nearly midnight.[71]

The very next morning, Wednesday, March 23, while the Senate was in session, a communication from the White House was placed before Vice-President Arthur. He read it and then sent it over to his fellow Stalwart, Senator Conkling. Lord Roscoe choked as he read, for Garfield had nominated Judge Robertson collector of the port of New York.[72]

A newspaper correspondent who was sitting next to Conkling had a peek at the note and said, "That ought to mean a fight?" Conkling paused for a moment and replied: "The nomination is the result, sir, of a perfidy without parallel. It should never be confirmed by an assemblage of American Senators— or gentlemen." Then he declined to talk any more.[73]

There is little doubt that the senator had reconciled himself to the prospect of Robertson's acquiring some post of honor, but his appointment as collector of the port of New York, a position absolutely necessary for political control of New York State, astounded him. Conkling, representing as he did the Stalwart tradition of loyalty to friends at whatever cost, had nothing left

[69] Chidsey, *Conkling*, p. 330.
[70] Caldwell, *Garfield*, p. 342.
[71] Garfield MSS, Diary, March 22, 1881.

[72] Chidsey, *Conkling*, pp. 331-32.
[73] *Ibid.*, p. 332.

to do but fight. He could not back out now. He must resist or be ruined.

The vice-president, the postmaster general, and the governor of New York petitioned the president to withdraw the nomination.[74] Both Conkling and Platt resigned their positions as United States senators.[75] The *New York Times,* the *New York Sun,* the *New York Herald,* and the New York *Nation* felt that the nomination was a purely political move for the purpose of handing the New York Republican machine over to Blaine's Half-Breeds.[76] Ex-President Hayes confided to his diary that Conkling and Platt made a strong point in claiming that to remove Merritt was a violation of the president's principles as laid down in his inaugural message, "and of all sound principles on the subject."[77] From Indianapolis the Stalwart J. R. Robinson wrote the president a frank letter in which he expressed his surprise at the appointment of an open enemy to an important office in New York. He reproved him for not consulting Senator Conkling in regard to the appointment of Robertson, as he had consulted Senator Harrison in regard to the appointment of Friedman as Indianapolis postmaster. "You must know," he declared, "and in fact you did know that the appointment of Robertson against the wishes of Conkling would bring on a fight."[78]

But Garfield was unyielding, and declared that they might take Robertson out head first or feet first but that he would not withdraw him.[79] The president was not alone in his crusade against Conkling. He received ample moral support from such

---

[74] *New York Herald,* May 17, 1881.

[75] Garfield MSS, Diary, May 16, 1881.

[76] *New York Times,* March 24, 1881; *New York Sun,* March 24, 1881; *New York Herald,* May 17, 1881; *Nation* 32:231-32, April 7, 1881.

[77] Hayes MSS, Diary, May 18, 1881.

[78] Garfield MSS, J. R. Robinson to Garfield, March 28, 1881.

[79] Caldwell, *Garfield,* p. 346.

capable editors as Whitelaw Reid, George William Curtis, Murat Halstead, and Joseph Medill.[80]

Garfield was greatly irritated when Conkling found out about Blaine's midnight visit just prior to the selection of Robertson. He was sure that "Some servant has leaked about the callers here . . . next leaker leaves."[81] His nomination of William E. Chandler for the office of solicitor general of the treasury was such an outright favor to Blaine that a storm of protest followed it. He was forced to call on Blaine, who agreed to have Chandler decline after he was confirmed.[82] The most he would do about the Robertson nomination, however, was to assume a political innocence which was hardly in accord with reality. As a politician General Grant had been frequently duped, but it is doubtful that he was deceived when Garfield wrote him that he had no reason to suppose that Robertson was regarded as a personal enemy by Senator Conkling.[83]

When the president on March 23 appointed Merritt consul general to London and Judge Robertson collector of the port of New York, he confidently wrote that this brought the contest to an early close and fully recognized the minority element.[84] The contest, however, rather than being brought to an early close, was unusually prolonged because the Senate was deadlocked for two months and unable to proceed to the consideration of executive business. The Robertson appointment seemed

---

[80] Garfield MSS, Whitelaw Reid to Garfield, March 24, 1881. Reid told Garfield of the interview with Platt which appeared in the *Tribune* and in other papers. He enclosed "the suppressed part of the interview." The part which Reid omitted to print revealed Garfield's promise to Conkling to make no changes in New York without first consulting the Empire State senators. See *Harper's Weekly* 25:390, June 18, 1881; *Cincinnati Commercial*, June 2, 1881; *Chicago Tribune*, March 24, 1881.

[81] Garfield MSS, Diary, March 30, 1881.

[82] *Ibid.*, March 26, 1881.

[83] Garfield MSS, Garfield to U. S. Grant, May 15, 1881.

[84] Garfield MSS, Diary, March 23, 1881.

but a secondary consideration as Republican senators sought to wrest the petty offices of the secretaryship of the Senate and sergeant at arms from the hands of the Democrats. Since both parties had exactly the same number of senators, the struggle resolved itself into a standstill. Finally, on May 4, Senator Dawes, leader of the Republican caucus, announced that the Republicans were ready to proceed to the consideration of the nominations submitted by the president of the United States.

By May 4 it had become clear to Senator Conkling that the name of Robertson would not be rejected. From his point of view there was only one way to save a desperate situation, and that was to confirm promptly the uncontested nominations of his Stalwart friends, and then to adjourn without any action in the case of Robertson.

The president, however, did not intend to be blocked by any maneuver of Conkling. As soon as he heard that the Republican caucus had approved Conkling's plan of adjournment and that one of the names from New York had already been confirmed, he promptly withdrew five of the New York appointments, thus leaving the name of Robertson standing alone.[85]

Conkling and Platt met this tactic of Garfield's by resigning from the United States Senate and appealing to the legislature of their home state for vindication. Garfield regarded this action as "a very weak attempt at the heroic," and thought it would be received "with guffaws of laughter."[86]

Two days after the dramatic resignation of Conkling and Platt, Robertson was confirmed without a roll call for the position of collector of customs of the port of New York. When on May 20, 1881 the Senate adjourned, Garfield was sure he had triumphed and wrote in his diary, "This is a great relief."[87]

---

[85] Caldwell, *Garfield*, pp. 344-45. The Republican caucus was a special committee on presidential appointments.

[86] Garfield MSS, Diary, May 16, 1881.

[87] *Ibid.*, May 20, 1881.

The relief proved to be but temporary; for while Conkling and Platt were in Albany seeking the solace of re-election, the Stalwart Charles Guiteau discharged his pistol into the president's back, crying out: "I am a Stalwart and Arthur is President now."[88] The scene of the attempted assassination was the Baltimore and Potomac railroad station in Washington. It occurred on July 2, 1881, at twenty minutes past nine o'clock, as President Garfield, accompanied by Blaine, entered the station. The president had intended to go to Williamstown for a reunion of the class with which he had graduated from Williams College in 1856. One bullet merely grazed his arm, but the other lodged itself in his back near the spine.[89]

Guiteau, former United States consul at Marseilles, France, had been thoroughly enraged over the Robertson appointment. He considered it sheer duplicity on Garfield's part.[90] Besides this, he had written the president on six different occasions in an unsuccessful attempt to obtain his own appointment to the Paris consulship.[91]

Henry Watterson, while expressing the hope that the attempt on the president's life was not the result of a conspiracy, declared that Mrs. Surratt was hanged "on less circumstantial evidence than occurs to the mind as to Roscoe Conkling and Chester A. Arthur." The editor of the *Louisville Courier Journal* rejoiced that the hand which dealt the blow was not that of a Southern man, for in that case Watterson was sure that there would have been a Stalwart outcry against the South from one end of the land to the other.[92]

---

[88] Josephson, *Politicos*, p. 315.

[89] T. C. Smith, *Garfield*, Vol. 2, p. 1179. The National Gallery of Arts is approximately the site of the former Baltimore and Potomac railroad station.

[90] *Ibid.*, p. 1185.

[91] Garfield MSS, Charles Guiteau to Garfield, December 31, 1880; April 18, 1881; May 10, 1881; May 13, 1881; May 16, 1881; May 23, 1881.

[92] *Louisville Courier Journal*, July 3, 1881.

On arrival at police headquarters Guiteau surrendered the following letter addressed to the White House, under date of July 2, 1881:

> The President's tragic death was a sad necessity but it will unite the Republican party. . . . I presume the President was a Christian and that he will be happier in Paradise than here. . . . I am a lawyer, a theologian and a politician. I am a stalwart of the stalwarts. I was with Gen. Grant and the rest of our men in New York during the canvass.[93]

Guiteau's action produced both a nationwide expression of sympathy for Garfield and a thorough detestation of Conkling and Stalwartism. Two weeks after the attack on the president's life the New York state legislature refused to vindicate Conkling and Platt, and replaced them with Senators E. G. Laplan and Warren Miller.[94]

The intense anxiety that gripped the country at the thought of the possibility of Garfield's death was adequately expressed by ex-President Hayes when he wrote in his diary: "Arthur for President! Conkling the power behind the throne, superior to the throne!" He believed that if Garfield lived he would have a hold on the hearts of the American people like that of Washington and Lincoln. The former chief executive was quite confident that a true and genuine reform of the civil service under Garfield was possible. He was certain that the extreme and savage partisanship which the Stalwarts had extolled as the cardinal virtue of a public man could now be abated.[95]

The mounting affection for the dying president was disturbing to William E. Chandler, who urged Mrs. Blaine to prevail upon her husband to do something about it. The press of the

---

93 *New York Times*, July 3, 1881.

94 *Ibid.*, July 23, 1881. Conkling and Arthur had to employ bodyguards for fear of assassination. See *Louisville Courier Journal*, July 6, 1881.

95 Hayes MSS, Diary, July 3 and 8, 1881.

country was in deep sympathy with the president and was almost deifying him. Chandler feared that this worship would make Garfield all-powerful if he lived.[96]

Roscoe Conkling wrote Attorney General Wayne MacVeagh that the "man who attempts the life of the President, if morally responsible, commits an offence which the nation ought to guard against and punish by the exertion of all the power civilized nations may employ." He begged MacVeagh to express to the president his deepest sympathy "in this hour which should hush all discords and enlist all prayers for his safe deliverance." He also offered his most respectful sympathy to Mrs. Garfield.[97]

President James Abram Garfield, after a seventy-nine-day fight for his life, answered the summons of his Maker at 10:35 P.M., September 19, 1881. Colonel D. G. Swain and an attendant were alone with the president when under the hand of death he cried out, "How it hurts here!" pressing his hand upon his heart. His last words were: "Swain, can't you stop this? O Swain!" Dr. D. W. Bliss came promptly to the president's side, and at 10:35 P.M. pronounced Garfield dead.[98]

Garfield's physical death signified Conkling's political demise. He never again held public office, attended a convention, or participated in politics. The announcement of the president's death increased the number of threatening letters Conkling had been receiving, but he paid them no heed. No longer, now, could he hope to explain himself. "How can I speak into a grave?" he would cry. "How can I do battle with a shroud? Silence is a duty and a doom!"[99]

---

[96] Blaine MSS, W. E. Chandler to Mrs. Blaine, July 18, 1881.
[97] Garfield MSS, Roscoe Conkling to Wayne MacVeagh, July 5, 1881.
[98] T. C. Smith, *Garfield*, Vol. 2, pp. 1200-01. According to Dr. Bliss, when Garfield heard that Conkling had not been returned to the Senate by the New York legislature, he said: "I am sorry for Conkling. He has made a great mistake in my judgment. I will offer him any favor he may ask, or any appointment he may desire" (*ibid.*, p. 1196).
[99] Stoddard, *As I Knew Them*, p. 114.

Three weeks before Arthur was sworn in as president of the
United States the faint beginnings of romance seemed to be entering his life. Perhaps it was fortunate for the American people
that Miss Julia Sands took it upon herself to write to Arthur,
for it might well be that she played a part in preventing Conkling from becoming "superior to the throne."[100] The Sand-
Arthur correspondence began on a rather austere note, with
Julia reminding Chester that the people's grief was not so much
because of the president's death as because he, Arthur, was to
be president. Julia, determined to tell Arthur the full truth as
she saw it, further reminded him that he was suspected of insti-
gating the foul act. Even his best friends, she continued, were
saying that he could not accept office with such a suspicion rest-
ing upon him. The fire of Miss Sand's conclusion could hardly
have failed to penetrate the political armor of the Stalwart vice-
president. She wrote:

> If there is a spark of nobility in you now is the time to let it
> shine. . . . If any man says: "With Arthur for President Civil Serv-
> ice Reform is doomed," prove that Arthur can be its firmest cham-
> pion. . . . It is for you to choose whether your record shall be
> written in black or in gold.[101]

Julia's inspiration may well have been one of the important
factors in the formation of Arthur's new political philosophy.
For Arthur, who had been a New York City spoilsman, became
as president a supporter of the merit system. In his first message
to Congress, that of December 1881, he declared that "original
appointments should be based upon ascertained fitness." He
gave his unhesitating support to the Pendleton Civil Service Reform bill, which many hailed as the Magna Charta of civil-

---

[100] Hayes MSS, Diary, July 3, 1881. Arthur's wife had died in January 1880, and
he was undoubtedly lonely at this time.

[101] Arthur MSS, Julia I. Sand to Chester A. Arthur, August 27, 1881. Miss Sand
was the daughter of the New York banker, Theodore V. Sand. When she
wrote the above letter she had not as yet met Arthur.

service reform. The Pendleton bill was passed by Congress on January 4, 1883.[102]

The weight of public opinion, as expressed in the American press, was a definite contributory element in the political transformation of Conkling's former lieutenant. The *Boston Transcript* echoed the editorials of hundreds of newspapers when it asserted that the conscience of the people told them that there was a radical evil in our system that made Guiteau's crime possible. Arthur was urged to clear away the evil which would still persist after Guiteau was hanged.[103]

The metamorphosis accomplished by Garfield's successor was so complete that George William Curtis, an old-time opponent of Arthur's, could write in praise of the new administration. Curtis declared that Arthur had not only "allayed all apprehension, but his pacific and temperate administration has gained the general approval of the country."[104]

Arthur's political triumph seemed to be on a par with his success in social affairs. Julia, discarding her former austerity, now addressed Chester as "My very bad friend," and chided him for letting so much time elapse without writing.[105]

---

[102] Rhodes, *United States*, Vol. 8, pp. 161-64.

[103] *Boston Transcript*, September 20, 1881.

[104] Howe, *Arthur*, p. 254.

[105] Arthur MSS, Julia I. Sand to Chester Arthur, September 13, 1882. "How atrocious!" the letter continues. "You are quite mistaken in supposing that I think you 'the gentlest mannered man that ever etc., etc. . . .' if you sent me a little sugary note from Newport . . . I should only have tossed it aside and said . . . Yes this is the way he talks to all my sex—in some form or other he has said this very thing twenty times this week to Mrs. E. D. Morgan and to Mrs. E. D. Jr.—to Mrs. John Jacob Astor and to Mrs. W. W.— to Mrs. Ellis and to his fiancee, Miss—excuse me but I really cannot remember which one you are engaged to at present!" The relationship between Miss Sand and Arthur is somewhat unclear. Professor George F. Howe, Arthur's biographer, stated in an interview with the author that Miss Sand was an invalid; that Arthur visited her at least once, in Professor Howe's opinion out of sympathy; that there is no evidence that they were in love; and that she opened the correspondence on her own initiative.

While the new president was achieving victory after victory in both the political and social spheres, Charles Guiteau was fighting desperately to avoid the hangman's noose. On November 14, 1881 Garfield's murderer was placed on trial for his life. More than two months later, on January 25, 1882, the jury brought in their verdict of guilty, and Guiteau was executed on June 30, 1882.[106]

The *New York Times* had intimated that Guiteau had discussed the murder with others before he perpetrated it. The *Times* also pointed out that on Friday, July 1, 1881, the day before the attempted assassination, Guiteau had absolutely no money, and yet on that very Friday he purchased the pistol which sent Garfield to a premature grave.[107]

In a letter marked "strictly private" Guiteau made a last personal appeal to President Arthur:

> My trial is about to close. . . . No one wants me hung save a few cranks. . . . I do not think there is an intelligent person in America that believes I would have shot Garfield on my own account. I certainly would never have shot him had I not been pressed into it. . . . A word from you to Mr. Porter will let me down easily.[108]

But Arthur maintained a discreet silence, the hangman did his work, and Guiteau joined Garfield to be judged by the only Judge who never makes a mistake.

Little Willie Madden had spoken far more truly than he could possibly have known when he wrote Garfield on November 2, 1880, "I am sorry Arthur has to be President when you die."[109] Willie's prophecy had come true. Garfield had won and lost.

---

[106] Caldwell, *Garfield*, p. 351.

[107] *New York Times*, July 4, 1881.

[108] Arthur MSS, Charles Guiteau to Chester Arthur, January 4, 1882. Porter was one of the two prosecuting lawyers at the Guiteau trial.

[109] Garfield MSS, Willie Madden to Garfield, November 2, 1880.

Countless editorials and personal letters of sympathy were written on the occasion of the death of the president. Among the editorials none was as beautiful or as true as that which appeared in the *Springfield Republican:*

> The prayers of the nation . . . have been poured forth incessantly. . . . Shall we say that God does not hear, that He does not care? That cannot be. He heard and He forbore to change His laws. . . . And now God's will not ours be done. All that man could, his whole heart's work, has been given; infinitely beyond his reach the decree has wrought, "And shouldering weights of pain, we hear submissive o'er the stormy main, chartered judgments walk forever more."[110]

Among the messages of sympathy that Mrs. Garfield received perhaps the most striking in that it best expressed the spirit of western civilization was that of Queen Victoria: "Words cannot express the deep sympathy I feel with you. May God support and comfort you as He alone can."[111]

---

[110] *Springfield Republican*, September 20, 1881.
[111] T. C. Smith, *Garfield*, Vol. 2, p. 1201.

---

1. Manuscripts and Documentary Sources

Chester A. Arthur MSS. Washington: Library of Congress.

Wharton Barker MSS. Washington: Library of Congress.

Thomas F. Bayard MSS. Washington: Library of Congress.

Chauncey F. Black MSS. Washington: Library of Congress.

Jeremiah S. Black MSS. Washington: Library of Congress.

James G. Blaine MSS. Washington: Library of Congress.

Benjamin F. Butler MSS. Washington: Library of Congress.

Simon Cameron MSS. Washington: Library of Congress.

William E. Chandler MSS. Washington: Library of Congress.
  The bulk of the Chandler papers are in the Library of Congress;
  however there are important Chandler letters in the New Hampshire Historical Society.

Roscoe Conkling MSS. Washington: Library of Congress.

Deutsch, Herman Julius. *Political Forces in Wisconsin 1871-1881.* Unpublished dissertation, University of Wisconsin, 1929.

Thomas C. Donaldson MSS. Fremont: Rutherford B. Hayes Memorial
  Library.

William M. Evarts MSS. Washington: Library of Congress.

Thomas Ewing MSS. Washington: Library of Congress.

Hamilton Fish MSS. Washington: Library of Congress.

Ganfield, Dorothy. *The Federal Influence of Wisconsin 1880-1907.* Unpublished dissertation, University of Wisconsin, 1928.

James A. Garfield MSS. Washington: Library of Congress.

Benjamin Harrison MSS. Washington: Library of Congress.

John Hay MSS. Washington: Library of Congress.

Rutherford B. Hayes MSS. Fremont: Rutherford B. Hayes Memorial
  Library.

Abram S. Hewitt MSS. New York: New York Public Library.
Robert G. Ingersoll MSS. Washington: Library of Congress.
Anson G. McCook MSS. Washington: Library of Congress.
William McKinley MSS. Washington: Library of Congress.
Manton Marble MSS. Washington: Library of Congress.
Louis T. Michener MSS. Washington: Library of Congress.
Justin S. Morrill MSS. Washington: Library of Congress.
Levi P. Morton MSS. New York: New York Public Library.
Carl Schurz MSS. Washington: Library of Congress.
John Sherman MSS. Washington: Library of Congress.
William T. Sherman MSS. Washington: Library of Congress.
John C. Spooner MSS. Washington: Library of Congress.
Allen G. Thurman MSS. Columbus: Ohio State Archaeological and His-
torical Society.
Samuel J. Tilden MSS. New York: New York Public Library.
Elihu B. Washburne MSS. Washington: Library of Congress.
Henry Watterson MSS. Washington: Library of Congress.
David A. Wells MSS. Washington: Library of Congress.

2. Printed Sources

Adams, Henry. "The Education of Henry Adams." In J. L. Davis, J. T.
Frederick, and F. C. Mott, editors, *American Literature*, Vol. 2,
pp. 354-58. New York: Charles Scribner's Sons, 1949.
Adams, Isaac E. *Life of Emery A. Storrs.* Chicago: Hubbard Broth-
ers, 1886.
Alexander, DeAlva S. *A Political History of the State of New York.*
4 vols. New York: Henry Holt and Company, 1890.
*Appleton's Annual Cyclopaedia and Register of Important Events of the
Year 1880*, Vol. 5. New York: D. Appleton and Company, 1881.
*Appleton's Annual Cyclopaedia and Register of Important Events of the
Year 1881*, Vol. 6. New York: D. Appleton and Company, 1882.
Badeau, Adam. *Grant in Peace: From Appomattox to Mount McGregor.
A Personal Memoir.* Hartford: S. S. Scranton and Company, 1887.
Bailey, Thomas A. *The American Pageant.* Boston: D. C. Heath and
Company, 1956.
Barker, Wharton. "The Secret History of Garfield's Nomination." *Pear-
son's Magazine* 35:435-43, May 1916.

Barnard, Harry. *Rutherford B. Hayes and His America.* Indianapolis: Bobbs-Merrill Company, 1954.

Barrows, Chester L. *William M. Evarts.* Chapel Hill: University of North Carolina Press, 1941.

Beale, Howard K. *The Critical Year.* New York: Harcourt, Brace and Company, 1930.

Bemis, Samuel F., editor. *The American Secretaries of State and Their Diplomacy,* Vol. 7. New York: Alfred A. Knopf, 1928.

Binkley, Wilfred E. *American Political Parties: Their Natural History.* New York: Alfred A. Knopf, 1945.

Biographical Dictionary of the American Congress 1774-1949. Washington: Government Printing Office, 1950.

Blaine, James G. *Twenty Years of Congress.* 2 vols. Norwich: Henry Bill Publishing Company, 1893.

Boutwell, George S. *Reminiscences of Sixty Years in Public Affairs.* 2 vols. New York: McClure, Phillips and Company, 1902.

Bowers, Claude G. *The Tragic Era.* Boston: Houghton Mifflin Company, 1929.

Brown, Roscoe C. E. *History of the State of New York.* 4 vols. Syracuse: Syracuse Press, 1922.

Buck, Solon J. *The Agrarian Crusade.* New Haven: Yale University Press, 1920.

Burgess, John W. *The Civil War and the Constitution.* 2 vols. New York: Charles Scribner's Sons, 1901.

———— *Reconstruction and the Constitution.* New York: Charles Scribner's Sons, 1902.

Burton, Theodore E. *John Sherman.* Boston: Houghton Mifflin Company, 1906.

Caldwell, Robert G. *James A. Garfield.* New York: Dodd, Mead and Company, 1931.

Campbell, Henry C. *Wisconsin in Three Centuries, 1634-1905.* 4 vols. New York: Century History Company, 1906.

Chidsey, Donald B. *The Gentleman from New York: A Life of Roscoe Conkling.* New Haven: Yale University Press, 1935.

Clapp, Margaret A. *Forgotten First Citizens: John Bigelow.* Boston: Little, Brown and Company, 1927.

Coleman, Charles H. *The Election of 1868: The Democratic Effort To Regain Control*. New York: Columbia University Press, 1933.

Congressional Globe. 31st Cong., 1st Sess. Vols. 22-25. Washington: Government Printing Office, 1851.

Congressional Record. 43d-46th Cong. Vols. 6-7, 21-23, 33-35, 40-45. Washington: Government Printing Office, 1881.

Cortissoz, Royal. *The Life of Whitelaw Reid*. 2 vols. New York: Charles Scribner's Sons, 1921.

Corwin, Edward S. "Stephen Johnson Field." In Allen Johnson and Dumas Malone, editors, *Dictionary of American Biography*, Vol. 6, pp. 372-76. New York: Charles Scribner's Sons, 1931.

Coulter, E. Merton. *The South during Reconstruction, 1865-1877*. Baton Rouge: Louisiana State University Press, 1947.

Cramer, Clarence H. *Royal Bob, The Life of Robert G. Ingersoll*. Indianapolis: Bobbs-Merrill Company, 1952.

"The Crédit Mobilier Report." In *House Reports*, 42d Cong., 3d Sess., no. 77. Washington: Government Printing Office, 1873.

Curran, M. P. *Life of Patrick Collins*. Norwood: Norwood Press, 1906.

Davis, J. L.; J. T. Frederick; and F. C. Mott, editors. *American Literature*. 2 vols. New York: Charles Scribner's Sons, 1949.

The Democratic Campaign Text Book for 1880. New York: John Polhemus Press, 1880.

Dennett, Tyler. *John Hay: From Poetry to Politics*. New York: Dodd, Mead and Company, 1933.

Dewey, Davis R. *Financial History of the United States*. New York: Longmans, Green and Company, 1912.

Documents Issued by the Union Republican Congressional Committee for the Presidential Campaign of 1880. Washington: n. p., 1880.

Dow, Neal. *The Reminiscences of Neal Dow*. Portland: Evening Express Publishing Company, 1898.

Dyer, Brainerd. *The Public Career of William M. Evarts*. Berkeley: University of California Press, 1933.

Eckenrode, Hamilton J. *Rutherford B. Hayes, Statesman of Reunion*. New York: Dodd, Mead and Company, 1930.

Ellis, John T. *The Life of James Cardinal Gibbons*. 2 vols. Milwaukee: Bruce Publishing Company, 1952.

Esarey, Logan. *A History of Indiana*. 2 vols. Indianapolis: B. F. Bowen and Company, 1918.

Ewing, Cortez A. M. *Presidential Elections from Abraham Lincoln to Franklin D. Roosevelt*. Norman: University of Oklahoma Press, 1940.

Faulkner, Harold U. *American Political and Social History*. New York: F. S. Crofts and Company, 1943.

Fite, Emerson D. *The Presidential Campaign of 1860*. New York: The Macmillan Company, 1911.

Fleming, Walter L. *Documentary History of Reconstruction*. 2 vols. Cleveland: Arthur H. Clark Company, 1906.

———— *The Sequel of Appomattox*. New Haven: Yale University Press, 1921.

Flick, Alexander C. *Samuel Jones Tilden: A Study in Political Sagacity*. New York: Dodd, Mead and Company, 1939.

Foulke, William D. *Life of Oliver P. Morton*. 2 vols. Indianapolis: Bowen-Merrill Company, 1899.

Fuess, Claude M. *Carl Schurz: Reformer*. New York: Dodd, Mead and Company, 1932.

Garfield and Arthur Campaign Song Book. Philadelphia: J. M. Armstrong and Company, 1880.

Hamilton, Gail. *Biography of James G. Blaine*. Norwich: Henry Bill Publishing Company, 1895.

Hancock, Almira Russell. *Reminiscences of Winfield Scott Hancock*. New York: Charles L. Webster and Company, 1887.

Handlin, Oscar and others, editors. *Harvard Guide to American History*. Cambridge: Harvard University Press, 1954.

Hatch, Louis C. *Maine: A History*. 3 vols. New York: American Historical Society, 1919.

Haworth, Paul L. *The Hayes-Tilden Election*. Indianapolis: Bobbs-Merrill Company, 1906.

Hayes, Rutherford B. *Diary and Letters*, edited by Charles R. Williams. 4 vols. Columbus: F. S. Heer Company, 1924.

Haynes, Frederick E. *James Baird Weaver*. Iowa City: State Historical Society of Iowa, 1919.

———— *Third Party Movements since the Civil War*. Iowa City: State Historical Society of Iowa, 1916.

Hesseltine, William B. *The Rise and Fall of Third Parties: From Anti-Masonry to Wallace.* Washington: Public Affairs Press, 1948.

———— *Ulysses S. Grant, Politician.* New York: Dodd, Mead and Company, 1935.

Hewitt, Abram S. *Selected Writings of Abram S. Hewitt,* edited by Allan Nevins, "Secret History of the Disputed Election, 1876-1877," pp. 155-94. New York: Columbia University Press, 1937.

Hicks, John D. *The American Nation: A History of the United States from 1865 to the Present.* 2 vols. Boston: Houghton Mifflin Company, 1943.

———— "James Baird Weaver." In Allen Johnson and Dumas Malone, editors, *Dictionary of American Biography,* Vol. 19, pp. 568-70. New York: Charles Scribner's Sons, 1936.

Hirsch, Mark D. *William C. Whitney: Modern Warwick.* New York: Dodd, Mead and Company, 1948.

Hoar, George F. *Autobiography of Seventy Years.* 2 vols. New York: Charles Scribner's Sons, 1903.

Holmes, Oliver W. "Augustus Schell." In Allen Johnson and Dumas Malone, editors, *Dictionary of American Biography,* Vol. 16, pp. 424-25. New York: Charles Scribner's Sons, 1935.

House Reports. 42d Cong., 3d Sess., no. 77. Washington: Government Printing Office, 1873.

Howard, Cecil H. C. *Life and Public Services of Gen. John Wolcott Phelps.* Brattleboro: Frank E. Housh and Company, 1887.

Howe, George F. *Chester A. Arthur: A Quarter-Century of Machine Politics.* New York: Dodd, Mead and Company, 1934.

Hudson, William C. *Random Recollections of an Old Political Reporter.* New York: Cupples and Leon Company, 1911.

Hunt, Gaillard. *Israel, Elihu, and Cadwallader Washburn: A Chapter in American Biography.* New York: The Macmillan Company, 1925.

Isely, Jeter A. *Horace Greeley and the Republican Party, 1853-1861.* Princeton: Princeton University Press, 1947.

Johnson, Allen and Dumas Malone, editors. *Dictionary of American Biography.* 20 vols. New York: Charles Scribner's Sons, 1928-1936.

Josephson, Matthew. *The Politicos: 1865-1896.* New York: Harcourt, Brace and Company, 1938.

Kent, Frank R. *The Democratic Party: A History.* New York: Century Company, 1928.

Lynch, Denis T. *Boss Tweed: The Story of a Grim Generation.* New York: Boni and Liveright, 1927.

McClure, A. K. *Our Presidents and How We Make Them.* New York: Harper and Brothers, 1900.

McGurrin, James. *Bourke Cockran: A Free Lance in American Politics.* New York: Charles Scribner's Sons, 1948.

McLaughlin, J. Fairfax. *The Life and Times of John Kelly: Tribune of the People.* New York: American News Company, 1885.

Marsh, John. *The Napoleon of Temperance.* New York: American Temperance Union, 1852.

Milton, George F. *The Age of Hate: Andrew Johnson and the Radicals.* New York: Coward-McCann Company, 1930.

———— *The Eve of Conflict: Stephen A. Douglas and the Needless War.* Boston: Houghton Mifflin Company, 1934.

Minor, Henry. *The Story of the Democratic Party.* New York: The Macmillan Company, 1928.

Mitchell, Robert S. *Horatio Seymour of New York.* Cambridge: Harvard University Press, 1938.

Morris, Robert. *William Morgan or Political Anti-Masonry: Its Rise, Growth and Decadence.* New York: Robert Macoy, Masonic Publisher, 1883.

Muzzey, David S. *James G. Blaine: A Political Idol of Other Days.* New York: Dodd, Mead and Company, 1934.

Myers, William S. *The Republican Party: A History.* New York: Century Company, 1928.

Nevins, Allan. *Abram S. Hewitt, with Some Account of Peter Cooper.* New York: Harper and Brothers, 1935.

———— *The Emergence of Modern America, 1865-1878.* New York: The Macmillan Company, 1927.

———— *Hamilton Fish: The Inner History of the Grant Administration.* New York: Dodd, Mead and Company, 1936.

Nichols, Jeannette P. "John Sherman." In Allen Johnson and Dumas Malone, editors, *Dictionary of American Biography,* Vol. 17, pp. 84-88. New York: Charles Scribner's Sons, 1935.

Oberholtzer, Ellis P. *A History of the United States since the Civil War.* 5 vols. New York: The Macmillan Company, 1917-1931.

Official Proceedings of the Democratic National Convention, Held in Cincinnati, Ohio, June 22-24, 1880. Dayton: Daily Journal Press, 1882.

Official Proceedings of the Democratic National Convention, Held in St. Louis, Mo., June 27-29, 1876. St. Louis: Woodward, Tiernan and Hale, 1876.

Official Register of the United States. Containing a List of Offices and Employees. Washington: Government Printing Office, 1879.

Paine, Albert B. *Thomas Nast: His Period and His Pictures.* New York: Harper and Brothers, 1904.

Platt, Thomas Collier. *The Autobiography of Thomas Collier Platt,* edited by Louis J. Lang. New York: B. W. Dodge and Company, 1910.

Proceedings of the Republican National Convention Held in Chicago, Illinois, June 2-8, 1880. Chicago: John B. Jeffery Company, 1881.

Randall, James G. *The Civil War and Reconstruction.* New York: D. C. Heath and Company, 1939.

———— *Lincoln the President.* New York: Dodd, Mead and Company, 1945.

The Republican Campaign Song Book for 1880. Washington: n. p., 1880.

The Republican Campaign Text Book for 1880. Washington: David H. Gildersleeve, 1880.

Republican Congressional Committee. *The Great Usurpation: The United States under the Confederate Senate and House of Representatives, An Oligarch.* Washington: Rufus H. Darby, Steam Power Printer, 1879.

Rhodes, James F. *History of the United States.* 9 vols. New York: The Macmillan Company, 1920.

Richardson, James D., editor. *A Compilation of the Messages and Papers of the Presidents.* 20 vols. Washington: Government Printing Office, 1896-1927.

Richardson, Leon B. *William E. Chandler, Republican.* New York: Dodd, Mead and Company, 1940.

Rogers, Cameron. *Colonel Bob Ingersoll.* New York: Doubleday, Page and Company, 1927.

Roseboom, Eugene H. *A History of Presidential Elections.* New York: The Macmillan Company, 1957.

Ross, Earle D. *The Liberal Republican Movement.* New York: Henry Holt and Company, 1919.

Schurz, Carl. *The Reminiscences of Carl Schurz,* edited by Frederic Bancroft and William A. Dunning. 3 vols. New York: McClure Company, 1908.

Seitz, Don C. *The Also Rans: Great Men Who Missed Making the Presidential Goal.* New York: Thomas Y. Crowell Company, 1928.

Senate Reports. 43d Cong., 1st Sess., no. 453. Washington: Government Printing Office, 1874.

Sherman, John. *Recollections of Forty Years in the House, Senate and Cabinet.* 2 vols. New York: Werner Company, 1895.

Smith, Charles Emory. "How Conkling Missed Nominating Blaine." *Saturday Evening Post* 173:2-3, June 8, 1901.

Smith, Theodore Clarke. *Life and Letters of James Abram Garfield.* 2 vols. New Haven: Yale University Press, 1925.

Southworth, Alvan Scott. *Life of Gen. Winfield Scott Hancock.* New York: American News Company, 1880.

Stanwood, Edward A. *A History of Presidential Elections.* Boston: Houghton Mifflin Company, 1896.

Stevens, Albert C., editor. *The Cyclopaedia of Fraternities.* New York: Hamilton Press, 1907.

Stoddard, Henry L. *As I Knew Them: Presidents and Politics from Grant to Coolidge.* New York: Harper and Brothers, 1927.

——— *Presidential Sweepstakes.* New York: G. P. Putnam's Sons, 1948.

Tansill, Charles C. *The Congressional Career of Thomas Francis Bayard, 1869-1885.* Washington: Georgetown University Press, 1946.

——— *The United States and Santo Domingo, 1798-1873.* Baltimore: The Johns Hopkins Press, 1938.

Tarbell, Ida M. *The Tariff in Our Times.* New York: The Macmillan Company, 1911.

Taussig, F. W. *The Tariff History of the United States.* New York: G. P. Putnam's Sons, 1909.

Thayer, William R. *The Life and Letters of John Hay*. 2 vols. Boston: Houghton Mifflin Company, 1915.

Tilden, Samuel J. *Letters and Literary Memorials of Samuel J. Tilden*, edited by John Bigelow. 2 vols. New York: Harper and Brothers, 1908.

Van Deusen, Glyndon G. *Thurlow Weed: Wizard of the Lobby*. Boston: Little, Brown and Company, 1947.

Walker, Francis A. *General Hancock*. New York: D. Appleton and Company, 1895.

Waterman, W. Randall. "Neal Dow." In Allen Johnson and Dumas Malone, editors, *Dictionary of American Biography*, Vol. 5, pp. 411-12. New York: Charles Scribner's Sons, 1930.

Watterson, Henry. *Marse Henry: An Autobiography*. 2 vols. New York: George H. Doran Company, 1919.

White, William A. *Masks in a Pageant*. New York: The Macmillan Company, 1928.

Williams, Charles R. *The Life of Rutherford Birchard Hayes*. 2 vols. Boston: Houghton Mifflin Company, 1914.

Wittke, Carl, editor. *The History of the State of Ohio*. 6 vols. Columbus: Ohio State Archaeological and Historical Society, 1941.

Woodward, C. Vann. *Reunion and Reaction: The Compromise of 1877 and the End of Reconstruction*. Boston: Little, Brown and Company, 1951.

The World Almanac and Encyclopedia. New York: Press Publishing Company, 1907.

279

denial by of desire for nomination,
119-20
effort of to conciliate factions in
Republican party, 181-92
effort of to enlist help of Conkling,
183-84
election of, 240-46, 249
Kelly's plan to contest election of,
243-44
letter of accepting nomination,
182-83
letter of to Grant on Robertson and
Conkling, 259
majority report on unit rule and,
92-93
meeting with of Grant and Conkling
at Mentor, 200-01
misdeeds of as described in *Democratic Campaign Text Book for
1880*, 222, 226-27
Morey letter and, 233-37, 251-52
nomination of, 108-10, 111
nomination of John Sherman by,
102-05
opinion of concerning conference
with New York Republicans,
186-87
opinion of on Hancock's nomination,
150
opposition of to Catholic Church,
215-16
press comment on election of, 248-52
promise of Halstead to support,
174-75
protest of against use of his name in
convention, 112-13
rumor of withdrawal by, 201
salary grab of 1873 and, 232 *note*
selection of Cabinet by, 252-54
Sherman's candidacy and, 36-38
speech of against unit rule, 91-92
speech of Grant for, 199
strategy of during convention of
1880, 102-05
unpopular appointment of in New
York, 256-57
winning by of senatorship, 102-03

Geiger, Joseph H., 104
Gibbons, James Cardinal, 40
Gibson, Randall L., 79
Gilmour, Richard, 40
Godkin, Edwin L., 8
Gorham, Arthur P., 256
Grace, William R., 238-39, 247
Grant, Mrs. Ulysses S., 86
Grant, Ulysses S.
  as candidate for Republican nomi-
    nation in 1880, 45-50, 85, 94
  assistance of to Butler, 48
  attack of on Hancock, 201-02
  attempts of to annex Dominican
    Republic, 7
  campaign speech of for Garfield, 199
  effect of early return from Europe on
    chances for nomination, 121
  election of in 1878, 4-6
  meeting of with Garfield and
    Conkling at Mentor, 200-01
  nomination of in 1868, 5
  opposition to at end of first term, 7
  permission of for withdrawal of
    name from 1880 convention, 86
  popularity of in South, 46
  position of in 1876 regarding third
    term, 10-11
  proposed to convention of 1880 as
    candidate for presidency, 98
  return of from European tour, 26-27
  third-term boom for, 27-28
  willingness of to withdraw as can-
    didate for nomination, 115
Gray, George, 132-33
Greeley, Horace, 7-9, 67
Green, Norvin, 77
Greenbackers, 157-64, 243
Grier, W. A. M., 109, 114
Grosvenor, William M., 110
Guiteau, Charles, 241, 261-62, 265, 266
Gumbleton, Henry A., 61

Hale, Eugene, 89, 90, 110, 169
Halstead, Murat
  letter of to Washburne, 42
  on Butler as Greenback nominee, 158